THE BAHA'I FAITH
IN AMERICA

THE BAHA'I FAITH
IN AMERICA

William Garlington

Foreword by Jeffrey J. Kripal

PRAEGER

Westport, Connecticut
London

Library of Congress Cataloging-in-Publication Data

Garlington, William, 1947–
    The Baha'i Faith in America / William Garlington ; foreword by Jeffrey J. Kripal.
        p. cm.
    Includes bibliographical references.
    ISBN 0–275–98413–3 (alk. paper)
        1. Bahai Faith—United States.   I. Title.
BP350.G37   2005
297.9'3'0973—dc22   2005013505

British Library Cataloguing in Publication Data is available.

Library of Congress Catalog Card Number: 2005013505
ISBN: 0–275–98413–3

First published in 2005

Praeger Publishers, 88 Post Road West, Westport, CT 06881
An imprint of Greenwood Publishing Group, Inc.
www.praeger.com

Printed in the United States of America

The paper used in this book complies with the
Permanent Paper Standard issued by the National
Information Standards Organization (Z39.48–1984).

10 9 8 7 6 5 4 3 2 1

In memory of Ray Meyer
whose life exemplified the words on his gravestone:
"Where there is love,
nothing is too much trouble,
and there is always time."

Contents

Foreword

Toward a More Mystical Monotheism

This is a very important book, but it is important for reasons that may not at first be obvious. Yes, there are few, if any, critically balanced histories of the Baha'i Faith that are at once accessible to the general reader and faithful to the norms of historical scholarship. Yes, William Garlington does an admirable job of clearly setting out the tradition's history, doctrine, institutional structure, and present American shape for his readers. Yes, the author provides an astute analysis of the moral, intellectual, and cultural debates that presently define the tradition's own sense (really senses) of direction and purpose. However, these are not the deeper reasons that such a book should be widely read. The deeper reason is this: the immediate future, stability, and welfare of civilization may very well depend largely on the topics of this book.

Of course, I express myself excessively, if not fantastically, here. Yet, I engage in such conscious hyperbole to make what I consider to be a very sane and quite serious point. Obviously, I do not mean to suggest that human civilization depends upon whether or not this particular book is purchased and struggled with or left to sit peacefully on the shelf (no author desires such peace). I personally would very much like many people to read this work, but I suspect that the welfare of human cultures does not depend upon these pages. What I do suspect, and suspect very strongly, is that the fundamental ethical and religious issues with which the Baha'i tradition so bravely struggles (even within itself) are the very same issues that presently threaten the social stability and physical safety of billions of human beings on this planet. Crudely put, that struggle is between two forms of religion. On the one hand, there is an exclusivistic monotheism (Jewish, Christian, or Islamic) that is structurally intolerant and often violent in its exclusionary claims to speak for the One True God,[1] closed off to other revelations of divinity and beauty, and willing to act on its apocalyptic fantasies. On the other hand, there is an inclusivistic or pluralistic mysticism that is, ideally, open to new truths and new ways of being human wherever and whenever they are found, self-reflexively aware of its own cultural and linguistic limitations, and celebratory of the inherent paradoxes of particularity and universality, of self and other, and of body and spirit. There are, of course, also mystical forms of monotheism in the history of religions. The Baha'i tradition is one of the most prominent and radical among them.

As I write this, our world is wracked by religious violence on a potentially terrifying scale. Human societies have long been plagued by religiously motivated violence, of course, but never in history have we possessed the technological means to carry out the Armageddons, holy wars, and final judgments that our scriptures imagine with such depressing consistency. We do now, and that makes all the difference. In our own time, this religious nightmare is spawned largely by a century-long, global and pan-religious outbreak of fundamentalism and now terrorism, much of it generated by the dualistic logic of monotheism and probably best thought of as a modern reaction to modernity itself.

Given the fundamentally religious motivations and intentions of these reactionary movements, it seems likely that other religious ideas and practices that are more liberal and humane might be especially effective in countering and eventually defusing these same reactions. We may or may not need spy satellites and smart bombs capable of locating and destroying hidden terrorist operations, but we most certainly need radical religious intellectuals, gifted visionaries, and new mystical theologies capable of accurately locating and peacefully deconstructing doctrines and practices that human reason (itself a reflection of God in many theological traditions) and a global humanity can only now begin to declare definitively dysfunctional and dangerous. As Mark Juergensmeyer has put it, religion itself has become a weapon of mass destruction, perhaps *the* weapon of mass destruction.[2] Until we can learn how to defuse such virtual bombs through their own technology (that is, more progressive and humane religious doctrine and spiritual experience), we can expect more, many more, physical bombs to shred our lovely bodies and reduce our astonishing cultural accomplishments to ugly rubble and yet more hatred.

There is a fundamental mistake that liberal thinkers (among which I would certainly count myself) make when it comes to the topic of religion. They consistently imagine that religious problems are not really religious, that religious language and doctrine encode deeper issues that are fundamentally political and economic in nature (which, of course, is also true). Human beings, they assume, are all basically working on the same assumptions, and so anyone who, say, flies a jumbo jet into a New York skyscraper or reduces a Texas compound or an Oklahoma federal building filled with men, women, and children to ashes must be "crazy" and must be operating entirely outside the parameters of their own religious subcultures. This, of course, is often simply not true. It is this same intellectual error that renders many liberal thinkers almost completely incapable of addressing effectively and imaginatively the deadly serious challenges of fundamentalism, terrorism, and religious violence.[3] Essentially, in our understandable concern to address social and economic issues (the triggers, if you will, that activate or catalyze the deeper and already existing theologies of exclusion and violence), we grossly underestimate the power of religious beliefs to guide, if not actually determine, human behavior, including and especially violent behavior. We thus miss the true root of the problem—religion itself.

To employ a technological analogy, which I would not want to take too far, religious doctrine and mythology are essentially the cognitive software that have been fed into the biological hardware of our brains for hundreds, sometimes thousands, of years now, partly in response to universal biological needs that are still very much with us (procreation, the rearing of children, the fear of death) but also in response to social circumstance and tribal necessities that no longer exist in any economically developed democratic society.[4] Perhaps these programs were functional, even helpful, at one time in the far-distant past. They certainly are no longer so, not at least on a global level. The religions are thus caught in an immense anachronism, essentially responding to new forms of knowledge and experience (about human sexuality, about democratic social practices, about modern science) with scriptural texts, interpretations, and laws that are embedded in now-defunct political systems and hopelessly naïve, prescientific models of the world. Indeed, I think we are beginning to realize, with some understandable grief and trepidation, that our religions too often function in a way that resembles far more a computer virus gone wild on the Internet (sometimes quite literally) than a helpful piece of programming that makes our lives richer, happier, and more peaceful. What makes these viruses so hard to counter is the (false) belief that *no one wrote them*; that is, that they are divinely revealed truths that can brook no criticism or accept no real change.

The fact that our very psychological and cultural identities, themselves often under considerable threat (if not in our political lives, then certainly in our approach to physical death), are intimately wrapped up with these same religious systems only makes the situation more dire. It is difficult indeed for a Hindu under colonialism or even after colonialism or a Muslim in a refugee camp to see the limitations, even dangers, of their own threatened ways of life. I am reminded here of the June 2002 California court ruling that declared the Pledge of Allegiance unconstitutional. Despite the utter reasonableness and legal consistency of such a ruling (what *is* "God" doing in a state-enforced ritual?), many members of Congress reacted with what can only be described as a fundamentalist nativism: they condemned the court and stood on the steps of Congress to recite the pledge before whirling cameras, literally shouting the phrase "under God." The historical context, of course, is everything: a post–9/11 America still reeling from the terrorist attacks. The reaction of the politicians is certainly understandable, even if it flows from some very dubious legal reasoning.

If we in America cannot step back and be critical of our own religious heritages amidst incredible wealth and privilege, how on earth can we expect Muslim populations that have lived in what are essentially refugee settlements for more than *fifty years* under constant threat or Hindus who are still hurting, even after fifty years of independence, from *two centuries* of humiliating European colonialism (not to mention centuries of previous Islamic colonialism) to be critical of their own? It seems obvious that freedom from religious oppression can only come after freedom from political oppression. Only free people can feel free to think critically about their own religions (and everyone else's). They must, and we must.

A cultural critic once noted that a satellite photo of the northeastern seaboard of the United States looks remarkably like a cancerous growth in a living tissue: both images are defined by an uncontrolled growth that will eventually kill the host organism, be it a human body or a planet, if not checked in time.[5] Nietzsche had said the same a full 100 years earlier, with one of those biting one-liners of his: "The earth, Zarathustra points out, has a skin, and this skin has diseases. One of these diseases, for example, is called 'man.'"[6] The lesson for us here is clear enough: it is remarkably difficult to name, understand, and treat a virus or cancer when we ourselves are the malady. I am not suggesting that human beings are the earth's cancer, but I am suggesting that many of our religious ideas come perilously close to the metaphor.

The critical discipline of religious studies as it is presently practiced in the universities is certainly no cure-all here, but it could certainly help, for what it is best at doing is showing how *all* mythologies, *all* doctrines, *all* rituals, for whatever else they may or may not be, are also human creations. One implication of this discovery is the realization that this religious software, like any software, can be rewritten or discarded, if we so choose—we are only the cancer or virus if we choose to be. The power of religious studies, in other words, lies partly in its ability to transcend a strict social determinism. We need not be puppets of our inherited religious beliefs, forever obedient to a God whose routinely despicable behavior in both sacred scripture and history (sacrificing sons, demeaning women, demanding holy wars, encouraging the hatred of minorities and other cultures or belief systems, blocking or seeking to control free thought and expression, attacking "the heathen," and so on) in any pluralistic civilized society would quickly land him in prison or, more likely, on death row. Perhaps that is just where he belongs.

This possibility might be profoundly disturbing to literalists and fundamentalists of every persuasion (and comparison can show that the Christian fundamentalist shares far more in common, in terms of process and thought pattern, with the Islamist radical or Hindu communalist than any of them would like to admit), but it is also a potentially healing truth for the future of our global community. At some point, we are going to have to admit to ourselves that some of our worst ideas are religious ideas and that there is no way to counter them effectively without radically and consistently challenging their *religious* bases. If your computer is crashing and the problem is a virus, you can clean the glass screen all you want, you can move the mouse here and there, you can pretend that your problems are the fault of the person who sold or shipped the computer (probably from the West), you can even take the computer apart and fiddle with the video card and mother board, but *nothing* will change, *nothing* will be fixed until you address the problem where it in fact exists; that is, in the internal mind or software of the system.

This is one of the many ways that we might come to appreciate the Baha'i tradition—as a kind of antivirus software for cultural systems (including and especially our own) that run on exclusivistic, monotheistic operating systems. The fundamental Baha'i doctrines that religious truth is relative and progressive, that humanity, not ethnicity or the nation-state, constitutes our fundamental unity, that spirituality and science need to meet and merge within a more integral vision, that all forms of prejudice need to be eliminated, and that all peoples deserve economic and social justice are precious gifts to a suffering, screaming planet and are well worth celebrating and encouraging wherever we find them. The American reader should also take serious note that a good share of Baha'i history is, in fact, tied up with American history, with American actors, and with the quintessentially American values of individualism, freedom, science, and pluralism. The reader, in other words, should take note that this is not only a Middle Eastern story; it is also an American story about America's rich religious pluralism and the country's indebtedness to and love of the Middle East. For good and for ill, we are all bound up with each other in our stories about each other. It is time now to imagine other stories about both one another and ourselves. With respect to the Baha'i sense of self and other, Garlington gently reminds both his readers and the tradition itself that, as with any religious tradition, there are problems here. Foremost among these are the tradition's struggle to free its remarkable understandings of revelation and religious progress from lingering gender and sexual discrimination, to embrace fully the findings of science (particularly in its evolutionary modes), and to recognize that intellectual freedom is not a human good that can be surrendered to any religious authority, including Baha'i religious authority.

The latter point is worth emphasizing here. If the world needs anything now, it is a thoroughgoing critical discussion of "religion" within and across every cultural boundary. Much, in other words, depends upon scholars and intellectuals *not* having to vet their thought with the religions they study and analyze. Such writers have, in effect, taken on a function in modern society that is analogous to that of the prophets and mystics of former times, calling into honest question all previous tradition and law for the sake of greater truth and justice, occasionally at considerable risk to their own personal safety and concern. There are few more important tasks today, I would suggest, than to encourage, support, and critically discuss such intellectual acts. Former societies often rejected the prophets of their own times; it would be a shame if we now rejected the prophetic and mystical truths of our present simply because we did not recognize them for what they are. The fact, moreover, that such radically healing truths are no longer inextricably tied to the personal charisma or authority of individuals but are now widely available on Internet sites and the physical shelves of every mega-bookstore renders them more, not less, attractive. Democracy and the free exchange of ideas have rendered even the prophet and the mystic common, indeed almost invisible.

William Garlington's personal spiritual path to and through a religious tradition that was originally "foreign" to his own birth culture and his public practice in the present book of a kind of hermeneutical and historical scholarship that is both appreciative *and* critical of the object of its study are classical characteristics of this same modern study of religion. So too are his mystical sensibilities for some of the more radical doctrinal features of Baha'i, which seek clearly to move beyond the Middle East's ancient and medieval Christian, Jewish, and Islamic faiths into a more hopeful future of peace and justice. Very much like some of the early Baha'i mystics, Garlington is willing to speak in his own modern idiom—which happens to be the idiom of scholarship—of a glimpsed religious truth that is not bound by any religious law, tradition, or history, but which manifests itself anew within every generation in the reflections and reflection of the human being.

William Garlington, in other words, is a "comparative mystic" in the sense that he employs a comparative imagination informed by the history of religions, a critical mind disciplined by modern theory, and a deeply sympathetic approach to religion honed by decades of his own spiritual practice in order to think with and through the Baha'i tradition.[7] In this, he thinks, writes, and exists in a long line of similarly oriented writers who, very much in the spirit (if never quite the letter) of the Baha'i genius, have opened themselves to radically new modes of being human by embracing paradoxical mystery and radical creativity over static "eternal" dogma and the dangerous certainties (illusions, really) of ethnic and religious immutability. As Beverly Lanzetta has so beautifully put it with reference to the "heresy" (read: originality) of mystical theology:

> Often the experience of mystery cannot be confined to the conceptual categories in which theology barters meaning. In this sense, every mystical act is itself a shift in paradigms and the stuff of "heresy." ... Those who have been guided into the annihilatory experience know that new theology continually unfolds both within a tradition and as the breakthrough of tradition. The mystical pioneers who have risked their visions of truth in often hostile climates, and who have offered us rare glimpses of a God who not only celebrates new ideas and new revelations, but who births them as well, provide hope for interreligious cooperation.[8]

Precisely because of this same animating spirit, Garlington's work is an occasion to celebrate and to hope: to celebrate the human spirit and its consistent refusal to be bound by any past cultural or religious system and to hope for a religious future that nourishes and liberates this same spirit rather than crushing it under the weight of more tradition, more unbelievable beliefs, and yet more fear.

May that spirit flourish here and everywhere. It is certainly time.

Jeffrey J. Kripal
J. Newton Rayzor Professor of Religious Studies
Rice University

Acknowledgments

This book could not have been written without the help of numerous people who have assisted me in one way or another. In Australia, Dr. Ray Meyer and Professor A. L. Basham encouraged me to start my academic work on the Baha'i Faith at a time when the field of Baha'i studies was virtually nonexistent. Over the years, the field has grown significantly. Baha'i scholars have focused their concerns beyond the Faith's early history in the Middle East to include its development in various parts of the world. In terms of the present work, I am greatly indebted to those scholars whose research endeavors in American Baha'i history have provided so much fruitful material. Prominent among this group are Peter Smith, Richard Hollinger, Gayle Morrison, Michael McMullen, Juan R. I. Cole, Peggy Caton, Loni Bramson-Lerche, Roger Dahl, Robert Stockman, William Collins, Moojan Momen, Deb Clark, and Jackson Armstrong-Ingram. Special gratitude is due to Anthony Lee, whose pioneering efforts in the publication of Baha'i academic work at Kalimat Press are without equal. I am also thankful to a number of individuals who commented on the manuscript at various stages of its completion. These include Steven Scholl, Robert Ballenger, Anthony Lee, David Langness, and Todd and Kimberly Garlington. It goes without saying that I am extremely grateful to Praeger Greenwood, and especially to my editor, Suzanne Staszak-Silva, for supporting my efforts and ensuring that the manuscript was up to the standards of publication. In addition, I would be remiss if I did not also declare my appreciation to my physical trainer, Susan Pyne, who helps me keep striving toward the Greek ideal of sound body and sound mind. Finally, words cannot adequately express the role that my wife Cris has played in bringing this work to fruition. For thirty-seven years, in innumerable ways, she has provided me with encouragement and support, and for this I will be forever grateful.

Introduction

On the shores of Lake Michigan, not far from where the North Canal meets the harbor at the Chicago suburb of Wilmette, stands the architecturally unique Baha'i House of Worship. With its ornately ornamented nine sides and majestic 150-foot-high dome, the temple has long been a major tourist attraction for the Chicago area. Since its completion in 1953, it has been estimated that some 5 million visitors have passed through the building's doors, and yet today very few Americans have any substantial knowledge of the religion it represents. To some degree, this has been the result of a lack over the years of both general publications on the Baha'i Faith and overall media coverage. Outside of the academic world, publications have primarily been limited to either in-house works, most of which have been designed to help spread the religion and are required to be submitted to an official Baha'i review process, or anti-Baha'i polemic. Thus a balanced, nonpartisan approach to the subject has been wanting. This book is an attempt to rectify the situation by presenting the reader with essential historical, doctrinal, and organizational information about the American Baha'i community while at the same time attempting to maintain an approach that neither seeks to glorify nor denigrate.

This raises the question of my own relationship to the Baha'i Faith. During the late 1960s, when I was still an undergraduate, I declared myself a Baha'i and became active in my local community. In the early 1970s, I moved with my wife and young son to Australia, where I entered a doctoral program at the Australian National University and wrote my dissertation on the topic of Baha'i mass teaching in Malwa, India. It was during those years of research that my personal religious commitment began to wane, essentially over theological issues related to revelation and infallibility. For a number of years following the completion of the dissertation, I officially remained part of the Baha'i community. Upon returning to the United States in the 1980s, my level of active participation declined, and eventually I formally withdrew my membership. Although I highly valued the Baha'i Faith's mystical dimensions and social principles, I found that I could no longer honestly consent to orthodox theological beliefs.

My years as a Baha'i enabled me to meet many wonderful people and see the religion from the "inside," so to speak. In terms of the current work, I believe that those years not only allowed me to gain specific understandings and insights into the workings of the Baha'i community, they also enabled me to develop a certain degree of what Wilhelm Dilthey called *verstehen* (sympathetic understanding). On the other hand, my later break with the community and consequent distance from the object of study, along with my academic training, puts me in a distinctive position. As noted above, most books about the Baha'i Faith have been written by either adherents or detractors. This effort attempts to speak both to those who are interested in the study of religion, and the universal approaches and terms that it uses, as well as to Baha'i adherents who value the attempt to represent as accurately as possible the points of view of Baha'i authors.

The book is divided into two parts. Part I contains a series of overview chapters designed to act as a general introduction to the Baha'i Faith. Here, such topics as the origins and historical development of the religion, its essential doctrines and teachings, and the nature of its community life and administrative structure are presented. The approach taken in Part I can best be described as normative. With the exception of the historical material, the various beliefs, practices, institutions, and modes of operation that are discussed therein are reflections of how Baha'i-produced literature ideally depicts them. Part II examines the historical development of the American Baha'i community from its earliest beginnings at the end of the nineteenth century until the present day. Its chapters not only examine the major events and personalities that comprise American Baha'i history, they also trace significant themes and issues that have characterized the community over the decades. In contrast to the normative approach taken in Part I, the chapters in Part II take what might be called a "realistic" approach to the material; that is, the various facets of Baha'i community life are examined from the perspective of how they have been expressed over time in actual social contexts rather than how they are idealized in Baha'i literature.

I do not make any substantial claim to original research. Except for some of the interview material found in its latter chapters, the work has relied for most of its information on the research carried out by those scholars mentioned in the Acknowledgments. Thus, at most, the current book can be seen as a modest attempt to both synthesize and analyze in a coherent manner the research findings of others.

Some comments on sources and the transliteration of Persian and Arabic words are required. In a number of instances, especially for contemporary issues, I have relied on Internet Web sites to obtain source material that is otherwise currently unavailable. The most helpful sites have been *Baha'i Library Online,* managed by Jonah Winters, and H-Net/H-Bahai–related sites such as *Occasional Papers in Shaykhi, Babi and Baha'i Studies,* edited by Juan R. I. Cole. While I am aware of the possible detriments of using Internet material, the stability and professionalism that characterize both these sites have given me the confidence to turn to them freely when necessary. Regarding the transliteration of Persian and Arabic words, I have used a modified version of the system of transliteration employed within the Baha'i community. The primary divergence from that system has been the elimination of diacritical marks in words that occur frequently within the text (that is, Babi instead of Bábí, and Baha'i instead of Bahá'í) and a greater use of Anglicized forms of terms and place names that have become common in Western usage. For those unfamiliar with diacritical marks as applied to Arabic and Persian words, the following examples hold: á = ball, í = meet, ú = tool.

One preliminary issue that needs to be raised is the question of Baha'i population figures. At the present time the Baha'i Faith claims between 5 and 6 million members worldwide and more than 150,000 believers in the United States. Challenges have been made to the validity of the American numbers, however, on the grounds that this figure does not take into account those individuals who have become inactive or left the community.[1] It may well be, therefore, that only half of the claimed believers in the United States maintain allegiance to the Baha'i administrative institutions. This does not mean, however, that those who are not active Baha'is have necessarily renounced their belief in Baha'u'llah (1817–1892), the prophet and founder of the Baha'i Faith, or negated the religious and social principles for which he stood. Just as there are many people who claim to be followers of Jesus Christ and yet are not official members of an established church, it seems fair to assume that there are a sizable number of individuals who identify with Baha'u'llah and his principles while remaining outside the established institutions of the Baha'i Faith. This would seem especially likely in the United States, where individualism in matters of religion is a prominent feature of social life. From the point of view of this study, the significant point is that at least 150,000 Americans have experienced enough identity with the Baha'i teachings to have made official written declarations of that belief. Moreover, when one adds to this number those people who may share much of the Baha'i worldview but have not felt the need to become official members of a religious organization, the overall figure of like-minded souls becomes much higher. Such a realization would lead us to believe that, beyond what the official Baha'i numbers represent, the growth of the American Baha'i community during the last century is indicative of a considerable number of Americans developing a worldview that is substantially different in outlook than the more traditional perspectives associated with American religiosity. This fact alone is justification for the need to better understand the teachings and goals of the Baha'i community.

What are the key components of this new worldview or paradigm shift that the American Baha'i community embodies? Foremost is the idea that religious truth is relative and progressive, that human history has seen more than one embodiment of divine revelation. Indeed, from a Baha'i perspective all the world's great religious traditions can trace their origins to One source, and hence they all reflect certain elements or degrees of truth. These truths, moreover, are periodically renewed and revised through the medium of revelation to meet the requirements of the age in which they appear. For Baha'is, the latest example of this divine/human connection is the message proclaimed by their prophet and founder, Baha'u'llah.

Directly related to the idea of religious unity is the belief in the Oneness of Humanity. In the words of Baha'u'llah, "Ye are all leaves of one tree and the fruits of one branch."[2] The implication of this premise is that humanity as a whole should receive mankind's highest allegiance, not the nation state or ethnic group. Baha'is, therefore, look forward to the day when there will be international bodies that supersede in authority the sovereignty currently granted to national governments, a sovereignty that some would add has been the cause of so many wars and atrocities. The exact role the Baha'i Faith will play in this evolutionary step is still being debated. Some of its leaders speak of a new type of theocratic model that will unite mankind, whereas others see the Baha'i institutions working in coordination with independent political authority. In both cases, however, there is a conviction that the process of globalization that is already taking place economically and technologically will continue in ways that will eventually make national and ethnic identities secondary, if not antiquated.

The third essential component of the Baha'i worldview is the belief in the equality of all human beings regardless of race, ethnicity, gender, or social class. Although this ideal has been proclaimed and extolled from the Declaration of Independence to the speeches of twenty-first-century politicians, its actualization in American life still leaves much to be desired. From a Baha'i perspective, until human equality becomes more adequately embodied in social reality, humanity will continue to experience the negative consequences brought about by the failure to do so.

Of course, it is one thing to advocate new patterns of thought and action and another to concretely express them. As the chapters in Part II indicate, the American Baha'i community has not been immune from shortcomings. Power struggles, short-sighted policies, and individual failures have marched hand in hand with examples of cooperative success, insightful leadership, and heroic self-sacrifice. We should not expect otherwise, for the mask the muse of history seems inevitably bound to expose is utopianism.

Part I

Introduction to the Baha'i Faith

1

Origins and Historical Development

The word "Baha'i" is a derivative of the Arabic *bahá* (light, glory). *Bahá* in turn refers to Baha'u'llah (the Glory of God), a title taken by the Persian nobleman, Mírzá Husayn 'Alí Núrí, who in 1866 publicly claimed to be the latest revealer of God's will for mankind. The story leading up to this declaration is an intriguing one and, as such, caught the attention of a number of contemporary European scholars including the renowned Cambridge University orientalist E. G. Browne (1862–1926). To trace its beginnings, we must return to mid-nineteenth-century Iran.

THE BABI PERIOD (1844–1850)

In the early 1840s, Iran, or Persia as it was generally known in the West, was a country experiencing profound social, political, and economic changes. Contact with Western colonial powers, as well as diverse internal pressures, had placed great strain on traditional institutions and resulted in a number of challenges to their authority. In the religious arena, there were certain messianic expectations related to the return of the Twelfth Imam, a mystical figure who according to some orthodox traditions of Twelver Shi'ism (the state religion of Iran) had mysteriously disappeared in the year 873 CE and would one day victoriously return to usher in a period of universal peace and justice. Indeed, as the 1,000-year anniversary of the disappearance of the Imam approached (1844 CE), speculation about his immediate appearance became more widespread. Such ideas, although often more symbolic than literal in interpretation, were particularly popular among the Shaykhí school of Twelver Shi'ism, whose two most prominent leaders were Shaykh Ahmad al-Ahsá'í (1743–1826) and Sayyid Kázim Rashtí (1793–1843).

Among the students who came under the influence of Rashtí was a certain Sayyid 'Alí Muhammad Shírází. Only in his early twenties, the young man had left his career as a merchant in the port city of Bushihr to journey to the holy cities of Karbala and Najaf (in present-day Iraq), and although he only remained at these sites for somewhat less than a year, his religious devotion and innocent demeanor impressed a number of the leading Shaykhís.[1]

Rashtí died in January 1844. 'Alí Muhammad was now living in his family's native city of Shiraz. Several months after the Shaykhí leader's death in May 1844, the youthful sayyid made his first messianic claim. He announced to a number of close associates that he was the Promised One and took the title Bab (gate), which indicated his association with the hidden Twelfth Imam. He subsequently directed some of his first disciples, referred to as Letters of the Living, to disperse and make his declaration known throughout the various provinces of Iran and Iraq. Then, in September 1844, he left on pilgrimage to Mecca.

During the Bab's stay in Mecca, one of his disciples was put on trial in Baghdad and found guilty of heresy for spreading his master's writings. Furthermore, opposition to the Bab's claim by leading Shi'ite religious leaders in the holy cities of southern Iraq (Karbala, Kufa, and Najaf) began to escalate. Perhaps for this reason, as well as the lack of general support for his declaration in Mecca, the Bab decided against going to Iraq and instead chose to return to his native homeland.

The Bab arrived in Shiraz in July 1845 and, for the next eighteen months, spent most of the time in the isolation of his own house. During this period, both the number of his followers and the level of antagonism from conservative religious leaders increased. Finally, in September 1846, the governor of the province of Fars ordered his arrest. During the ensuing chaos, which included a simultaneous outbreak of cholera in the city, the Bab was released on condition that he depart the province.[2] He immediately left for Isfahan, which now harbored a growing and well-organized Babi cell. There he received momentary refuge from persecution by gaining the protection of Isfahan's governor, Manúchihr Khán, who died shortly after, in February 1847. His successor did not share the deceased governor's sympathy for the Bab. By this time, the growing commotion surrounding the young man and his followers had become a concern for the monarchy in Tehran, where Muhammad Sháh and his chief minister, Hájjí Mírzá

Áqásí, feared the political consequences of continuing upheaval. Consequently, a month after Manúchihr Khán's death, the royal minister ordered the new governor to send the Bab to the capital under armed escort. The Bab, however, was not destined to reach Tehran. During the journey, his guards received further orders that he be taken to the fortress of Mákú, located in the mountains of northwest Iran near the Russo-Ottoman frontier. He remained at Mákú for nine months until he was transferred a little further south to the castle-prison of Chiríq. It was here, in what he called "the grievous mountain," that the Bab would spend most of what remained of his short life.[3]

Three months after his arrival at Chiríq, the Bab was summoned to the city of Tabriz to be examined by a panel of religious leaders in front of the crown prince. Much of the trial was designed to mock the young sayyid. After being asked a series of questions, which in addition to those related to his religious claims included queries concerning Arabic grammar and medicine, the panel concluded that only the question of his sanity caused the postponement of his immediate execution and should this doubt be removed in the future, the sentence of an apostate (death) would without hesitation be placed upon him.[4] His feet were then beaten, and he was returned to Chiríq.

Several important consequences resulted from the Bab's permanent imprisonment in northwestern Iran. First, it was during this time that he began to elaborate upon and expand his claims. Most importantly, he now professed to be the Imam Mahdi (also known as the *Qá'im*—"He who will arise"), a messianic figure who would bring about the Day of Resurrection and alone had the power to abolish Islamic law.[5]

Second, the more extreme elements of the Babi community began to emerge and advance their positions. The most striking example of such developments took place during the months of June and July 1848 at the small village of Badasht in north-central Iran when a number of radical Babis, including the poetess Táhirih, announced that they were no longer under the authority of Shi'ite legal ordinances. In an open demonstration of defiance, Táhirih publicly removed her veil.

Finally, the Bab's isolation created an escalation in the instances of violent confrontation between his followers and the general populace. Throughout the realm, Babis were increasingly attacked. Similarly, Babi militants began to call for the use of force. The turning point came just after the Badasht Conference when a group of Babis under the command of one of the Bab's earliest and closest disciples, Mullá Husayn Bushrú'í, unfurled a symbolic black flag and set out toward Chiríq for the purpose of rescuing their imprisoned leader. Not far from the town of Bárfurúsh, they were confronted by a hostile mob. A fight broke out in which both a number of Babis and townspeople were killed. Afterward, the Babis took refuge in the nearby shrine of Shaykh Tabarsí. A lengthy siege followed that eventually involved government troops and the use of mortar bombardment. After seven months of fierce fighting, the starving and decimated Babis surrendered, only to be killed or enslaved. During the first half of 1850, similar conflicts occurred in both the southern city of Zanján and the northern town of Nayríz.

Muhammad Sháh died in September 1848, and his son, Násiri'd-Dín Sháh, succeeded to the royal throne. As crown prince, Násiri'd-Dín Sháh had presided over the earlier examination of the Bab at Tabriz, and now that he was monarch, he was anxious to prevent any further spread of the movement. In the mind of his chief minister, Amír Kabír, it was the figure of the Bab that provided the required solution. According to a prominent historian of the Babi period, Yale Professor Abbas Amanat: "Amir Kabir had already come to the conclusion that his execution was the only way to prevent future Babi insurgencies. The religious intensity of the Babi resistance in Tabarsí and Nayríz, as well as the ongoing uprising in Zanjan, convinced him as to the symbolic place the Bab reserved in the mind of his followers."[6] Consequently, on July 9, 1850, together with one of his young disciples, the Bab was brought before a firing squad in Tabriz and executed.

With many of its notable followers killed at Tabarsí and Zanján and now its proclaimed messiah eliminated, what remained of the Babi community started to splinter. Lacking cohesive organization, the movement lost its dynamism and began to decline. Under these circumstances, in August 1852, an assassination attempt was made on the life of Násiri'd-Dín Sháh. The ill-conceived plan failed and produced severe governmental reprisals in which at least thirty to forty prominent Babis were slain, some in a most cruel fashion.[7] The nominal leader of the Babi community, Mírzá Yahyá Núrí, whose title was Subh-i-Azal (Morn of Eternity), responded by going into hiding.

BAHA'U'LLAH AND THE EMERGENCE OF THE BAHA'I COMMUNITY (1852–1892)

Although the Bab penned a large number of verses, which spoke to a variety of religious themes,[8] the shortness of his life (most of which was spent in relative isolation) resulted in the movement's lack of a coherent belief system. It would appear that the community demanded a charismatic leader to accomplish such a task. In this regard, the Bab himself had made references in several of his later writings to a specific messianic figure called *Man-yuzhiruhu'lláh* (He whom God shall make manifest) who would arise at some time in the future to provide divinely inspired direction. The powerful psychological need for the prompt appearance of such a figure within the shattered Babi community can be measured by the fact that although one of Babism's leading modern scholars has concluded that the Bab saw *Man-yuzhiruhu'lláh* as appearing later rather than sooner (sixty-six years at minimum and probably more than six hundred years),[9] in the period immediately following the Bab's death, at least twenty-five such claims were made.

One of the prominent Babis able to avoid death during the reprisals of 1852 was Mírzá Husayn 'Alí Núrí, the half brother of the above-mentioned Subh-i-Azal, who since the Badasht Conference had been known by the title Baha'u'llah. Although he had no direct involvement in the assassination conspiracy, Baha'u'llah was arrested, given a life sentence, and confined to the infamous underground Síyáh Chál prison in Tehran. Because of the pressure his distinguished family was able to muster, as well as the staunch support of the Russian ambassador, after four months Baha'u'llah was released from the dungeon and, by order of the shah, exiled to the city of Baghdad. On January 12, 1853, together with several members of his immediate family, he began a two-month journey westward.

As part of the Ottoman Empire, and thus beyond the direct political control of Tehran, Baghdad had become a primary destination for Babi exiles. During his first year there, Baha'u'llah began to attract a following within the Babi community, and he soon found himself in conflict with Subh-i-Azal. In response to the increasing unease within the community, in April 1854 Baha'u'llah decided to leave the city and shortly thereafter departed for the mountains of Kurdistan where for two years he left aside Babi politics and associated instead with a number of the region's prominent Sufi mystics. He later recounted this period as follows: "We betook ourselves to the wilderness, and there, separated and alone, led for two years a life of complete solitude.... Alone, We communed with Our spirit, oblivious of the world and all that is therein ... until the hour when, from the Mystic Source, there came the summons bidding Us return from whence We came."[10]

Baha'u'llah returned to Baghdad in March 1856 and once again started to play an active role within the Babi community. The prior tensions with Subh-i-Azal resurfaced, and over the next few years, they continued to increase. In addition to this internal conflict, the Persian foreign minister in Baghdad began to interpret Baha'u'llah's rise to prominence as a security threat to his government, and he consequently convinced the shah to put political pressure on the Ottoman government to return the Babi leaders to Iran, where their activities could be more closely monitored. Eventually the Ottoman authorities agreed to order Baha'u'llah and Subh-i-Azal to leave Baghdad, but since both men had by this time obtained Ottoman citizenship, they were not sent back to their native country but invited instead to go to Istanbul.

Baha'u'llah's last twelve days in Baghdad were spent in the Najíbiya Garden on the outskirts of the city. Future Baha'is would later celebrate this period as the Twelve Days of Ridván (paradise), during which Baha'u'llah is believed to have first indicated to family and certain chosen disciples that he was He whom God shall make manifest.

Along with members of their immediate families and a number of close disciples, the half brothers arrived in Istanbul on August 16, 1863. Because of further political intrigue between the Iranian and Ottoman governments, four months later they were sent to Edirne (approximately 150 miles north-west of Istanbul). It was here that the breach that had begun between them in Baghdad widened into an unbridgeable break. Thus, in the period from August 1865 through February 1866, the Babi community split into two definite factions. In the latter year, Baha'u'llah made his leadership claim public, and the majority of Babis both in Edirne and Iran became Baha'is. Most of those who rejected him aligned themselves with Subh-i-Azal and became known as Azalis.

The continuing hostility between Baha'is and Azalis, as well as the con-stant stream of pilgrims who came to see Baha'u'llah, raised new concerns among government officials. Eventually it was decided that Baha'u'llah and his inner circle would be banished to the Syrian penal colony of Akká, situated on the bay north of Haifa, where murderers and political prison-ers from throughout the Ottoman Empire were consigned, while Subh-i-Azal and his close followers were sent to Famagusta, Cyprus. On August 12, 1868, the already twice-banished band of Persians once again began journeys into exile.

The Baha'is reached Akká on August 31. Until October 1870, they were kept under closed confinement in the citadel barracks. During this period, several followers became ill and died, and Baha'u'llah's youngest son was killed when he fell through a skylight. The group was then transferred to a local inn, while Baha'u'llah and his family were lodged in a small house. For the next seven years, severe restrictions of movement were enforced. After that time, Baha'u'llah was allowed to live outside of the city proper. The last years of his life were spent in a large house known as the Mansion of Bahjí, where he granted audiences to his followers and a few special visitors, including the aforementioned E. G. Browne.

The impression Baha'u'llah made upon the Cambridge scholar is worth noting: "The face of him upon whom I gazed I can never forget, though I cannot describe it. Those piercing eyes seemed to read one's very soul; power and authority sat on that ample brow; while the deep lines on the forehead and face implied an age which the jet black hair and beard flowing down in indistinguishable luxuriance almost to the waist seemed to belie."[11]

In both Edirne and Akká, Baha'u'llah wrote numerous tablets. These writings can be classified into roughly four categories: laws and ordinances, prayers and meditations, scriptural interpretations, and discourses and exhortations. Among these, two compositions stand out as significant: the *Kitáb-i Aqdas* (*The Most Holy Book*) and the *Súrat al-Múluk* (*Tablet to the Kings*). The former was composed in Akká in 1873 and set down the laws and precepts that were to govern the Baha'i community. It also established a line of succession and ordained certain institutions designed to ensure the community's future unity. The *Súrat al-Múluk*, written in Edirne in 1867, collectively addressed the world's monarchs and religious leaders. This overture was later supplemented by letters sent to individual rulers from Akká. Included in the list of recipients were: 'Álí-Páshá (the grand vizier of the Ottoman Empire), Napoleon III (the French emperor), Alexander II (tsar of Russia), Victoria (queen of England), and Pope Pius IX. In these tablets, Baha'u'llah called upon the "kings" to reduce their armaments, to put the beneficial needs of their subjects before their own personal desires, and to protect the peace by accepting the principle of collective security.

When Baha'u'llah died in May 1892, he left a dynamic and growing community. Written correspondence with groups of believers, as well as personal contact with individual pilgrims, had provided unifying links between shepherd and flock that, in turn, had fostered an enthusiastic spirit for spreading the word. The large majority of Baha'is resided in Iran where, despite periodic examples of persecution, the new religion continued to expand. As a result of emigration and directed Baha'i missionary activity, Baha'i communities had also been established outside of Baha'u'llah's homeland, in Ottoman Iraq, Syria, Egypt, the Sudan, India, and Burma. The Asian communities could trace their existence back to several of the Bab's relatives who had set themselves up in business in Bombay in the 1860s. Somewhat later (1875), Baha'u'llah personally commissioned the Baha'i Sufi scholar, Jamál Effendi, to travel to India and help stimulate missionary activities. After touring the length and breadth of the subcontinent, Jamál Effendi journeyed to Burma, where he helped create a Baha'i community in Rangoon.

Baha'u'llah's teachings will be considered at some length in subsequent chapters. For the moment, suffice it to say that in claiming to be He whom God shall make manifest, Baha'u'llah was not just speaking to Shi'ite Muslims. As his letters to the kings and rulers indicate, he was asserting that he was the latest of God's earthly spokesmen and that his message was a universal one that was destined to unite the nations of the earth into a new world commonwealth.

THE LEADERSHIP OF 'ABDU'L-BAHA (1892–1921)

Following Baha'u'llah's death, the leadership of the Baha'i community passed to his eldest son, 'Abbás Effendi, who was designated the sole interpreter of his father's writings. Despite the refusal of Baha'u'llah's younger son ('Abbás Effendi's half brother, Mírzá Muhammad-'Alí) to recognize him and the subsequent opposition of all but two of Baha'u'llah's immediate family, the large majority of Baha'is accepted their new leader. At this time, 'Abbás Effendi took the title for which we would later be known throughout the Baha'i world: 'Abdu'l-Baha (the servant of Bahá).

While still remaining a prisoner of the Ottoman government, in 1894 'Abdu'l-Baha gave his approval to a Syrian Christian convert, Ibrahim George Kheiralla, to introduce the claims and teachings of Baha'u'llah into the United States. Kheiralla had initial successes in New York City, Chicago, and Kenosha, Wisconsin, so that by the year 1900, some 2,000 Americans had become Baha'is. Although Kheiralla would later turn against the 'Abdu'l-Baha and side with the backers of Mírzá Muhammad-'Alí, most of the leading Americans whom he brought into the Baha'i community remained loyal to 'Abdu'l-Baha. Some, such as Phoebe Hearst, the wife of Senator George F. Hearst, made pilgrimages to the Holy Land to visit their new master. Others were instrumental in introducing the Faith into Europe. For example, May Bolles established the first Baha'i Center on the European continent in Paris.[12]

In the aftermath of the Young Turk Revolution and the fall of 'Abdu'l-Hamíd's Ottoman government in July 1909, 'Abdu'l-Baha was released from captivity. He was sixty-five years old and was now free to move beyond the confines of Akká and its immediate surroundings. Though he was in poor health, he chose to depart Akká for Haifa, where local Baha'is built him a house. In the future, he would seldom return to the city that had been his prison for more than forty years.

In August 1910, the Baha'i leader went to Egypt. He remained there for approximately one year before leaving for Europe aboard the SS *Corsica*.

The establishment and growth of a number of Baha'i communities in both Europe and North America had made him determined to travel westward, and now that his health was much improved, he felt ready to take up that task. One month later, he found himself addressing the congregation of the City Temple in Holborn, London, whose minister, the Reverend R. J. Campbell, was well-known for his liberal attitudes. In this, his first public address in a western country, 'Abdu'l-Baha referred to the gift of God in this age as being the knowledge of the oneness of mankind and the oneness of religion.[13] A week later, he addressed the congregation of St. John the Divine at Westminster. On this occasion, Archdeacon Wilberforce read the English translation of his talk. Over the next few weeks, similar presentations were made at a variety of different London venues, including Annie Beasant's Theosophical Society.

In early October, 'Abdu'l-Baha traveled to the continent, where he spent the next two months in Paris making a number of public presentations related to his father's teachings. Many of these talks were recorded and later published under the title *Paris Talks*. Though not considered scripture, *Paris Talks* would eventually become a very popular and oft-quoted Baha'i source that would go through numerous editions. As in London, his Paris addresses focused on the theme of religious unity. Thus, on November 10, at Avenue de Camoens, we find him claiming that "we must abandon the prejudices of tradition if we are to find the truth at the core of all religions."[14]

After wintering in Egypt, 'Abdu'l-Baha again journeyed westward, this time to visit the new Baha'i communities in the United States and Canada. Like his European venture, the trip was primarily designed to stimulate missionary activities. An added reason for the American tour was 'Abdu'l-Baha's desire to bring closure to the rift that had occurred in many of those communities as a result of Kheiralla's falling-out with the Baha'i leader. Upon docking in New York on April 11, 1912, 'Abdu'l-Baha set out in earnest to accomplish these goals.

'Abdu'l-Baha's 239-day stay in North America will be examined in some detail in Part II. During this period of time, he visited more than twenty major cities including: New York City, Washington, Chicago, Pittsburgh, Cleveland, Montreal, Minneapolis, Cincinnati, San Francisco, and Oakland. Wherever he went, he met with local Baha'is and did his utmost to help foster a new sense of community unity and purpose. He also made numerous public appearances and, for the most part, was well received by both his audiences and the press. For example, following his speech at Stanford University on October 8, the *Palo Altan* wrote: "Those who pray for the coming of the kingdom of God on earth may see in Abbas Effendi one who dwells in that kingdom consciously, and creates an environment pulsating with the peace that passeth ordinary understanding."[15]

In reading the accounts of early American Baha'i reactions to 'Abdu'l-Baha's visit, one is struck by the charismatic impact he had on his followers. He was continually referred to as "Lord" or "Master," and to many he seems to have become an object of devotion. While he never failed to uphold the figure of his father as God's spokesman for this age, the appeal of Baha'u'llah's message appears to have been emotionally identified with 'Abdu'l-Baha himself. Some spoke of him as "the Return of Christ," and despite his repeated denial of this position, for many early American believers there remained an aura of the supernatural around him.[16]

On December 5, 'Abdu'l-Baha left New York City for a return trip to Europe. Most of his time was again spent in Britain and France, but near the end of his stay on the continent, he traveled by train to Germany, Austria, and Hungary, stopping briefly in Stuttgart, Esslingen, Wangenburg, Vienna, and Budapest. After a final brief period in Paris, 'Abdu'l-Baha boarded ship in Marseilles, and four days later he arrived in Port Said. Because of failing health, he stayed in Egypt for six months, and it was not until December 5, 1913, that he finally returned to Haifa.

'Abdu'l-Baha remained in or near Haifa for the remainder of his life. While he desired to visit other Baha'i communities, particularly those in Asia, the outbreak of war in 1914 and poor health prevented him from doing so. Instead, he sent personal envoys to convey his message. Thus, two of his most faithful attendants, Mírzá 'Alí-Akbar-i-Nakhjávání and Mírzá Mahmúd-i-Zarqání, were sent to the Caucasus and India, while Emogene Hoagg was directed to Italy. Although the Baha'i leader could no longer visit his flock, both before and after the war numerous pilgrims from several continents came to see him and receive his blessing. They in turn acted as sources of information and inspiration to their local Baha'i communities.

It was during the war years that 'Abdu'l-Baha wrote *Tablets of the Divine Plan*, in which he outlined a "teaching campaign" (a Baha'i term for proselytizing or missionary activity) designed to take the message of Baha'u'llah to some 120 countries, territories, and islands. At this time, Baha'is resided in thirty-five countries, and it would not be until 1937, when the religion's administrative institutions were better developed, that the project would be initiated, but even the dark hours of World War I could not diminish 'Abdu'l-Baha's vision.

'Abdu'l-Baha's humanitarian qualities were also exemplified during this period. The disruption of normal life that the war caused led to food shortages and the fear of famine. The Baha'i leader responded by supplying

Akká and Haifa with wheat from family-owned lands in the Jordan Valley and near the shores of the Sea of Galilee. For this effort, he was invested with the insignia of Knighthood of the British Empire on April 27, 1920.

On November 28, 1921, 'Abdu'l-Baha died. For twenty-nine years he had been the recognized leader of the Baha'i Faith. While it is not believed that he received revelations from God in the manner of his father, Baha'is do accept that he was divinely inspired and guided. Consequently, Baha'is believe that in him "the incompatible characteristics of a human nature and superhuman knowledge and perfection have been blended and are completely harmonized."[17]

SHOGHI EFFENDI AND THE RISE OF THE ADMINISTRATIVE ORDER (1921–1957)

Some time before his death, 'Abdu'l-Baha wrote his *Will and Testament*. In it he designated his grandson, Shoghi Rabbání, as "the Guardian of the Cause of God"; that is, the Baha'i Guardian. The validity of the will was subsequently challenged by both the followers of Mírzá Muhammad-'Alí, who argued that, through blood lines, 'Abdu'l-Baha's half brother was the rightful heir to leadership of the Baha'i community, and later by several American Baha'is, the most prominent being Ruth White, who claimed the document was a forgery. The former were able to cause some disruption in a number of Baha'i communities, and the latter attracted a small group of supporters in the United States and Germany, but among the majority of Baha'is, their claims went unheeded.

Shoghi Rabbání, or Shoghi Effendi as he is popularly known to Baha'is, was only twenty-four years old when he learned that he had been appointed by 'Abdu'l-Baha to lead the small but expanding Baha'i world community.[18] Perhaps because of his youth or the extreme stress of such a daunting task, the initial years of Shoghi Effendi's leadership were marked by periodic withdrawals from Haifa. Both in 1922 and 1924, he remained in Europe for periods lasting up to eight months. During the 1922 absence, he even left the direction of all Baha'i affairs in the hands of 'Abdu'l-Baha's sister, Bahiyyih Khánum. Only after 1926 does it appear that he was finally able to completely accept the leadership responsibilities that had suddenly been cast upon him.

Shoghi Effendi set two main goals for the Baha'i community: first, that its various national and local bodies evolve from a loosely knit conglomeration of semi-independent units into a unified and coordinated administrative system, and second, that the Baha'i Faith establish itself as an independent religion. The first required the construction of viable local, national, and international institutions that could provide the religion's scattered communities with an established basis of legitimate authority. The second goal involved clearly distinguishing the faith of Baha'u'llah from the religion of Islam.

During 'Abdu'l-Baha's lifetime, a national institution that administered the affairs of the various communities under its jurisdiction had been introduced in the United States and Canada. Under Shoghi Effendi's directive, in 1927 the American community adopted a Baha'i National Constitution, which gave its National Spiritual Assembly a firm basis in law. By 1934 the Baha'i Guardian had created national spiritual assemblies based on the American model in the following countries/regions: Iran, Iraq, India-Burma, Great Britain, Germany, Egypt-Sudan, and Australia-New Zealand. Likewise, *The By-Laws of the Spiritual Assembly of the Baha'is of the City of New York*, which was drafted in 1931, served as a model for local communities around the globe.

The Guardian's organizational designs ran into immediate difficulties with the rebellion of 'Abdu'l-Baha's former secretary and interpreter, Ahmad Sohrab, who believed that Shoghi Effendi was killing the spirit of the Baha'i cause by making it overly authoritarian in structure. Arguing for a more inclusive vision, he joined with others in 1929 to form the New History Society. Shoghi Effendi responded by pronouncing the organization distinct from the Baha'i community. The conflict resulted in Ahmad Sohrab being declared a "covenant-breaker," a designation equivalent to excommunication, with the addition that the individual is to be shunned by all Baha'is.

Shoghi Effendi's effort to create an independent Baha'i identity started with his own lifestyle. A prime example lay in the fact that whereas 'Abdu'l-Baha regularly visited a mosque, the Baha'i Guardian never entered one. According to his wife, Rúhíyyih Rabbání, "What local people had suspected—that the Baha'i Cause was really something quite different—became blatantly clear."[19] To his mind, there were no Muslim Baha'is, Christian Baha'is, or Zoroastrian Baha'is; there were only Baha'is. His endeavor was unexpectedly aided on May 10, 1925, when an Egyptian law court in Beba, after hearing a divorce case involving Baha'is and their Muslim wives, concluded that because of its peculiar laws and institutions the Baha'i Faith was not to be considered part of Islam.

In 1937 Shoghi Effendi launched the first of three systematic teaching campaigns designed to spread Baha'u'llah's message across the entire planet. In so doing, he was finally initiating the first phase of the scheme set down in 'Abdu'l-Baha's *Tablets of the Divine Plan*. Known as the Seven

Year Plan, the campaign was directed mainly toward the American communities. Its goals included the establishment of at least one Baha'i community in every state of the United States, province of Canada, and republic of Latin America. All countries in which Baha'i communities already existed were called upon to extend teaching activities, increase the translation of Baha'i literature, develop educational courses, and work toward the purchasing of properties or buildings to be used as future national centers. By the time of its completion in April 1944, the goals of the plan related to the Americas were achieved, and numerous Baha'i communities throughout the world had grown and been strengthened.

After a two-year respite, the Second Seven Year Plan was initiated. Like its predecessor, the new campaign called on the Baha'i communities in various countries to continue to expand their activities in the vital areas of teaching, publication of literature, and community education. Moreover, it outlined a methodical teaching campaign for Europe similar in its objectives to the previous operation in the Americas.

The latter years of the Second Seven Year Plan saw the introduction of two new institutions designed to fortify the Baha'i administrative structure on the international level: the International Baha'i Council and the Hands of the Cause. The former, composed of eight members appointed by the Guardian and intended to be the forerunner of a future Baha'i international court, initially served the purpose of providing a liaison between the Faith and the new state of Israel. The second was a group of nineteen individuals (later expanded to twenty-seven), also appointed by Shoghi Effendi, who were given the responsibilities of overseeing teaching activities and protecting the community from internal strife and division. The Hands also became vital links of communication between national Baha'i communities and the Guardian in Haifa.

The success of the Second Seven Year Plan was marked by the creation of four new national spiritual assemblies. These administrative bodies were formed in the regions of Central America, South America, Canada, and Italy-Switzerland,[20] bringing the total number of such institutions in the Baha'i world to twelve. At the conclusion of the plan in 1953, Shoghi Effendi felt that the movement was now strong enough to launch his most ambitious program of expansion.

Four international teaching conferences held successively in Kampala, Uganda; Wilmette, Illinois; Stockholm, Sweden; and New Delhi, India, signaled the beginning of the Ten Year Crusade. Shoghi Effendi notified all Baha'i communities around the world that the time was right for a "world-embracing Spiritual Crusade involving the simultaneous initiation of twelve national Ten Year Crusades and the concerted effort of all

National Spiritual Assemblies of the Baha'i world aiming at the immediate extension of Baha'u'llah's spiritual domain as well as the eventual establishment of the structure of His administrative order in all remaining Sovereign States, [and] Principal Dependencies ... scattered over the surface of the entire planet."[21] The major objectives of the Ten Year Crusade included almost doubling the number of countries in which the Baha'i Faith was established from 131 to 236, doubling the amount of translated literature, and quadrupling the number of national spiritual assemblies to forty-eight.

It was also during the years of Shoghi Effendi's Guardianship that two significant architectural goals were accomplished. The first was the completion of the American House of Worship (*Mashriqu'l-Adkhár*) in Wilmette, Illinois, on the shores of Lake Michigan. The ground breaking for the temple had occurred on May 1, 1912, in a ceremony attended by 'Abdu'l-Baha. Construction, however, did not begin in earnest until 1920, and it was not until May 1, 1953, that the building was officially dedicated. The second was the raising of the golden-domed superstructure to the Shrine of the Bab on Mt. Carmel in Israel, which housed the remains of 'Alí Muhammad. In time, both buildings would become internationally significant symbols of the burgeoning Baha'i world community.

THE FAITH UNDER THE LEADERSHIP OF THE HANDS OF THE CAUSE (1957–1963)

In the midst of the Ten Year Crusade, Shoghi Effendi suddenly died. In November 1957, he succumbed to a heart attack in London after being bedridden by a case of the Asian flu. The Baha'i world was in an initial state of shock, and the dismay only deepened when it was revealed that their Guardian had not left a will nor appointed a successor. To avert a leadership crisis, the Hands of the Cause met two weeks later in Haifa, and on November 25 they issued a statement to the Baha'i world announcing that until such time that the supreme legislative institution (referred to in the writings of Baha'u'llah, 'Abdu'l-Baha, and Shoghi Effendi as the Universal House of Justice) could be elected, a group of nine Hand members would guide the Faith. Twenty-six of the twenty-seven Hand members signed a document to this effect, and all the national and regional assemblies agreed to recognize their authority.

In November 1958, the Council of Hands announced that the Universal House of Justice would be elected in April 1963. A year later, they also proclaimed that in 1961 the heretofore appointed International Baha'i Council would be replaced by a new council elected by the members of all national spiritual assemblies. At this point, Mason Remey, a Hands of the Cause member and president of the International Baha'i Council, responded by declaring that, according to 'Abdu'l-Baha's *Will and Testament* and Shoghi Effendi's later pronouncements, the Guardianship had to continue in order for the Baha'i Faith to receive divine guidance. He subsequently claimed that, because of his position as president of the International Baha'i Council and his close relationship with Shoghi Effendi, he should be the new Guardian. He then openly made an appeal to the world's Baha'is to accept his claim. The Hands of the Cause reacted by eventually declaring him and his scattered followers covenant-breakers. Thereafter, Remey went on to establish what he called the Orthodox Baha'i Faith, remnants of which still exist today.

Despite the loss of Shoghi Effendi and the disruption surrounding Remey's activities, most of the goals of the Ten Year Crusade were accomplished. By 1963 Baha'is resided in 259 countries and territories, and fifty-six national spiritual assemblies had been formed. In addition, three new temples had been constructed in Uganda, Australia, and West Germany. Perhaps the most significant development during this period was the introduction of a new technique for spreading Baha'u'llah's message. To Baha'is it came to be known as "mass teaching."

The mass teaching technique differed from previous policy in that it did not require an individual to have extensive knowledge of the Baha'i teachings, laws, or administrative apparatus before becoming a member of the community. Acceptance of Baha'u'llah's religious claims was deemed sufficient. In practice this meant that becoming a Baha'i could be a reaction of the heart as much as a response of the head. Specific doctrines, laws, and administrative procedures could be learned, but love for Baha'u'llah was considered primary. Thus, while at one time it might take individuals weeks or months, perhaps even years, to declare themselves believers, with the advent of mass teaching, people could be enrolled after an initial contact with a Baha'i teacher.

The initial use of the mass teaching approach can actually be traced back to the final years of Shoghi Effendi's Guardianship and the efforts of two individuals: Enoch Olinga and Dr. Rahmatu'llah Muhájir, both of whom would be appointed Hands of the Cause during the Guardian's final year. In Uganda, Olinga enrolled several dozen members of the Teso ethnic group in this manner and then expanded his work into the Cameroons with similar results. In 1954, Dr. Muhájir was successful in bringing into the Baha'i community large numbers of believers on the Indonesian island of Mantawai, where he was acting as a physician in the Indonesian Ministry of Health.

It was in India, however, in the early 1960s, that mass teaching accelerated and thereafter became characteristic of Baha'i teaching efforts in many parts of the world. Two events signaled the beginning of the process that was destined to fundamentally change the demographics of the Baha'i world community, and both involved the efforts of Dr. Muhájir, now a member of the Hands of the Cause. One was a visit by a Baha'i teacher to a Bhilala tribal village in the state of Madhya Pradesh, and the other was a teaching conference held in a nearby village that was dominated by members of a Hindu caste of low social standing, who were referred to as "untouchables." In both instances, hundreds of villagers declared themselves Baha'is. An intensive teaching campaign by local Baha'is was launched throughout a number of rural districts in Madhya Pradesh, and during the next few months the Indian Baha'i community expanded its membership from less than 1,000 to more than 89,000.[22] A new day in the field of Baha'i missionary activity had dawned.

THE UNIVERSAL HOUSE OF JUSTICE (1963–PRESENT)

In April 1963, some 300 members of the world's national spiritual assemblies met in Haifa, Israel, to elect the first Universal House of Justice. After the nine-member, all-male body had been selected, the delegates journeyed to London. There, along with 7,000 Baha'is from throughout the world, they celebrated the centenary of Baha'u'llah's initial disclosure in Baghdad that he was He whom God shall make manifest. From this point forward, supreme authority in the Baha'i community was to be vested in the Universal House of Justice. The body was to be elected every five years, and its legislative decisions were to be considered infallible.

To help them in their administrative role, over the years various Universal Houses of Justice have created several additional institutions whose structure and scope of responsibility will be discussed in Chapter 4. In general, these bodies have been given the task of assisting national institutions in spreading and defending the Faith and acting as channels of communication between those national institutions and the Baha'i World Center in Haifa.

In the manner of the former Guardian, Houses of Justice have designed a number of worldwide teaching plans ranging in length from two to nine years. In their own words, the driving aim of the plans was "to carry the message of Baha'u'llah to every stratum of society, not only in the towns and cities, but also in the villages and country districts where the virus of materialism has had much less effect on the lives of men."[23] Although the plans did not always meet their specific goals, for the most part they produced a continual growth rate that by the time of the new millennium allowed Baha'i leadership to claim a world community of some 5 million believers.

Four main dynamics have characterized the nature of the Baha'i world community during the last quarter of the twentieth century. The first has been the substantial growth in believers as a result of the continuation of mass teaching, especially in areas of Asia, Africa, and South America. Here India again took the lead, and with a reported 2 million declarations became the largest Baha'i national community in the world. Sizable increases were also seen in Vietnam, Kenya, Bolivia, South Africa, the Philippines, and Congo. Even though the American community remained one of the wealthiest and most influential in the Baha'i world, numerical progress there was not as dramatic; as of the year 2000, Baha'is claimed 150,000 followers in the United States. The same can be said for Europe, where in 1997 Baha'is numbered a little more than 50,000. In the Middle East, whatever growth has taken place has been primarily a result of natural internal increases. This has led a prominent Baha'i sociologist to observe that by the late 1980s the Baha'i Faith had changed from an essentially Middle Eastern community into one that was predominantly third world in composition.[24]

Another major factor that needs to be mentioned at this time is the impact that the Iranian Revolution had on the Baha'i world community. During its short history, the Iranian Baha'i populace has experienced periodic outbursts of persecution, but starting in 1960 during the reign of Mohammed Reza Shah Pahlavi there was relative calm. The situation drastically changed following the 1979 February Revolution and the establishment of the Islamic Republic of Iran. All Baha'i institutions were closed down, numerous Baha'is were arrested, many lost their jobs or had their financial assets taken over, and some community leaders were executed. The reasons given for such hostility ranged from apostasy to never-proved charges of spying for either the United States, Great Britain, or Israel. Baha'i communities around the world responded by petitioning their own governments to officially condemn the attacks, and thus the persecutions acted as a rallying point for Baha'i unity. Furthermore, the dispersion of Iranian Baha'i refugees to a number of Western Baha'i communities resulted in the appearance of a new social dynamic. Despite the common element of faith shared by their members, many local Baha'i communities now had to face issues that resulted from the introduction into their midst of distinct cultural perspectives. This is a significant theme that will be discussed in greater detail in Part II, when it can be examined in the context of several specific American local communities.

A third dynamic that has characterized Baha'i activities around the world since the early 1980s has been the introduction of social and economic development projects into the religion's teaching and consolidation plans. By 1983, Baha'i leadership had come to realize that if the Faith was going to have any significant impact on the social fabric of life, it could not remain primarily a religion of words. Rather, it would have to reach out and openly display its principles in the form of specific programs that spoke to the social and economic needs of its members. Thus, in its 1983 Ridván message, an annual address sent every April, to the Baha'i world, the Universal House of Justice stated:

> We may therefore be utterly confident that the new throb of energy now vibrating throughout the Cause will empower it to meet the oncoming challenges of assisting, as maturity and resources allow, the development of the social and economic life of peoples, of collaborating with the forces leading towards the establishment of order in the world, of influencing the exploitation and constructive uses of modern technology, and in all these ways enhancing the prestige and progress of the Faith and uplifting the conditions of the generality of mankind.[25]

Two examples of such projects are the Indore Baha'i Vocational Institute for Rural Women in India, and the Guayami Cultural Center in Panama. The Indore Institute was founded in 1984 for the purpose of providing both basic education and technical training to rural women, especially those of tribal origin. Besides operating a radio station, the Guayami Cultural Center also trains secondary school teachers and circulates information on health care and farming. By the mid-1990s, there were some 1,300 Baha'i-sponsored social and economic development projects operating in more than 100 countries worldwide, most of them small in both scope and scale but dedicated to the actualization of Baha'i principles.

Finally, the last few decades have seen the completion of several architectural projects designed in part to better visually acquaint the public with the Baha'i Faith. At least one Baha'i house of worship now exists on each of the populated continents, and Akká and Haifa have become the home of a number of significant structures including the Shrine at Bahjí, where Baha'u'llah is buried, and the administrative buildings of the Universal House of Justice. In terms of public awareness, three locations stand out: the Wilmette, Illinois, House of Worship, the New Delhi House of Worship and the terraced gardens on Mt. Carmel. The first has become the main symbol of the Baha'i Faith in the West. The second, which was completed in 1986 and is more commonly known as the Lotus Temple, has been the recipient of several architectural awards and admits up to 2.5 million visitors a year. On some Hindu holy days it has attracted as many as 100,000 visitors. The Baha'i gardens in Haifa, which surround the Shrine of the Bab, are composed of nineteen separate terraces with fountains and promenades stretching from the top of Mt. Carmel to its foothills. Like both the Wilmette and New Delhi Houses of Worship, the Baha'i gardens have become a major tourist attraction.

At the beginning of the third millennium, the Baha'i Faith stands poised to enter a new phase in its historical development. Having evolved over the last 150 years from an obscure sect within Iranian Shi'ism into what some sociologists might term a new religious movement, it seems well positioned to turn into a full-fledged world religion. Like other religions, it faces the challenge of accommodating the forces of modernity to the standards of tradition. In this vein, Baha'i leadership not only has to resolve certain questions related to Baha'i identity, it must also come to terms with such issues as the male-only restriction to membership on the Universal House of Justice, the growing tension between a number of Baha'i scholars and administrators, and its position regarding the future relationship between religion and state. One thing, however, is certain: namely, that millions of believers and non-Baha'is alike have been drawn to the beliefs and principles espoused by Baha'u'llah and his son, 'Abdu'l-Baha. It is now time to examine these ideas in greater detail.

2

Beliefs and Principles

During his years in captivity, Baha'u'llah composed a large number of treatises and tablets that have become the foundation for Baha'i beliefs and principles. 'Abdu'l-Baha's extensive writings have also been added to the Baha'i canon, as have Shoghi Effendi's interpretations and elucidations. The beliefs and principles discussed below are those that are currently held by the Baha'i world community as expressed in official Baha'i literature and commented upon by scholars working in the field of Baha'i studies. Since ideas change over time as a result of reinterpretation, historical variations in Baha'i doctrine will be noted when applicable.

THE TRANSCENDENCE OF GOD

In *Gleanings from the Writings of Baha'u'llah*, the prophet and founder of the Baha'i Faith states the following: "Exalted, immeasurably exalted, art Thou above the strivings of mortal man to unravel Thy mystery, to describe Thy glory, or even to hint at the nature of Thine Essence."[1] Hence, God's essence is conceived as unknowable and absolutely transcendent. God is indivisible, unchanging, and all powerful—above all names and free from all human likeness. In the *Kitáb-i Íqán* (*Book of Certitude*), Baha'u'llah claims: "To every discerning and illumined heart it is evident that God, the unknowable Essence, the divine Being, is immensely exalted beyond every human attribute, such as corporeal existence, ascent and descent, egress and regress.[2]

Like the Bab before him, Baha'u'llah taught that God created the universe through an act of will. Unlike most Judeo-Christian conceptions, creation does not appear out of nothing (ex nihilo) but is seen to be continually flowing out of the divine realm (though always absolutely distinct from God), and thus, like its source, it is eternal. The argument is made that since God has always been and the creative will is part of God's essence, it necessarily follows that there can never have been a time when there was no creation. Consequently, all existent things are seen by Baha'u'llah to have entered into creation as part of the dynamic natural grace of their Ultimate Source.

While the God of which Baha'u'llah speaks is in essence beyond all human understanding, that God is also a personal God who is capable of communicating with creation. In this sense the Baha'i notion of deity follows the pattern found in many religions whereby even when portrayed in the most abstract of ways, God maintains a personal, I-Thou relationship with mankind:

> O Son of Man! Veiled in My immemorial being and in the ancient eternity
> of My essence, I knew My love for thee; therefore I created thee, have
> engraved on thee Mine image and revealed to thee My beauty.[3]

Moreover, God has numerous attributes, such as mercy, compassion, power, and justice, and it is by knowledge of these attributes that man can be said to have knowledge of God. It was Baha'u'llah's conviction that it is through the divine attributes that mankind can relate personally to a God who is not a person.

THE CONCEPT OF MANIFESTATION (*MAZHAR-I ILÁHÍ*)

Since it is impossible for created beings to comprehend God's essence, Baha'u'llah taught that periodically God sends forth prophets or messengers, who he referred to as Manifestations of God. The nature of a Manifestation in Baha'i theology is different, however, from the traditional understanding of prophet or messenger in that in his person are found all the names and attributes of God. Beyond displaying the divine qualities, Baha'u'llah goes so far as to claim that the essence of the Manifestation is completely unique; he is a distinct category of creation to whom other human beings cannot even be compared. Though he inhabits a human body, the body of the Manifestation is to ordinary human bodies as diamond is to stone.[4] It should be made clear, however, that the Manifestation is not viewed as divine incarnation. While no creature can even claim to exist when compared with the Manifestation, a clear distinction is always made between the Manifestation and God. The Manifestation acts like a mirror; he reflects the sun, but he is not the embodiment of the sun.

Essentially, the Manifestation fulfills three purposes. First, he reflects the glory of God in the realm of creation. Here he serves what might be termed a spiritual/aesthetic purpose. Second, since he embodies the names and attributes of God, he becomes the communicative link between God and mankind. Whatever mankind can know of God is grasped through the person and message of the Manifestation. In this regard, Baha'u'llah claims that the first duty of every human being is the recognition of the Manifestation for his age. Third, the Manifestation acts in the capacity of a divine physician. His example and teachings form the foundation for human progress, and the failure to recognize and follow him results in social decay. As 'Abdu'l-Baha stated: "The world of humanity is sick, but that skilled Physician hath the healing remedy ... and the dressing for every wound."[5]

Although the Manifestation has a divine side to his nature, he experiences the same bodily and cultural limitations as other human beings. He is subject to hunger and thirst and is restricted in terms of worldly knowledge. For example, he does not inherently know languages other than those in which he has been raised or educated. Consequently, at one level the Manifestation is a humble servant of God, and at another he mirrors the divine perfections to a wayward mankind.[6]

PROGRESSIVE REVELATION AND THE PRINCIPLE OF RELIGIOUS UNITY

Throughout the writings of Baha'u'llah and 'Abdu'l-Baha, reference is made to a number of previous Manifestations of God. For example, Baha'u'llah speaks of Moses, Jesus, Muhammad, and the Bab in this manner, and, according to Shoghi Effendi, 'Abdu'l-Baha understood both Buddha and Krishna to be in this category. Moreover, the Manifestations are not viewed as purely independent entities. Just as the sun that rises and sets each day is in reality the same sun, so the Manifestations are understood to be one and the same. 'Abdu'l-Baha uses the mirror analogy to explain this doctrine: "The Divine Manifestations are so many different mirrors, because they have a special individuality, but that which is reflected in the mirrors is the same sun."[7] Where Manifestations differ is in the intensity, not the quality, of the light they reflect.

The body of ideas within Baha'i theology that explains the appearance and impact of the Manifestations of God is known as Progressive Revelation. In general, this doctrine holds that the world's religions have all been part of a dynamic historical process whose driving force has been the Manifestations. From the dawn of human history to the present day, Manifestations have revealed to mankind the laws and commandments of God that have subsequently become the catalysts for the development of civilization. Over time the initial creative forces within each religion begin to weaken, and there follows a period of slow but inevitable decline. The resulting religious and cultural deterioration creates the need for a renewed discharge of spiritual energy, which, in turn, is supplied by the appearance of the next Manifestation. Ironically, the new Manifestation is generally rejected and often persecuted by contemporary religious and political leaders, but his teachings nevertheless become the seeds for an eventual spiritual rebirth. Baha'is believe, therefore, that despite the initial dismissal of Baha'u'llah's message by the kings and princes of his time, as the latest Manifestation of God, his religion will eventually result in the establishment of a new world order. Thus, when it comes to an understanding of the dynamics of civilization, Baha'i scriptures adhere to a cyclical but progressively unfolding view of history. In this vein, one is tempted to compare the Baha'i view to certain aspects of the rise-and-fall model of civilizations employed by the British historian Arnold Toynbee in his voluminous book, *A Study of History*.

The paradigm of Progressive Revelation leads naturally into the principle of religious unity. Also known among Baha'is as the Oneness of Religion, this concept declares that since they have a common divine source, all the world's great religious traditions share fundamental and essential features. Here a distinction is made between the universal truths found in all religions and the diversity of expression that they express as a result of specific historical and cultural factors. The former "consist of faith in God (or in non-theistic terms, Ultimate Reality), existential truths of life, the awakening of human potential and the acquisition of spiritual attributes or virtues."[8] Examples of the historical and cultural expressions of religions are their theological dogmas, specific rites and rituals, ecclesiastical organizations, and traditional mores. It is in relationship to these nonessential components that the Baha'i view of religion can be said to be culturally relative in orientation, for it is at this level of content that the unique features of different religions reside.

As an example of this belief in the twofold nature of every religion, we can briefly inspect the Baha'i approach to Christianity. Holding to the conviction that Jesus of Nazareth was a Manifestation of God, Baha'is assume that Christianity was a major instrument in the overall advancement of spiritual civilization. The religion's essential characteristics were (and are) the faith and trust in God that Jesus maintained, as well as the essential virtues that he taught as found in the Sermon on the Mount. Less objective in nature, but still fundamental, is the sense of spiritual meaning and purpose that he gave to those who proclaimed to follow him. The nonessential aspects of Christianity would include: specific elements related to historical Christology, for example, the doctrine of the trinity and the literal interpretation of the virgin birth; numerous ritualistic components, such as the mass or baptism; the ecclesiastical hierarchies of the churches; and certain cultural mores that were incorporated into its system over time. Regarding the latter, priestly celibacy or various restrictions related to women's social and religious roles come to mind. Needless to say, a similar attitude and approach would apply to the world's other religious traditions.

When it comes to specifics concerning exactly which of the world's religions are to be included within the Baha'i framework of the Oneness of Religion, there is some degree of ambiguity. The more conservative approach is the one that cites Shoghi Effendi's 1936 list of nine existing religions: the Baha'i Faith, the religion of the Bab, Hinduism, Buddhism, Zoroastrianism, Judaism, Christianity, Islam, and the religion of the Sabians.[9] The limitations of such an approach are obvious: certain individual figures such as Confucius, Lao Tzu, and the founder of Sikhism, Guru Nanak, are not included. What is more, the classical Greek and Roman religions and the world's numerous native traditions are excluded. Within this more exclusivist understanding, attempts have been made to broaden the field by referring to some individuals as "minor prophets" who, while not classified as Manifestations of God, are still believed to have been divinely inspired. A case in point is the Hindu avatar, Rama. In a similar vein, the idea of cross-cultural influence has been introduced; for example, the suggestion that Socrates was influenced by the Jewish prophets who in turn represented the Manifestation Moses.

Those who hold to a more inclusive interpretation of the Oneness of Religion see the references in Baha'i scriptures to "all religions" and "all prophets" as being literal while at the same time understanding Shoghi Effendi's reference to nine religions as being symbolic. Since nine is the Baha'i symbol for completeness, its use by the Guardian in this instance can be seen as metaphorically referring to all religions. A similar approach is to interpret the Sabian religion as representing all religions not mentioned in the Qur'an. A good example of the inclusivist approach can be seen in the following statement by the Baha'i philosopher Dann May:

> Clearly then, the Baha'i writings recognize the existence of vast numbers of Manifestations who have appeared in all cultures throughout the history of the human

race. Thus, given such references, the phrase "all the Prophets" is best interpreted as broadly and open-endedly as possible. Such an interpretation would include all known historical prophets, messengers, and founders of the world's religions, whether of the past, present, or future, together with all those whose identity has now been lost. Similarly, the phrase "all religions" should be interpreted in the widest possible context to include all known existing religions together with those that are no longer practiced.[10]

In line with such thinking is the recent position taken by some Baha'i thinkers that Native American prophets could be accepted into Baha'i doctrine.[11]

Regardless of the model used by contemporary Baha'is to determine religious legitimacy, one thing is certain: the Baha'i holy figures vigorously opposed the idea of religious exclusivism. The belief that any one religion contains the sole truth or provides the only path leading to salvation was expressly denied.

THE NATURE AND PURPOSE OF MAN

In a series of table talks in Haifa with American Laura Clifford Barney, later published under the title, *Some Answered Questions*, 'Abdu'l-Baha stated that what made man unique in the world of creation is his possession of a human spirit or rational soul—a nonmaterial reality connected to the body through the functions of the mind. Like the animals, man has a physical body and senses that allow him to experience such things as hunger, thirst, heat, and cold, but his superior intelligence, which is a quality of his soul, permits him to understand in varying degrees himself, the world around him, and the spiritual realities of existence. The soul comes into existence, 'Abdu'l-Baha explained, when the body is created, but it is independent of the body and survives after its death. Although functionally related to the body and the mind, the soul is in essence separate from both and cannot be affected by the infirmities of either.

Whereas man's soul allows him to understand various aspects of reality, according to Baha'u'llah it is the knowledge and love of the source of all existence, that is, God, that is the sole aim of his having been created.[12] All human beings, therefore, have the capacity to know and love God in varying degrees, but to do so they need a teacher who will bring out their potential. This teacher must be a perfect guide; he must possess those divine attributes (names of God) that allow him to be a spiritual educator. This perfect teacher is none other than the Manifestation of God.

Once human beings begin to know the attributes of God through belief in the Manifestation, they must express their love and knowledge in the realm of action. Accordingly, Baha'i doctrine holds that all individuals have free will; although their environment may influence their attitudes, it is through their own volition that they can reach their potential. The emphasis placed on action in the Baha'i writings demonstrates that the world is not to be renounced. Rather, as 'Abdu'l-Baha indicated, man should develop his spirituality by participating in the building of an ever-advancing civilization: "If we are true Baha'is speech is not needed. Our actions will help in the world, will spread civilization, will help the progress of science, and cause the arts to develop. Without action, nothing in the material world can be accomplished, neither can the words unaided advance a man in the spiritual Kingdom."[13] In this sense, the Baha'i worldview contains an element of what the famed German sociologist, Max Weber, termed "inner-worldly asceticism," whereby the world is seen to be a workshop for God's activities. However, unlike the Christian variety of this phenomenon, namely, the Calvinistic form of Puritanism, from a Baha'i perspective the primary aim of work in the world is not the winning of individual salvation but the uplift of all humanity.

Since the human soul is created with the quality of pure potentiality, there is no room in Baha'i thinking for the idea that it is tainted by original sin. Whatever sinful actions the soul may manifest are a result of its refusal to express the divine attributes. Furthermore, the existence of independent and positive evil is denied. 'Abdu'l-Baha stated: "Briefly, the intellectual realities, such as all the qualities and admirable perfections of man, are purely good, and exist. Evil is simply their nonexistence.... Then it is evident that all evils return to non-existence. Good exists, evil is non-existent."[14]

When the body dies, the soul is neither reincarnated nor consigned to a permanent spiritual abode such as heaven or hell. In accord with the dynamic and evolutionary approach to existence found in other areas of Baha'i thought, the worlds of God are seen to be countless, and the soul traverses them in a process that is never ending.

A Baha'i belief directly related to the nature of the human soul is the idea that as a category of creation, man has always existed. Recalling Baha'u'llah's teaching that God and creation both exist eternally, it follows that as "the gem of creation," man has always been. What has changed over time is the physical form man has taken. It would therefore appear that Baha'i doctrine holds to a position somewhere between contemporary notions of evolution and creationism. As a "species essence," man is a timeless reality and part of God's eternal creation; as a biological species, man has gone through numerous physical changes and adaptations in time and space. The exact relationship between these two dimensions is a question that Baha'i scholars are currently debating.[15]

THE UNITY OF RELIGION AND SCIENCE

The spiritual foundation upon which Baha'u'llah and 'Abdu'l-Baha's thinking was built was the belief that behind or beyond the material forms of creation lies a timeless and eternal sphere of reality. While the principles of this reality can be rationally explained, an understanding of its deeper truths is primarily a result of inspiration or, in the case of Baha'u'llah, divine revelation. From the perspective of modern science such abstract speculation is considered out of bounds, as there is no way to universally verify its conclusions. Yet, one of the elemental themes stressed by 'Abdu'l-Baha during his visits to Europe and North America was the unity of science and religion. How can this assertion be accounted for?

In effect, 'Abdu'l-Baha posited a dualistic framework. In the world of creation, scientific truth is to be prized, for it is based on universally accepted methods of observation and measurement as well as rational thinking. In this realm, if religious teachings are found to contradict sound science, then it is religion that must give way. Thus the ideas that the earth is only several thousand years old or that pairs of all existent animals were placed by Noah on an ark are to be considered false. The value that such traditional beliefs might have would be strictly allegorical; their content should not be taken literally. Similarly, religious stories containing miracles, whereby the laws of nature are contradicted, should not be claimed to be literally true. Rather, their symbolic meaning should be sought. However, when it comes to the eternal realm, 'Abdu'l-Baha, like his father, believed that scientific knowledge was limited. While it could point beyond the realm of creation, science alone could not grasp the divine truths nor create essential human values. This was the domain of the manifestations and prophets.

In the manner of modern scientific thinking, Baha'u'llah and 'Abdu'l-Baha taught that the entire universe is unified by interlinking laws and processes. Moreover, they held to the notion that reason and the human intellect could probe the mysteries of creation to ever-expanding degrees of depth and insight without exhausting the extent of those mysteries. In this sense, they saw science not only as a practical tool but as an artistic venture that in the final analysis culminated in the glorification of God.

In general, therefore, Baha'is have found little difficulty in accepting the findings of modern science. The one major exception has been in relationship to the question of evolution, where, as mentioned above, there is an ongoing debate regarding 'Abdu'l-Baha's commentary on the human species as "having always been distinct." The significance of this debate goes beyond mere theoretical disagreements concerning the evolutionary process and strikes at the heart of Baha'i thinking. More conservative interpretations would see 'Abdu'l-Baha's pronouncement as divinely inspired and therefore true, whereas a more liberal perspective would see any scientific statement made by 'Abdu'l-Baha as being bound by the very principles that he supported.

THE ONENESS OF MANKIND

At the core of Baha'i social philosophy lies the principle of the Oneness of Mankind. 'Abdu'l-Baha designated it the foundation of the Faith of God, and Shoghi Effendi referred to it as the most vital of all the principles found in Baha'u'llah's tablets. According to this ideal, all people, regardless of race, ethnicity, gender, religious background, or social standing, are believed to be equal in the eyes of God. They may differ in their potential capacities and will of necessity attain to different intellectual and economic stations in life, but they are all children of the same creator. The Baha'i Faith's social principles, therefore, can be viewed as an extension of its theological beliefs. The emphasis placed on the oneness and unity of the Godhead results in a corresponding drive toward unity in the human sphere. In the words of Baha'u'llah: "Ye are the fruits of one tree, and the leaves of one branch."[16]

The primary adjunct to the principle of the Oneness of Mankind is the ideal of the elimination of all prejudice: racial, ethnic, nationalistic, religious, or gender. Both Baha'u'llah and 'Abdu'l-Baha emphasized that since God loved all human beings equally, no individual had the right to glorify himself over another or look upon another with scorn and contempt. Ideally this means that Baha'is should be constantly striving to abolish all notions of basic human inequality within their communities.

One of the most striking examples of the ideal of equality among the faithful is the lack of any type of priesthood or body of scholars who are considered bearers of special knowledge or guides to spiritual enlightenment. With the death of Shoghi Effendi, official interpretation of Baha'i scriptures came to an end. While the Universal House of Justice "elucidates" upon the writings, all believers should have the right to read and understand the writings for themselves with the qualification that no individual can claim his or her understandings to be authoritative. According to Baha'u'llah, in this day men and women are meant to investigate truth for themselves.[17] No body of clerics can guide them, and they should not blindly follow the path of tradition.

In essence, then, the principle of the Oneness of Mankind involves Baha'is accepting a level of individual identity that is based upon an

unprejudiced view of human reality. That identity reaches beyond traditional group associations. A Baha'i should see himself or herself primarily
as a member of mankind and only secondarily as belonging to a specific
nation, class, race, or ethnic group.

THE EQUALITY OF MEN AND WOMEN

An important corollary to the Baha'i principle of the Oneness of Mankind is the equality of men and women. In his 1998 study of Baha'u'llah's
thought and its relationship to the modern world, the University of
Michigan historian Juan R. I. Cole suggested that a theological grounding
for the Baha'i prophet's positive view of women came from feminine
descriptions of God found in his mystical poetry.[18] Together with the
impact of certain reformist influences, both Western and Middle Eastern
in origin, this theology formed the basis for much of Baha'u'llah's thinking from the 1870s onward. While it was not completely unique within
modernist Islamic thought, it certainly challenged many Middle Eastern
social norms regarding gender issues. Even more radical in terms of potential interpretation were the Baha'i prophet's several references to women
"being as men." Here Baha'u'llah appears to have detached notions of
masculinity and femininity from their strictly biological understanding and
instead viewed them as types of spiritual qualities that are distributed
among both genders.[19] For example, bravery, which was traditionally associated with masculinity, is depicted by Baha'u'llah as being present in
many women while being absent in many men.

'Abdu'l-Baha shared his father's views concerning the expansion of
women's roles, and he likely had those opinions bolstered by his contact
with a number of strong-willed Western females. In a tablet to the women
of the East, he referred to their Western counterparts as having won the
prize of excellence from men in the teaching of the Faith and then went
on to add: "Soon they will soar like the birds of the Concourse on high
in the far corners of the world and will guide the people and reveal to
them the divine mysteries."[20]

Baha'u'llah and 'Abdu'l-Baha's views on women have meant that female
believers in contemporary Baha'i communities have obtained a fairly high
degree of individual freedom. This statement must be understood as being
relative to the cultural values encompassing individual communities, but
in general it is probably fair to say that the social roles available to women
have increased. Education for girls is supported, women are encouraged
to seek professions, worship is not segregated along gender lines, and
administrative positions are open to all. The one seeming anomaly to this

situation is the male-only restriction for membership on the Universal House of Justice, which is based on the fact that Baha'u'llah used the masculine term *rijál* (men) when referring to the institution's members. The restriction has been maintained since the time of the House's inception in 1963, though recently a number of Baha'i scholars have pointed out that Baha'u'llah's use of *rijál* in other contexts was such as to go beyond gender. Since this issue would seem to be a significant one for Baha'i communities, especially those in Europe and North America, it will be addressed in Part II.

Symbolically speaking, it is the Babi poet, Táhirih, who has come to represent for Baha'is the ideal of women's equality. Baha'i legend has it that just before she was strangled to death in 1852, she told her assassins that while they might kill her, they would never be able to stop the emancipation of women.

WORLD GOVERNMENT AND UNIVERSAL EDUCATION

In a tablet written to the descendants of the Bab (who are known as *Afnán*), Baha'u'llah stated that although at one time love of country was considered an essential element of the Faith of God, "The Tongue of Grandeur hath, however, in the day of His manifestation proclaimed: 'It is not his to boast who loveth his country, but it is his who loveth the world.'"[21] The sentiment behind this declaration would lead one to believe that Baha'u'llah envisioned for mankind a higher political allegiance than that of the nation state. It should be of no surprise, then, to find that among other peace-oriented admonitions, he called for a union of the nations and a system of collective security. 'Abdu'l-Baha likewise spoke of the necessities of a parliament of man and a supreme tribunal, but it was Shoghi Effendi who wrote most succinctly on this issue. It is worth quoting him at length:

> The unity of the human race, as envisaged by Baha'u'llah, implies the establishment of a world commonwealth in which all nations, races, creeds and classes are closely and permanently united, and which the autonomy of its state members and the personal freedom and initiative of the individuals that compose them are completely safeguarded. This commonwealth must, as far as we can visualize it, consist of a world legislature, whose members will, as the trustees of the whole of mankind, ultimately control the entire resources of all the component nations, and shall enact such laws as are required to regulate the life, satisfy the needs and adjust the relationships of all races and peoples.[22]

Although the Baha'i community supports the United Nations and has established the Baha'i International Community United Nations Office, which cooperates as a nongovernmental organization and participates in regular sessions of several of the organization's commissions, it is evident from the content of Shoghi Effendi's statement that he was not referring to the current United Nations. At present, the exact formulation and structure of this world commonwealth remains speculative, but it is generally expected to evolve out of future conditions and events. Some Baha'i scholars assume that the new system will be based on a theocratic model, while others believe that it will maintain the separation of church and state.[23] Whatever the understanding, belief in the eventual establishment of a new world order has become part and parcel of Baha'i historical thinking.

The writings of the Baha'i holy figures also demonstrated that they understood the necessary relationship between education and the ideal of world citizenship. Without an educated populace whose decisions could be informed by reflective reason rather than rigid tradition or mere superstition, there would be little or no hope for mankind to move toward this new, more expanded sense of identity. Consequently, Baha'u'llah and 'Abdu'l-Baha advocated the implementation of universal education, with 'Abdu'l-Baha giving special emphasis to the necessary instruction of females. Both men agreed that the primary purpose of education should be the realization that "all men are as one soul." All other knowledge, even that which is derived from the more practical sciences, should be seen as secondary in significance. One might term this approach "spiritual pragmatism," since it sees knowledge as valuable only when it acts in the service of religious ideals. It is in this context that one should understand Baha'u'llah's dictum that only those sciences should be studied that are conducive to human progress.

The importance given to education in the Baha'i texts has resulted in many Baha'i communities giving special emphasis to this aspect of social life. The historical record is replete with examples of Baha'i-sponsored support for educational institutions, from the establishment of a school for girls in Tehran at the beginning of the twentieth century to the current operations of educational institutions on nearly every continent. Moreover, in recent decades education has become the focal point of many of the religion's social and economic development projects, and in those countries in Asia, Africa, and the Pacific Islands where mass teaching has become prominent, the establishment of village primary schools has often been a major goal.

Along with the sciences, Baha'u'llah believed that the learning of a world language should be an essential element of the educational process. Linguistic differences not only limit effective communication among peoples, they also help support notions of ethnic and national superiority. In this vein, Baha'u'llah recounts in his *Epistle to the Son of the Wolf* the advice given to Kamál Páshá in Istanbul: "It beseemeth you and the other officials of the Government to convene a gathering and choose one of the divers languages, and likewise one of the existing scripts, or else to create a new language and a new script to be taught children in schools throughout the world."[24] Given this attitude, it is not surprising to find that the relationship between the Baha'i community and the Esperanto movement has had a long and established history. Esperanto, a universal language, was highly praised by 'Abdu'l-Baha, and since the time of its introduction, many Baha'is have learned the language and actively supported its establishment. For example, in the 1920s and 1930s, a number of outstanding individual Baha'is, such as Martha Root, Lidia Zamenhof, and Hermann Grossmann, were involved in the Esperanto movement, and the Baha'i Esperanto League was later founded at the beginning of the 1970s. Along similar lines, in October 1995, the Baha'i International Community United Nations Office made a number of proposals as to how the United Nations could be reformed, one of which included the selection of one of the living languages (or an artificial language) to become a primary instrument of communication in all of the international body's affairs.[25]

As much as Baha'u'llah, 'Abdu'l-Baha, and Shoghi Effendi opposed blatant nationalism, the Baha'i ideal of world citizenry should not be taken to infer that the Faith's members are not meant to demonstrate loyalty to their individual governments. On numerous occasions, Shoghi Effendi reiterated that Baha'is must follow the laws of the countries in which they reside and that any overt political activity on their part was strictly forbidden. While Baha'is are permitted to vote in elections and voice their own political opinions, they are not allowed to join in partisan politics by becoming members of political parties or running for political office. The only exception to governmental obedience is in those cases where Baha'is are required to renounce their belief in Baha'u'llah.

THE ELIMINATION OF THE EXTREMES
OF WEALTH AND POVERTY

One of the paramount virtues extolled in the Baha'i writings is justice. In *The Hidden Words*, Baha'u'llah goes so far as to say that it is the best-beloved of all things in his sight.[26] Justice, moreover, was not merely understood by the Baha'i prophet to refer to individual relationships. Structural justice involves the elimination of political and social policies that result in human exploitation and the unfair distribution of resources.

Baha'u'llah was appalled by the extremes of poverty and wealth he observed during his stay in Istanbul, and he understood that much of the cause of the inequities had to do with government policies and corruption. 'Abdu'l-Baha was likewise committed to the economic side of social justice. While he did not criticize wealth per se, especially when it was accumulated as a result of an individual's own labor, he did comment that wealth was really commendable if the entire population was wealthy and that the true purpose of wealth was not self-indulgence but the dedicated use of its fruits in the maintenance of the welfare of society.[27]

When it came to specific economic mechanisms that would bring about an alleviation of the extremes of poverty and wealth, Baha'u'llah was less direct. As Shoghi Effendi later commented in a letter to an individual believer: "The contribution of the Faith to this subject is essentially indirect, as it consists of the application of spiritual principles to our present-day economic system. Baha'u'llah has given us a few basic principles which should guide future Baha'i economists in establishing such institutions which will adjust the economic relationships of the world."[28]

'Abdu'l-Baha did elaborate somewhat on several practical economic polices, which included a graduated income tax, profit sharing, community-provided work for all, and welfare for the sick and disabled. He also commented on the problems of industrial relations, where he opposed the confrontational approaches of strike and lockout that created a zero-sum game and proposed instead the introduction of consultative decision-making processes. However, like his father, 'Abdu'l-Baha believed that the real answer to economic problems lay not in specific mechanisms but in men's hearts. To this end, he advocated the voluntary sharing of wealth: "This voluntary sharing is greater than (legally imposed) equality, and consists in this, that one should not prefer oneself to others, but rather should sacrifice one's life and property for others. But this should not be introduced by coercion so that it becomes a law which man is compelled to follow."[29] It is this type of thinking that leads Baha'is to claim that the solution to the world's economic problems is spiritual in nature.

It is fair to say that to this point in its historical development Baha'i leadership has not made an attempt to initiate any substantial economic reforms within its own communities. Shoghi Effendi stated on several occasions that the time had not yet come to bring about such a fundamental change in the economic structure of society, and the Universal House of Justice has followed a similar path. The closest Baha'is have come to influencing economic change is through the development projects that they have initiated in several parts of the developing world. A good example of such a project is the New Era Development Institute (NEDI) founded in 1987 in Panchgani, India. Over the years, NEDI has become known primarily as a center for rural education with a mission of providing both vocational and developmental training to male and female villagers. Vocational skills taught at the Institute range from diesel mechanics to primary education. Over the past decade, NEDI has also implemented a number of small-scale projects in several villages near Panchgani. Examples of such projects include poultry raising, carpentry training, the creation of village grain banks, and the development of bio-gas energy systems.

While the scope of its beliefs and associated social principles are essential to a religious community's self identity, they are by no means the only, or perhaps even the most important, components of spiritual life. It is often sacred objects, rituals, modes of worship, and legal rules and regulations that become primarily significant in providing a group with a sense of internal unity and cohesion. These elements of Baha'i community life will be the focal point of Chapter 3.

3

Aspects of Baha'i
Community Life

When individuals become Baha'is, they are doing more than just accepting Baha'u'llah's claim to be a Manifestation of God or asserting specific religious beliefs and social principles. They are joining a living community in which membership involves a commitment to a variety of behaviors and modes of social interaction. The degree to which these activities become manifest in a Baha'i's life depends on several variables including level of personal maturity, size and location of the local community, and the standard of community leadership. In the following pages, certain aspects of Baha'i life as they are presented in Baha'i literature will be briefly examined.

THE NINETEEN DAY FEAST

The focal point of Baha'i community life is the Nineteen Day Feast. As its name implies, this local meeting of the faithful takes place every nineteen days, at the beginning of each Baha'i month (see Table 1). The origin of the Feast goes back to the time of the Bab, when it was related to the providing of food and water for guests (hence the name, Feast). Baha'u'llah continued this sharing of food, as did 'Abdu'l-Baha. There was certainly a symbolic aspect to these occasions because 'Abdu'l-Baha often referred to them as the "Lord's Supper."

It was during 'Abdu'l-Baha's ministry that the Feast took on the semblance of a regular monthly meeting with both devotional and social functions,

Table 1   Baha'i Feasts and Dates

Name	Date	Name	Date
1. Splendor	March 21	11. Will	September 27
2. Glory	April 9	12. Knowledge	October 16
3. Beauty	April 28	13. Power	November 4
4. Grandeur	May 17	14. Speech	November 23
5. Light	June 5	15. Questions	December 12
6. Mercy	June 24	16. Honor	December 31
7. Words	July 13	17. Sovereignty	January 19
8. Perfection	August 1	18. Dominion	February 7
9. Names	August 20	19. Loftiness	March 2
10. Might	September 8		

and thereafter it became identified with Baha'i unity. "The aspect of the feast most stressed in the writings of 'Abdu'l-Baha was the creation of an atmosphere of spirituality, unity and prayer."[1] During the period of the Guardianship, Shoghi Effendi added an administrative portion to the Feast, so that today it is comprised of three parts: (1) devotional—involving readings from the Baha'i sacred writings, (2) administrative—a period for the believers to consult on a variety of community matters, and (3) social—a time when food is shared. Only Baha'is are allowed to attend the devotional and administrative portions of the Feast, but visitors are welcome to take part in the social gathering.

If the community is of sufficient size to have a Baha'i center, the Feast would be held in that building.[2] In smaller communities it usually takes place at the homes of individual Baha'is. Attendance at the gathering is desirable but not obligatory, and there is no sanction taken against believers who fail to attend. Although the basic format of the Feast is similar throughout the Baha'i world, there is considerable variation in the details depending on the cultural background of the community and the personal inclinations of the host.

WORSHIP

Worship, or devotional activity, plays a vital role in most religious communities, and in this regard the Baha'i Faith is no exception. In his letters to the kings, we find Baha'u'llah declaring: "Worship none but God, and, with radiant hearts, lift up your faces unto your Lord, the Lord of all names."[3] Hence, the object of all Baha'i worship should be God alone, whose likeness cannot be represented by any form. In practical terms, this means that the *word* as expressed in Baha'i scriptures comes to play the primary role in Baha'i devotional life, since it is believed to be the essential medium of communication between mankind and the divine realm. This raises the question as to the scope and content of the official Baha'i canon.

Unlike Judaism, Christianity, or Islam, the Baha'i Faith does not have one primary book that its followers revere as sacred. During his lifetime, Baha'u'llah penned numerous treatises, tablets, prayers, and meditations, all of which are considered to be revealed scripture. These have been published in various languages in the form of both independent books and compilations. In addition, a large number of his writings still remain untranslated and unpublished. Baha'u'llah's core text, the *Kitáb-i Aqdas* (*Most Holy Book*) contains the laws and ordinances that are the spiritual and legal bedrock of the Baha'i community; his *Kitáb-i Íqán* (*Book of Certitude*) is an explanation of the allegorical nature of revealed scriptures; the *Haft Vadi* (*Seven Valleys*) and the *Chahar Vadi* (*Four Valleys*) are examples of his mystical prose; and *The Epistle to the Son of the Wolf,* which was his last major work, restates the circumstances surrounding his claims and repeats the basic tenets set forth elsewhere in his writings. However, in terms of devotional sources, it is a number of compilations that have become the most significant. Chief among these is a volume titled *Gleanings from the Writings of Baha'u'llah.* Moreover, a large number of Baha'u'llah's devotional selections have been published in a variety of prayer books.

The writings of 'Abdu'l-Baha are also believed to have a sacred character to them. Although they are not considered revelation, 'Abdu'l-Baha's position as the official interpreter of Baha'u'llah's texts and the perfect exemplar of his teachings accounts for their elevated status. Many of these documents took the form of personal correspondence. A large number of such letters have been compiled into distinct volumes such as *The Tablets of 'Abdu'l-Baha Abbas.* Outstanding among 'Abdu'l-Baha's independent works are *The Secret of Divine Civilization*, which deals with the science of politics, and the previously alluded to collection of his table talks on theological and philosophical issues titled *Some Answered Questions.* Added to these are several collections of his prayers and meditations.

Shoghi Effendi also wrote voluminously, and his writings are believed to have been divinely inspired when it came to his role as official interpreter of both Baha'u'llah's and 'Abdu'l-Baha's texts, but they are not considered part of Baha'i scripture. Shoghi Effendi always insisted on this distinction, going so far as to forbid the reading of his writings during the devotional portion of the Nineteen Day Feast.

Baha'i worship is expressed primarily in the form of prayer. Baha'is believe that there is a language of the spirit by which man can communicate with God. 'Abdu'l-Baha described this connection as a state in which "man turneth his face towards His Highness the Almighty seeking his association and desiring his love and compassion."[4] The attitude of prayer should be devotional in nature. God is the beloved whom the believer longs to praise, and in so doing receives the spiritual benefit of returned grace. The ideal devotee is detached from the bondage of self and seeks his or her joy in glorifying God. Consequently, Baha'i prayers are not viewed as magical mantras whose repetition alone can bring about a state of communication with the divine. Rather they are "spiritual poetry" that helps elicit the devotional sentiment necessary for such communion.

Individual prayer consists in the believer finding a quiet spot, calming the mind, and then chanting, reading, or meditating upon verses of the Bab, Baha'u'llah or 'Abdu'l-Baha. Self-created prayers are also acceptable, although they are not considered to have the spiritual potency of those revealed by the holy figures. As in Islam, daily individual prayer is considered obligatory, but whereas Muslims are required to pray five times a day, Baha'is are commanded to pray at least once.

Baha'u'llah established three obligatory prayers from which individual Baha'is are free to choose. The most commonly used obligatory prayer is the short prayer that is to be recited at noon:

> I bear witness, O my God, that Thou hast created me to know Thee and to worship Thee. I testify at this moment to my powerlessness and Thy might, to my poverty and Thy wealth. There is none other God but Thee, the Help in Peril, the Self-Subsisting.[5]

Both the medium and long obligatory prayers are much more elaborate in content and also require the believer to assume a number of specific bodily postures and hand positions. In addition to the three obligatory prayers, several specific prayers by Baha'u'llah are considered to be especially powerful. These include the "Fire Tablet," the "Long Healing Prayer," and the "Tablet of Ahmad." The latter contains within its verses the promise that should one who is in affliction read it with absolute sincerity, "God will dispel his sadness, solve his difficulties, and remove his afflictions."[6]

Baha'i communal worship at the Nineteen Day Feast involves the believers chanting prayers or reading selections from the scriptures. There is no congregational worship; that is, there is no formal prayer that is recited in unison or in the accompaniment of a prescribed ritual. Neither is there an official prayer leader whom the faithful follow. The host or hostess at any given feast may select certain passages to be read by specific community members, but anyone in attendance is free to make their own devotional offering.

Although the essential form of Baha'i devotional practice involves the use of Baha'i scripture, during the Faith's short history there have been examples at both the national and local levels of indigenous forms of worship being introduced into devotional life. For example, during the first half of the twentieth century a Christian-style hymnody became an essential element in American Baha'i worship.[7] For reasons that are not completely clear, the hymns were eventually phased out, so that except for those American Baha'is who experienced them as children, they have become virtually forgotten. A contemporary example is the use in India of a traditional devotional song known as a *bhajan*. Since these songs not only provide a good illustration of devotional diversity in Baha'i history but are also an excellent illustration of the use of non-Baha'i symbols in a Baha'i context, they will be examined more closely.

Bhajans have long been popular among devotional sects in India. Even today many wandering bards perform these songs in towns and villages, recounting in the process the glorious deeds of numerous gods, saints, and heroes. When a *bhajan* is performed in a group setting, one of the devotees stands and sings the various verses while the entire assemblage joins in unison to sing the words of the refrain. During the 1960s and 1970s, Baha'i teachers and administrators in central India began to make use of *bhajans* for both educational and devotional purposes. In so doing, they incorporated traditional Hindu symbolism into the Baha'i message. For example, the songs made continual references to the god Vishnu's incarnations (avatars), Rama and Krishna, as well as to the holy text the Bhagavad Gita and the messianic figure Kalki, whose future appearance is mentioned in a number of sacred Hindu books. Thus, we find the following lyrics in a *bhajan* titled "The Kalki Avatar":

> Refrain: Arise O children of India, the Kalki *avatar* has come.
> Vishnu's *avatar* has come with the name Baha'u'llah.
> Nowhere in the entire world can the influence of religion be seen.
> The wicked have obtained everything,
> The truthful have lost everything,
> According to the Bhagavad Gita the time of Vishnu's *avatar* has come.
> Awake (refrain)
> The *Gita* has said when circumstances are such
> Religion will once again be reestablished, just as it is happening today.
> In order to save righteousness Kalki *avatar* has come.
> Awake (refrain)

Foolish people have not recognized that Vishnu's *avatar* has come again.
Radha and Arjuna knew that Baha'u'llah was the Lord's new abode.
The eternal has once again manifested himself
Awake (refrain)[8]

Numerous *bhajans* similar to the above were sung during teaching excursions, feasts, and village conferences. Whether they will be fully incorporated into Indian Baha'i devotional life or go the way of American Baha'i hymnody remains to be seen.

Before turning our attention to Baha'i ritual, it should be noted that both Baha'u'llah and 'Abdu'l-Baha partially redefined worship in a Baha'i context by considering any form of work done in the service of humanity as equivalent to worship. As the latter stated during one of his presentations in Paris: "The man who makes a piece of notepaper to the best of his ability, conscientiously, concentrating all his forces on perfecting it, is giving praise to God. Briefly, all effort and exertion put forth by man from the fullness of his heart is worship."[9]

RITUAL

If ritual is defined as a fixed form of religiously oriented performance, then it is appropriate to say that the Baha'i Faith is virtually lacking in ritual. This judgment was confirmed by Shoghi Effendi when he spoke of Baha'u'llah having reduced all ritual and form in his faith to an absolute minimum. On several occasions the Guardian warned national Baha'i leadership to take care lest any uniform procedures or rigid rituals be imposed upon the believers. He was also quick to point out that the concept of ritual uncleanness as practiced in certain religious communities had been abolished by Baha'u'llah.

In effect, there are only three aspects of Baha'i religious life that can be considered ritualistic in content: actions related to the obligatory prayers, the required pronouncement in the marriage rite, and certain aspects of the funerary observance including the recitation of the "Prayer for the Dead" and associated procedures regarding the proper preparation and disposal of the corpse.

Examples of the ritualistic component of the obligatory prayers include such acts as preprayer washing of the hands, sitting, standing, bowing, and facing toward Akká at certain points during the prayer, and periodically reciting the Greatest Name (*Yá Bahá'u'l-Abhá*; that is, O Glory of the All-Glorious). In this sense, the Baha'i obligatory prayers exhibit a direct resemblance to certain Islamic devotional rituals.

The Baha'i marriage ceremony contains a single ritualistic element; namely, the required recitation by both bride and groom in front of two witnesses of the words: "We will all, verily abide by the will of God." Otherwise the celebrants are free to choose the form and content of their wedding, although they should not be married in a church nor any other acknowledged place of worship identified with another faith.

The procedures related to the means of preparing and disposing of a deceased believer's corpse are more elaborate. The dead are to be buried, and there is a prohibition against cremation. Since it is believed that internment should take place as soon after death as circumstances permit, there is also a rule against carrying the body more than one-hour's journey away from the place of death. The believer should be wrapped in a shroud of either cotton or silk, and a ring should be placed upon his or her finger bearing the inscription: "I came forth from God, and return unto Him detached from all save Him, holding fast to His Name, the Merciful, the Compassionate."[10] Before burial, the body should be placed in a coffin of stone or hard wood. At the grave site, the "Prayer for the Dead" is to be recited by one of those present while the remainder of the party stands in silence. It is the only congregational prayer prescribed by Baha'i law.

Recently some believers have argued that the Baha'i community has taken Shoghi Effendi's prohibition against rigid ritual too far. Instead of concentrating on rigidity, it has eliminated virtually all ritual and thereby deprived the religion of a necessary form of expression.[11] Baha'is who continue to oppose the introduction of additional ritualistic elements maintain that they can easily degenerate and become meaningless or that they can act as deterrents to cultural diversity by overly formalizing Baha'i worship and devotion.

The current antiritualistic attitude would lead one to suspect that the rituals described above are not widely practiced throughout the Baha'i world, especially considering the fact that a very large number of declared Baha'is live in the developing nations where literacy rates are low and local traditions are still very influential. One obvious example would be the funerary ritual in India. Since cremation is the standard method for disposing of the dead among the subcontinent's Hindu population, and burial is rarely a viable option except for perhaps a small number of Indian Baha'is whose background is non-Hindu, Baha'i burial rituals would seem for the moment to be irrelevant. Although there is little empirical and no statistical evidence to confirm it, our presumption is that Baha'i rituals are regularly practiced primarily in urban communities and that the inclusion of the ritualistic elements related to obligatory prayers would be essentially limited to two groups: Baha'is from Middle Eastern background, where both Baha'i and local tradition support such behavior, and long-standing Baha'is who have been thoroughly educated into the finer aspects of their religious heritage.

HOLY DAYS

There are a significant number of occasions within the Baha'i year that are ceremonious in nature. On most of these holy days, believers are meant to suspend work and gather in their local communities to commemorate specific events in Baha'i history that are considered to be sacred. The holy day observances generally involve the reading of appropriate passages from Baha'i scriptures and the recitation of prayers, but once again there is no prescribed format or standardized content. However, each holy day does have its own peculiar theme and tone. Brief descriptions of the Baha'i holy days follow.

Naw Rúz

The feast of Naw Rúz takes place on March 21 and signifies both the end of the Baha'i period of fasting (see below) and the beginning of the new year. This event is one of the most joyous of Baha'i holy days and is occasioned by the sharing of food, song, and general merriment. Like other new year celebrations found throughout the world, Naw Rúz commemorates the passing of the old and the advent of the new.

The First, Ninth, and Twelfth Days of Ridván

The Ridván holy days (April 21, April 29, and May 2) mark the twelve-day period in 1863 just prior to Baha'u'llah's departure from Baghdad. Shoghi Effendi referred to the Ridván period as the holiest and most significant of all Baha'i festivals. Of the three days, the first is the most sacred, since it marks the day on which Baha'u'llah revealed to his family and a number of close followers that he was He whom God shall make manifest. The Baha'i prophet defined the attitude with which his followers should approach this observance when he wrote: "Rejoice with exceeding gladness, O people of Bahá, as ye call to remembrance the Day of supreme felicity, the Day whereupon the Tongue of the Ancient of Days has spoken ... [and] shed upon the whole of creation the splendors of his name, the All Merciful."[12]

The Declaration of the Bab

Two hours and eleven minutes after sunset on May 22 signals the beginning of the anniversary of the Declaration of the Bab.[13] On this evening, local believers gather to hear a recounting of the meeting between the Bab and his first disciple, Mullá Husayn. At this time, they are reminded of the Bab's position as a Manifestation of God and his role in the unfolding of God's plan for mankind. This is a time for exalted joy and fellowship.

The Ascension of Baha'u'llah and the Martyrdom of the Bab

The two most solemn of Baha'i holy days take place on May 29 and July 9. The former memorializes the passing of Baha'u'llah, while the latter recalls the execution of the Bab. Although they are not mournful events in the manner of the Shi'ite commemoration of the Martyrdom of Husayn (when men, young and old, often beat themselves with whips), the expectant moods of reverence and sorrow mark them off as essentially different in tone and character from other Baha'i holy days. The Martyrdom of the Bab also has the potential for evoking a sense of the supernatural, since both Baha'i and non-Baha'i accounts alike report the strange occurrence of the Bab's "disappearance" after the firing squad initially discharged its bullets. Following a search of the grounds, the young sayyid was found and returned to the scaffold, where after a second firing he was pronounced dead.[14] For some Baha'is, this occurrence is regarded as a sign from God that the Bab was one of his "chosen ones."

The Birth of the Bab and the Birth of Baha'u'llah

On October 20 and November 12, Baha'is celebrate the births of their religion's "twin founders." There is not a great deal of information about the Bab's birth, but tales of his childhood are common, and they provide ample material for such an occasion. These accounts often have a touch of the miraculous to them. The same can be said for Baha'u'llah, who is often depicted in Baha'i lore as being no ordinary child: for example, there are stories that as a baby he never cried and that as a young boy he had numerous prophetic dreams. In addition to such sacred storytelling, both occasions are generally characterized by feasting and various forms of entertainment.

The Day of the Covenant

On November 26, Baha'is gather to remember the appointment of 'Abdu'l-Baha as the Center of the Covenant, or the legitimate source of authority in the Baha'i community following Baha'u'llah's death. Since the date of 'Abdu'l-Baha's birth was the same as The Declaration of the Bab (May 23), the Baha'i leader told his followers that the May date was to be exclusively associated with the martyred prophet and not himself. According to 'Abdu'l-Baha's biographer, Hasan Balyuzi: "But as the Baha'is begged for a day to be celebrated as His, He gave them November 26th, to be observed as the day of the appointment of the Centre of the Covenant."[15] As a sign of deference to his father, 'Abdu'l-Baha directed the Baha'is not to give up working on this day.

The Ascension of 'Abdu'l-Baha

The final holy day on the Baha'i calendar is The Ascension of 'Abdu'l-Baha, which is commemorated on November 28. The occasion is a solemn one during which a variety of accounts relating to 'Abdu'l-Baha's life and death are generally read. A common reading comes from the pen of Shoghi Effendi and reports 'Abdu'l-Baha's last moments:

> At 1:15 A.M. He arose, and, walking to a table in His room, drank some water, and returned to bed. Later on, He asked one of His two daughters who had remained awake to care for Him, to lift up the net curtains, complaining that He had difficulty in breathing. Some rose-water was brought to Him, of which He drank, after which He again lay down, and when offered food, distinctly remarked: 'You wish Me to take some food, and I am going?' A minute later His spirit had winged its flight to its eternal abode, to be gathered, at long last, to the glory of His beloved Father, and taste the joy of everlasting reunion with Him.[16]

SACRED PLACES

As mentioned in Chapter 1, two of the most sacred spots in the Baha'i world are the Shrine of the Bab on Mt. Carmel and the Tomb of Baha'u'llah in nearby Bahjí. In addition, Baha'u'llah mentions that his house in Baghdad and the house of the Bab in Shiraz should be considered holy spots. Since these sites will be briefly discussed in the upcoming examination of Baha'i pilgrimage, another Baha'i sacred space, the *Mashriqu'l-Adhkár*, will be examined here.

Mashriqu'l-Adhkár, which means Dawning-place of the Praise of God, is the name given to Baha'i houses of worship. The initial *Mashriqu'l-Adhkár* was constructed in 'Ishqábád, in Russian Turkestan, between the years 1902 and 1907 and became a model for the future American temple. During the Russian Revolution, the building was confiscated by the state. In 1968 it suffered severe damage from an earthquake and was subsequently demolished. Today there are seven Baha'i houses of worship located respectively in Wilmette, Illinois; Kampala, Uganda; Sydney, Australia; Frankfurt, Germany; Panama City, Panama; Apia, Western Samoa, and New Delhi, India. There are also plans to construct a house of worship in Chile in the near future. Although the various houses of worship have their own unique architectural designs, they are all characterized by the nine-sided, circular shape that is symbolic of the principle of religious unity referred to in Chapter 2. In keeping with this principle, the houses of worship are not confined to Baha'i use only; at certain times, members of any religion or persuasion are free to enter and worship therein.

The *Mashriqu'l-Adhkár* as envisioned by 'Abdu'l-Baha was more than just a place for devotional expression. Accordingly, the Baha'i leader advised that houses of worship should be associated with a complex of buildings, each dedicated to social, humanitarian, educational, or scientific pursuits. In this way, they would exemplify the Baha'i ideal that worship is also service. According to Baha'u'llah, in the future Baha'i houses of worship will be constructed in every town and village.[17]

The Baha'i House of Worship in Wilmette, Illinois, will be dealt with in Part II, where the history of its origin and construction will be discussed in some detail. The New Delhi House of Worship will serve as an example of the design and contemporary use of the *Mashriqu'l-Adhkár* as sacred space.

Plans for a Baha'i House of Worship in the subcontinent can be traced back as far as the 1920 All-India Baha'i Conference, but it was not until the late 1970s, when the land and financing had been secured and the architectural design settled upon, that building could commence. The 26.6-acre site that was to become the temple's home was located on the outskirts of south New Delhi in an area now called Bahapur. The architect, Fariburz Sabha, designed the structure on the pattern of a popular Indian flower, the lotus. Construction began in 1979, and it took six years and eight months to complete the project. The forty-meter-high house of worship is composed of twenty-seven freestanding marble-clad petals, arranged in clusters of three to form the traditional nine sides found on all Baha'i temples. The dedication ceremony on December 24, 1986, was attended by more than 8,000 people from 125 countries and brought enormous press coverage to the Indian Baha'i community. Known commonly throughout India as the Lotus Temple and at times referred to as the Taj Mahal of the twentieth century, the New Delhi House of Worship soon won praise in numerous architectural and engineering journals. For example, *Twentieth Century Architecture*, an anthology that noted the most outstanding structures of the twentieth century, lists the Lotus Temple as one of the three major architectural achievements of the year 1987.[18]

It has been estimated that during its short history the Lotus Temple has drawn more than 50 million visitors. As with all Baha'i houses of worship, it is open to people of every culture and religious background. Within its prayer hall the scriptures of the world's major religions are read or recited according to specifically arranged programs. There are no lectures given in the hall, nor are any ritualistic performances permitted. At certain times, all members of the public are welcome to meditate and pray in silence. Future plans call for the temple to be surrounded by a number of institutions such as schools and libraries for spreading education, hospitals to serve the ailing, orphanages to look after the needs of neglected children, and homes to care for the destitute and aged.

For the majority of believers the continental *Mashriqu'l-Adhkárs* represent the prime examples of Baha'i sacred space that they are likely to visit. For those who can afford such an undertaking, Baha'i scriptures encourage the making of at least one pilgrimage to the holy places in the Middle East.

PILGRIMAGE AND THE FAST

The origin of Baha'i pilgrimage to the Holy Land can be traced back to Baha'u'llah's incarceration in Akká. From 1868 onward, Baha'i pilgrims regularly converged on the city to meet with or catch a glimpse of their imprisoned leader. Baha'u'llah subsequently included the obligation of pilgrimage in his *Kitáb-i Aqdas*, thereby formalizing it in the manner of the Islamic pilgrimage (hajj). It was during the time of 'Abdu'l-Baha's leadership that the first European and North American Baha'is began making trips to the Middle East, and today thousands of Western Baha'is take part in the rite each year.

Baha'u'llah designated three places of pilgrimage: the residence of the Bab in Shiraz, his own former residence in Baghdad, and the Shrine at Bahjí.[19] The Bab's residence was destroyed during the Islamic Revolution in Iran and has not yet been rebuilt. Furthermore, pilgrimages to Shiraz and Baghdad have been suspended because of unfavorable political conditions. This means that for the moment Haifa is the center of Baha'i pilgrimage.

As in Islam, the central purpose of Baha'i pilgrimage is to worship at the "most holy spot" and its associated locations, namely, the aforementioned Tomb of Baha'u'llah at Bahjí and several related sites, the most significant of which is the Shrine of the Bab on Mt. Carmel. The pilgrimage lasts nine days and is organized by officials at the Baha'i World Center. On the first day, the pilgrims visit the Shrine of the Bab. On the second day, they go to the Tomb of Baha'u'llah, and on succeeding days, they visit such places as the barracks in Akká where Baha'u'llah was initially kept, his two residences in that city, the residence and Shrine of 'Abdu'l-Baha, the Monument Gardens, and the Buildings of the Arc. Although there is no formal ritual that is part of Baha'i pilgrimage, several practices have become common, including the circling of the shrines and recitation of the "The Tablet of Visitation."[20]

The Tomb of Baha'u'llah is housed in one of the rooms of the Bahjí mansion, which in turn is surrounded by a small garden from which the city gets its name (al-bahjah; that is, place of delight). The following inscription in Arabic appears above the mansion's main doorway: "Greetings and salutations rest upon this Mansion which increaseth in splendour through the passage of time. Manifold wonders and marvels are found therein, and pens are baffled in attempting to describe them."[21]

Because of its golden dome and its location on Mt. Carmel, the Shrine of the Bab may be the most famous of all Baha'i buildings. As early as 1909, this location had taken on a sacred character when the remains of the Bab, which according to Baha'i tradition had been hidden since the time of his execution, were placed there under the direction of 'Abdu'l-Baha. Shoghi Effendi's Guardianship saw the construction of the building's superstructure, and by 1953 the shrine had assumed its current configuration. The shrine's interior is decorated with Persian carpets, menorahs, and illuminated passages from Baha'i scripture.

When Baha'i pilgrims worship at these two sacred spots, they do so with the belief expressed in the words of 'Abdu'l-Baha: "Holy places are undoubtedly centres of the outpouring of Divine grace, because on entering the illumined sites associated with martyrs and holy souls, and by observing reverence, both physical and spiritual, one's heart is moved with great tenderness."[22]

Another example of the Baha'i Faith's Islamic heritage can be found in the annual period of fasting that Baha'u'llah made mandatory for all believers 15 years of age and older. Exceptions are made for travelers, the sick, and women who are pregnant or nursing. Just prior to the fast, which encompasses the Baha'i month of 'Alá (Loftiness), there are four days (five in a leap year) of gift-giving and festivities known collectively as Intercalary Days. The fast proper begins at dawn on the second day of March and ends at sunset on March 20. During this period, believers are meant to abstain each day from sunrise to sunset from the intake of food and drink (including smoking). Both can be consumed during the evening hours, but moderation is advised.

The fast is essentially a period of meditation and prayer, a time for spiritual refreshment and reinvigoration. The prescribed manner of starting and ending each day involves the offering of prayers of thanksgiving and praise. Baha'is are also encouraged to offer their own prayers throughout the day. In this manner, the fast not only acts as a reminder to individuals of their dependence on the gifts of life, it also provides a unifying social function in that it joins Baha'is throughout the world in a common purpose and course of action. The fast ends with the celebration of the Naw Rúz festival.

LAWS AND ORDINANCES

The majority of Baha'i laws and ordinances are found in the *Kitáb-i Aqdas*. It appears that the book began as an initial tablet of laws recorded sometime during the first years of Baha'u'llah's imprisonment in Akká and that it was then supplemented over time with verses written in response to specific questions put to the Baha'i leader by various followers. Thus, the *Aqdas* not only contains prescriptions and procedures related to prayer, pilgrimage, fasting, burial of the dead, and inheritance but also statutes that prohibit, among other things, the public confession of sins, gambling, and the use of intoxicants. In addition, like other sacred and/or legal documents, the laws of the *Aqdas* condemn such overt antisocial behavior as murder, rape, arson, theft, and adultery. As official interpreters of Baha'u'llah's writings, both 'Abdu'l-Baha and Shoghi Effendi had the authority to interpret the *Aqdas* and did so on several occasions. Today the Universal House of Justice is the sole Baha'i institution with legislative powers.

Within the *Aqdas*, there are a number of laws and ordinances that concern the family. Especially significant are those related to marriage and divorce. Baha'u'llah was raised in a culture in which polygamy was considered a social norm. Consequently, it should not be surprising to find that in the *Aqdas* he allows for a man to have two wives. Perhaps as a result of the negative impact this ordinance might have had in countries outside of the Middle East, 'Abdu'l-Baha later interpreted Baha'i marriage relations to be monogamous in structure, arguing that Baha'u'llah had insisted that polygamy be based on complete fairness and that such fairness was impossible to fulfill.

Marriage in the Baha'i community should neither follow the tradition of arranged marriage, in which a bride- and groom-to-be have no say regarding their future spouses, nor should it be based completely on the independent choices of the couple. In this respect, Baha'u'llah requires that before a man and a woman can be married, all living biological parents need to give their permission in writing. This means that should any living parent not agree, under Baha'i law the marriage ceremony cannot be performed. Should the couple proceed with the marriage in another setting, both face the sanction of losing their Baha'i voting rights (see Chapter 4). This law applies regardless of the ages of the individuals in question.

Baha'is are permitted to marry non-Baha'is, but again the above conditions regarding parental permission pertain. Since it is a requirement that Baha'is have a Baha'i marriage ceremony, in the case where one of the partners is not a Baha'i, the Baha'i ceremony must still be performed, although there is no prohibition against two separate ceremonies taking place.

Divorce is allowed but not encouraged, and women are as free as men to ask for a separation. However, before a divorce can be granted, the couple must go through "a year of patience," during which time they remain married but live apart. It is hoped that during this twelve-month period they will be able to reconcile their differences and thereby save the marriage. If the year of patience is completed without reconciliation having taken place, the local Baha'i administrative body grants a divorce, and the couple are then free to seek a civil dissolution.

When it comes to some of the more controversial issues related to human sexuality and the family, such as abortion and homosexuality, Baha'i tradition has a number of things to say, but since these issues will be dealt with in some depth in Chapter 8 ("Priorities and Issues in the Modern American Baha'i Community"), they will be passed by here.

One of the striking features of Baha'u'llah's law code is that it eliminates holy war, or *jihád*, as a category of behavior. As early as 1863, the Baha'i leader had spoken out against religious strife, and the teaching of peace became a continuous theme in many of his later writings. Near the end of his life Baha'u'llah categorically stated in *The Epistle to the Son of the Wolf*: "We have abolished the law to wage holy war against each other."[23] In terms of contemporary Baha'i ethics, this has meant that in relationship to military service Baha'is request noncombatant status and carry a weapon only upon command. Thus, during those conflicts where a military draft has been enforced, such as World War II and the Vietnam War, American Baha'is have served in noncombatant roles, and a number of the faithful have distinguished themselves as field medics.[24]

The penalties for breaking Baha'i laws range from monetary fines for minor offenses to more severe forms of punishment for crimes such as theft, arson, and murder. The punishments for theft include imprisonment or exile and, upon a third offense, the application of a mark upon the brow; arson and murder can result in either life imprisonment or the death penalty, depending on the discretion of the judges. Since Baha'i courts are currently nonexistent, such matters are designed for future conditions. At present, the loss of community voting rights is the only penalty available to Baha'i institutions.

Baha'u'llah provided a basis for both the financial security of his community and the establishment of a future welfare program by creating the *Huqúqu'lláh* (the Right of God). The *Huq*, as it is commonly known, is essentially a donation that believers with sufficient means make to the Head of the Faith—which since the death of Shoghi Effendi has been the Universal House of Justice. It is somewhat similar to the Shi'ite *khums*, in which one-fifth of an individual's wealth is bestowed upon the community. Baha'u'llah reduced the size of the "gift" to 19 percent of one's discretionary income (the money left over after all debts have been subtracted). At this point in time, the *Huq* is voluntary in that each individual calculates the amount and pays it only when he or she chooses. In addition to the *Huqúqu'lláh*, Baha'is are encouraged to make financial contributions to the Baha'i Fund throughout the year. Only Baha'is are allowed to make such contributions.

In the opening paragraphs of the *Kitáb-i Aqdas*, Baha'u'llah says: "Think not that We have revealed unto you a mere code of laws. Nay, rather, We have unsealed the choice Wine with the fingers of might and power."[25] In an interesting paper titled "Choice Wine: The Kitáb-i Aqdas and the Development of Baha'i Law," the Baha'i scholar Anthony Lee maintains that unlike the Islamic doctrine of the fixed and unchanging nature of the Qur'an, Baha'u'llah intended his holy book to be resilient and open to interpretive flexibility.[26] Whether such an evaluation is accurate will remain to be seen.

TEACHING

An essential activity for every Baha'i community is spreading the Faith. The significance of this aspect of Baha'i life was indicated by the Universal House of Justice when it wrote: "The cornerstone of the foundation of all Baha'i activity is teaching the Cause."[27] The Baha'i Faith, therefore, can be said to be missionary in spirit, although the expression of that attitude is generally less overt than the house-to-house canvassing or direct-confrontation methods employed by such groups as the Mormons or Jehovah's Witnesses. Indeed, Baha'is generally deny that they proselytize, preferring instead the term "teaching."

Perhaps the most popular form of teaching in American Baha'i communities is the Fireside. The meeting received its name from 'Abdu'l-Baha, who during his visit to the United States would often teach groups of people in large living rooms with stone fireplaces. At an American Baha'i Fireside, local believers bring their friends (or "contacts") to hear a presentation on the basic history and beliefs of the Faith. The emphasis in these talks is given to the religious claims made by Baha'u'llah, often in terms of their relationship to Christian prophetic expectations. The presentation is followed by a discussion period in which guests are free to ask questions. If anyone shows sufficient interest or enthusiasm, he or she may be asked to sign a declaration card, although during earlier periods of Baha'i history, when more emphasis was given to knowledge of the Faith as a prerequisite for Baha'i enrollment, it was unlikely that such an immediate conversion would have been encouraged. As mentioned previously, it was not unusual for individuals to take weeks or months to declare their faith.

Baha'i communities often put on public proclamation events. Such occasions are generally expressive of a given Baha'i principle and are often presented in coordination with a specific holiday or associated commemoration. For example, on such occasions as United Nation's Day or Dr. Martin Luther King Jr.'s birthday, Baha'i groups across the United States present programs that support world government and racial equality. Inevitably, these programs will also include mention of the Baha'i Faith and its basic teachings.

During the 1960s and 1970s, the more direct form of teaching, known as "mass teaching," was introduced into the American Baha'i community. As recounted in Chapter 1, the origin of this technique of short evocative presentations to large numbers of people in public places can be traced to an approach used in India and several other developing nations. In mass teaching, formal meetings were abandoned for the spontaneity of the moment. As will be discussed later, South Carolina became a focal point for such teaching in the United States.

Mass teaching in the United States has not been without its Baha'i critics. To some the approach is viewed as being too aggressive, while to others it is seen as bringing individuals into the community who have not had sufficient time to reflect on the seriousness and implications of their declarations. The fact that many who announced their belief under such conditions subsequently left the community gives support to this appraisal, and while one still hears within the context of Baha'i teaching work such slogans as "entry by troops," it is probably fair to say that in recent years mass teaching in the United States has lost the momentum it had developed during previous decades.

Although Baha'is do not go on teaching missions in the sense that Mormons do, they are encouraged to "pioneer." A Baha'i pioneer is a person who leaves his or her home for the purpose of settling in a country or region where the numbers of believers are low or where an international teaching plan has called for the establishment of additional local communities. Pioneering is a topic frequently mentioned in Baha'i texts. For example, a number of passages in the writings of 'Abdu'l-Baha and Shoghi Effendi are devoted to encouraging Baha'is to relocate their residences in order to further the Baha'i teaching mission. Homefront pioneers are those Baha'is who relocate within their own country, while international pioneers take overseas assignments. Many Baha'is who have risen to positions of national and international leadership have at one time or another acted as Baha'i pioneers.

The aspects of Baha'i community life discussed here are extremely important in providing believers with a sense of Baha'i identity. As with any other religion, being a Baha'i is a communal as well as an individual experience. However, Baha'i communal identity goes beyond commonly shared beliefs, modes of worship, and legalized behavior. It also includes involvement in, and association with, a distinct administrative structure known to Baha'is as the Administrative Order. The functioning of this system will be the next topic of investigation.

4

The Baha'i Administrative Order

A significant part of the Baha'i conversion process involves the incorporation of believers into the working dynamics of a number of administrative institutions that were created and developed by the religion's founders and their duly appointed successors. These institutions are part of an internationally linked system whose present form is seen to be the embryonic stage of a world social order referred to in Baha'i literature as the World Order of Baha'u'llah. At the present stage of the religion's development, the primary functions of such institutions include the guidance of its teaching and consolidation plans and the monitoring of the general needs of its members. The administrative institutions are organized on three levels: local, national, and international (see Table 2).

LOCAL ADMINISTRATION

The foundational administrative institution in the Baha'i Faith is the local spiritual assembly. In any local Baha'i community (an incorporated town or city) where nine or more adult Baha'is reside, a local spiritual assembly composed of nine individuals is elected by democratic vote. As in all Baha'i elections, neither nominations nor campaigning are allowed. Rather, all adults in the community simply write down the names of the nine people they feel will best serve the group. The nine individuals who receive the most votes thereafter become members of the assembly. Following the Baha'i principle of fairness, should two members of the

Table 2   The Baha'i Administrative Order

Elected Positions	Appointed Positions
ΔThe Universal House of Justice	ΔHands of the Cause
(elect. All NSAs)	(appt. Shoghi Effendi)
• Secretariat	
• Research Department	
ΔNational Spiritual Assemblies	ΔInternational Teaching Center
(elect. Convention delegates)	(appt. UHJ)
• National Committees	
ΔRegional Baha'i Counsels	ΔContinental Boards of Counselors
(elect. Regional LSAs)*	(appt. UHJ)
ΔLocal Spiritual Assemblies	ΔAuxiliary Boards
(elect. local communities)	(appt. Continental Boards)
	• Assistants

*Members of some regional counsels are appointed.

community share the same number of votes, the one who represents a minority group within society at large should be awarded the position. The election of the local spiritual assembly takes place every year on the first day of Ridván (April 21). Following their election, assembly members select their own chairman and secretary.

The institution of the local spiritual assembly was established by Baha'u'llah, and he made it incumbent upon the members of these bodies "to take counsel together and to have regard for the interests of the servants of God, for His sake, even as they regard their own interests."[1] Consequently, when discussing community business, assembly members are meant to harness their egos and openly consult in a prayerful and tranquil manner on the issues at hand. An ideal definition of Baha'i consultation would include the acceptance that all ideas are to be considered as belonging to the assembly as a whole and not to the specific individuals who suggest them.

Assembly meetings are held on a regular basis, generally once a week. A meeting can only take place when all members have been notified of its time and location, but five members at any given meeting constitute a quorum, and a majority vote of those present is sufficient for conducting business. To maintain the proper atmosphere, all meetings should be opened and closed with a prayer. In larger Baha'i communities, local spiritual assemblies are often assisted by a number of specific committees, each chaired by an assembly member. For example, committees related to teaching, child education, public relations, and finance are common.

During the business portion of the Nineteen Day Feast, the chairman of the assembly makes a report to the believers. The report is followed by community discussion and consultation. At this time, individual Baha'is are free to make specific recommendations to their elected leaders, but before any recommendation can constitute a resolution to be considered by the assembly, it must be adopted by a majority vote of those present.

In terms of decision making, a majority vote by assembly members constitutes a verdict, and once arrived at, it should become the decision of the entire body. In other words, in the Baha'i administrative system there is no room for minority opinion; the majority decision is to be considered the decision of all, and community members are not supposed to publicly criticize or act contrary to it. Shoghi Effendi reinforced this position when he stated that "every Assembly elected in that rarefied atmosphere of selflessness and detachment is, in truth, appointed of God, that its verdict is truly inspired, that one and all should submit to its decision unreservedly and with cheerfulness."[2]

In performing their administrative duties, members of local spiritual assemblies are not responsible for their decisions in the way this term is understood in most contemporary political systems. They are not bound to represent any specific constituency but are called upon to base their decisions on nothing but the admonitions of their own consciences.[3] Nevertheless, they are pledged under all conditions to follow the dictates of justice.

When it comes to conflict resolution within the community, perhaps the most common problems brought before assemblies are those that involve marital dispute, but any issue that is not directly under the auspices of civil or criminal law can also come under assembly examination. Individual confidentiality is protected in such encounters by the fact that assembly minutes are closed to the community.

As representatives of the Baha'i community, members of local spiritual assemblies are relegated such additional responsibilities as protecting their religion from external attack, assuring that the community is not disrupted by internal conflict and division, and maintaining regular contact with other institutions within the administrative hierarchy. The communicative link is a two-way process. On the one hand, local assemblies provide the administrative channel through which the national and international institutions communicate with individual believers. At the Feast, assembly secretaries relay to their communities any communications or directives their local body has recently received. On some occasions, prerecorded tapes from the National Center (in the United States, Wilmette, Illinois) are played. Conversely, the assemblies serve as a means for adherents to make suggestions to the National Spiritual Assembly. If a recommendation is passed at the Feast, a given assembly may, at its discretion, forward the suggestion to the national body. This chain of communication is considered of vital importance in terms of strengthening the capacity of all Baha'is to understand the relation of the local community to the rest of the Baha'i world.

Another administrative process that involves the participation of the members of local Baha'i communities is the selection of the delegates who act as electors of the National Spiritual Assembly. In every country where there exists a national administrative body, delegates, whose number and apportionment are determined by Baha'i population patterns, are annually selected by means of democratic election to attend the Baha'i National Convention. The method of choosing delegates varies according to country. In countries where the Baha'i population is small, delegates are often directly chosen by local communities, each community being assigned a specific number of delegates according to its relative size. In countries like the United States, where the number of Baha'is is relatively large, delegate positions are allocated on the basis of population density, with different geographical areas receiving a certain number of seats. In both cases, whether directly or indirectly, the votes of individual local Baha'is determine who will represent them at the National Convention.

The ability to vote in Baha'i elections is a right granted to each person upon his or her declaration of faith. Voting rights, however, can be removed at the discretion of a national spiritual assembly. A sanction of this type can be applied for such things as flagrant disobedience of Baha'i laws, direct involvement in partisan politics, or actions that are seen to undermine the authority of Baha'i leadership.

NATIONAL ADMINISTRATION

Baha'i national administration is guided by the National Spiritual Assembly. Like its counterpart at the local level, the National Spiritual Assembly is composed of nine members who are chosen each year at the Baha'i National Convention. The first election of the National Spiritual Assembly in the United States took place in 1925. The institution's present-day headquarters is in Wilmette, Illinois.

The National Convention is held every April. At that time, delegates from throughout the country assemble to elect their national leaders. Each delegate is free to write down the names of any nine people he or she chooses, and the nine individuals who receive the most votes become the new members of the next national assembly. In case of a tie for the ninth position, there is a second ballot cast. As in the case of local elections, there is no electioneering allowed, although, as statistical analysis has shown, prior membership on the National Spiritual Assembly acts as its own campaigning mechanism in that it gives the individuals concerned greater national exposure.

In addition to electing the National Spiritual Assembly, in the words of Shoghi Effendi, the National Convention should "also fulfill the functions of an enlightened, consultative and cooperative body that will enrich the experience, enhance the prestige, support the authority, and assist the deliberations of the National Spiritual Assembly."[4] Accordingly, convention delegates can use this opportunity to raise issues from their local communities that they deem worthy of consultation. In turn, the newly elected national body should reveal to the delegates its hopes and concerns and also familiarize them with various matters of national significance that will have to be considered during the upcoming year.

Once elected, the members of the National Spiritual Assembly select their own officers, the most important of which are the positions of secretary and treasurer. The office of the secretary of the National Spiritual Assembly is doubtless the most significant Baha'i office in any given country, and historically, many influential believers have held this position. Originally a part-time position of service, in large Baha'i communities it has become a full-time, paid office, and although theoretically a new secretary can be selected each year, in the United States there has been a tendency for one person to hold the office for prolonged periods of time.

The essential purpose of the National Spiritual Assembly as outlined by Shoghi Effendi is to unify and coordinate, through constant communication with the Holy Land, the activities and general affairs of both the local spiritual assemblies and individual Baha'is under its jurisdiction.[5] More specifically, these duties are to be realized through the institution's promotion of devotional and public meetings, educational conferences, and Baha'i publications. The body is also given management over the construction of Baha'i centers and other buildings designed to unite and advance the religion.

Since national assembly members live in various parts of any given country, there is a natural problem concerning the frequency of meetings. Shoghi Effendi was very aware of this issue and encouraged all national spiritual assemblies to meet as often as possible. He also suggested that some individuals could communicate their opinions through written correspondence and that it was therefore unnecessary for all members to be present at every session. His main concerns were that national activities not be allowed to suffer in any way and that the institution's work not be retarded or postponed because of secondary considerations.

To aid them in carrying out their delegated functions, national spiritual assemblies annually appoint a variety of committees. These committees are given such vital assignments as the translation and publication of official literature, the management of the House of Worship, and the supervision of national teaching campaigns. Two of the most important committees in any national community are the National Teaching Committee and the Publishing Trust.

The National Teaching Committee is "the vital right arm of the National Spiritual Assembly."[6] While it remains under the supervision of the Assembly, it is essentially given the power to manage the overall teaching program for the entire country. Each year the committee is required to submit a general plan for the accomplishment of its tasks to the national secretary, who then presents it to the National Spiritual Assembly for approval. To assist it in carrying out its various projects, the National Teaching Committee generally has a number of auxiliary committees under its command whose members are likewise appointed by the National Spiritual Assembly.

Baha'i Publishing Trusts are responsible for the creation, regulation, and marketing of Baha'i literature. Books, pamphlets, study guides, and audio and video tapes all come under their purview. The Baha'i Publishing Trust for the United States is based at the National Center in Wilmette, Illinois. In addition to its regular publishing tasks, the committee produces a quarterly journal titled *World Order*. Closely associated with the Publishing Trust are a number of departments that are responsible for such things as the production of *The American Baha'i*, a monthly newspaper sent to all registered believers in the country, and the development and coordination of research activities. The latter is the domain of the Research Department. This department is also in charge of the policy of Baha'i literature review.

Baha'i literature review, which requires that all individual Baha'is submit to a committee any writings, scripts, or films dealing with the Baha'i Faith that are meant for publication or public viewing, began during the time of 'Abdu'l-Baha and was continued in a more systematic fashion under the leadership of Shoghi Effendi. The Universal House of Justice has likewise kept this policy in place and has made several statements as to its purpose. In a memorandum dated September 8, 1991, the institution relayed:

> At this early stage in the development of the Baha'i Faith, which is striving against great odds to establish itself in a world that is highly critical, often antagonistic towards new ideas, and whose communications media tend to emphasize negative information, it is important that Baha'i authors, scriptwriters and filmmakers endeavour to present the Faith with accuracy and dignity.... Therefore, a Baha'i author is expected to ensure to the extent possible a correct representation of the Faith in his work; as an aid he draws upon the reviewing facilities provided by Baha'i institutions.[7]

The communiqué went on to say that submission to Baha'i review should be seen in the same light as the submission for prepublication review of a scientific paper and that Baha'i authors should respect the function of review in the Baha'i community. Nevertheless, there have been some believers, especially within the Baha'i scholarly community, who have found the requirement to be outdated and have made their feelings public. This discussion will be addressed again in Chapter 8.

The expansion of the Baha'i world community and the growing complexity of the issues that faced national spiritual assemblies in certain countries led in June 1997 to the creation by the Universal House of Justice of a new group of institutions known as regional Baha'i councils. The councils were meant to act as intermediaries between local and national bodies and thereby help establish a balance between centralized and decentralized approaches to administration. They were structured so as to take on certain characteristics of both local and national spiritual assemblies. In essence, the councils were meant to implement the policies of the national spiritual assemblies in particular regions. While they were not meant to replace the functions of national teaching committees and remained responsible to national spiritual assemblies, the councils were designed to develop their own autonomous strategies and programs.

Since 1997 the main task of regional Baha'i councils has been to devise and execute expansion and consolidation plans in close collaboration with the local spiritual assemblies within their areas of jurisdiction. This has included efforts to help create and maintain strong local spiritual assemblies as well as to appoint committees to handle such issues as the translation, publication, and distribution of Baha'i literature. They have also been asked to arrange and supervise the unit elections for delegates to the National Convention, formulate annual budgets for their regions, and encourage believers within their areas of jurisdiction to contribute to various Baha'i funds.

Regional council members are selected by means of a dual process of election and appointment. In those regions where election has been considered appropriate, members of all the local spiritual assemblies cast ballots on May 23 (the anniversary of the Declaration of the Bab). They are free to vote for any nine adult Baha'is who reside within the region. Voting is accomplished through the submission of sealed, mailed ballots. Tie votes are broken by means of lot, and any vacancy during the year is filled by the person who had the next-highest number of votes on the ballot in the preceding election. In other regions, it is left to the National Spiritual Assembly to decide whether the number of members on the council is to be five, seven, or nine. Similar to the elected councils, balloting takes place among members of the local spiritual assemblies in the region, but the outcome of the voting only constitutes a nomination list for the National Spiritual Assembly, which then appoints council members from among these nominees.

INTERNATIONAL ADMINISTRATION

At the apex of the Baha'i administrative structure stands the Universal House of Justice, whose headquarters is at the Baha'i World Center in Haifa, Israel. This body of nine men is elected every five years by the members of all national spiritual assemblies. The first House was elected in 1963, and the world's Baha'is are now being governed by the ninth such assembly. The Universal House of Justice claims its authority from Baha'u'llah's "Tablet of Ishráqát": "The affairs of the people are in charge of the men of the House of Justice of God. They are the trustees of God among His servants and the sources of command in His countries."[8] Elaborating on this theme, 'Abdu'l-Baha wrote: "By this House is meant that Universal House of Justice which is to be elected from all countries ... after the manner of the customary elections in Western countries such as those of England."[9]

In the same manner as the selection of both local and national spiritual assembly members, no campaigning is supposed to take place during the election process. Likewise, House members are not responsible to their electors nor any other Baha'i constituency. Their decisions should be based entirely on the principles of justice derived through prayer and consultation. In fact, since the Universal House of Justice is believed to be under the influence of divine guidance, all decisions within its area of jurisdiction become, in effect, unanimous and are to be accepted by believers as being "free from all error."

As the supreme institution in the Baha'i world, the Universal House of Justice has the power to legislate on any matter not found in the Baha'i writings. Again, this right is based on scriptural authority: "It is incumbent upon the Trustees of the House of Justice to take counsel together regarding such laws as have not been expressly revealed in the Book. Of these whatever they deem advisable and proper must they enforce."[10] The Constitution of the Universal House of Justice describes the institution's duties as including: the analysis and classification of Baha'i scriptures, the defense and protection of the Baha'i community, the teaching of its message, the expansion and consolidation of its institutions, the enactment of laws and ordinances not found in its scriptures, and the arbitration of disputes between Baha'i institutions and/or individual believers.[11]

The House's most active work has been in the arenas of community expansion and consolidation. The numerous systematic teaching plans that have characterized the Baha'i community's missionary efforts since 1963 have been conceived and guided by the House and its various subsidiary institutions. As an example of such guidance, in December 1995 the Universal House of Justice wrote to the Baha'is of the world announcing its Four Year Plan. This letter not only set out specific goals, such as the number of new local spiritual assemblies to be established during this period, it also outlined various requirements for the project's success. These included: (1) a renewed vitality among individual believers in teaching the Faith to others, (2) the obligation of all believers to uphold the authority of the Faith's institutions, (3) a commitment on the part of local and national assemblies to develop more rapidly as community builders and planners, and (4) an enhancement of patterns of behavior by both individuals and institutions that demonstrate the unity and fellowship of Baha'i life.[12] Such communiqués accompany the launching of every international Baha'i teaching plan.

The House also acts as a source of support for the various national spiritual assemblies under its guidance. Since its inception, there has been a regular flow of correspondence from the World Center to the national bodies (and through them to the local assemblies and individual believers). While, on occasion, it has had to discipline national spiritual assemblies, the overall attitude of the House appears to have been one of tolerant encouragement for the national institutions.

Periodically, the Universal House of Justice delivers special messages to the Baha'i world. These statements generally focus on an overarching theme found in the Baha'i writings and are often meant to be presented to influential individuals and institutions, both religious and political, within society at large. An example of this type of communiqué was the House's 1985 Peace Message to the peoples of the world titled *Promise of World Peace*. Here, the supreme Baha'i institution expressed the belief that world peace is not only possible but that it also is the inevitable next stage in the social evolution of the planet. The real question, the House maintained, is whether peace will be reached by the path of suffering resulting from humanity's clinging to old patterns of behavior or through a fresh act of consultive will. The House's latest message of this kind was sent in April 2002 to the world leaders of religion. After noting that one of the fundamental obstacles to the achievement of the goal of human unity has tragically been organized religion, the message challenged religious leaders to see beyond the limitations of nationalism, racial- and ethnic-based identities, gender inequalities, and religious bigotry.

When it comes to acts of legislation that can be considered infallible in nature, there have only been seven occasions when the Universal House of Justice has made such enactments.[13] Included in these were its declaration in 1963 that no future Guardian could be appointed, the establishment of its constitution in 1972, and the creation of regional Baha'i councils in 1997. There is, however, an ongoing discussion within the community regarding the nature and extent of the institution's infallibility. The debate revolves around whether infallibility is limited to the specific acts of legislation mentioned above or if it also applies to more general pronouncements such as the prohibition against women serving on any future Universal House of Justice.

Running parallel to the elected administrative institutions of the Baha'i Faith are a number of appointed positions. In descending order of authority they are: the Hands of the Cause, the Continental Boards of Counselors, and the Auxiliary Boards.

The Hands of the Cause were a select group of believers whose main function was to help spread and protect the Baha'i Faith at the international level. The origin of this institution can be traced back to the time of Baha'u'llah, who appointed four such individuals. 'Abdu'l-Baha did not name any Hands during his years of leadership, but he testified to their position in his *Will and Testament* and provided for their selection by Shoghi Effendi. Hence, in December 1951, the Guardian chose twelve Hands, and by the time of his death in 1957, he had elevated forty-three individuals to this rank. One of the most important powers given to the Hands by Shoghi Effendi was the authority to expel and reinstate covenant-breakers. Today only one Hand remains alive: Dr. 'Ali-Muhammad Varqa (born 1911).

Since the Universal House of Justice decided that it did not have the scriptural authority to appoint additional Hands of the Cause, with the continual decrease in their number it became necessary to create a new institution. Hence, in June 1968, the Continental Boards of Counselors were brought into being. Members of the Boards were appointed by the House and were assigned many of the former functions carried out by the Hands. They were also given charge over the auxiliary boards (see below). In July 1969 and April 1970, further increases in the numbers of counselors were made. Today there exist five continental boards and eighty-one continental counselors.

With the creation of numerous regional Baha'i councils in 1997, consultation with these bodies became one of the counselors' major responsibilities. Specifically, the Universal House of Justice directed them to help the regional councils formulate individual teaching and consolidation plans within the framework of the various worldwide plans that were issued from Haifa. In this process, the counselors often make use of members of another appointed institution: the Auxiliary Board.

The institution of the Auxiliary Board was created by Shoghi Effendi for the purpose of aiding the Hands of the Cause in their assigned duties. At that time, two categories of auxiliary boards were brought into existence: the Auxiliary Boards for the Propagation of the Faith and the Auxiliary Boards for the Protection of the Faith. Later, the Universal House of Justice made both types of boards subservient to the needs of the various Continental Boards of Counselors. Although they are distinct entities and have been assigned different areas of focus, the Universal House of Justice has stressed that many of the functions of the two auxiliary boards are held in common, especially as seen in the areas of consolidation and educational "deepening."[14] To help facilitate relationships between local spiritual assemblies and these auxiliaries, counselors have made an effort to assign board members to regions in which they personally reside.

The responsibilities of the propagation boards include such tasks as stimulating community enthusiasm for spreading the Faith, bringing to the attention of local believers the goals of the current national or international teaching plan, helping organize local and regional proclamation events, and encouraging financial contributions to various Baha'i funds. In this capacity, board members are not supposed to be given any administrative assignments. Rather, their function is solely to serve as advisors to the elected institutions.

As their title indicates, members of the protection boards have been given the specific task of safeguarding Baha'i communities. Perhaps as a result of its history of persecution in Iran, as well as the internal disruptions that have characterized each transition of leadership, Baha'i administrative thinking has developed the category "enemy of the Faith." This notion finds one of its most acute expressions in the following letter from the Universal House of Justice, dated October 10, 1976:

> The need to protect the Faith from attacks of its enemies is not generally appreciated by the friends because such attacks, particularly in the West, have so far been intermittent. However, we know that these attacks will increase and will become concerned and universal. The writings of our Faith clearly foreshadow not only an intensification of the machinations of internal enemies, whether religious or secular, as our beloved Faith pursues its onward march towards ultimate victory ... the Auxiliary Boards for Protection should keep "constantly" a "watchful eye" on those who are known to be enemies or to have been put out of the Faith, discreetly investigate their activities [and] warn intelligently the friends of the opposition inevitably to come.[15]

As mentioned above, auxiliary board members play an important role in relationship to regional Baha'i councils. Regular meetings between councils and their auxiliary board members are required. At such meetings, the discussion of teaching strategies should predominate, although a free exchange of general information and ideas is also encouraged. In addition to these scheduled meetings, whenever counselors feel it necessary or desirable, they are free to deputize auxiliary board members to represent them in consultations with a regional Baha'i council.

Just as auxiliary board members act as assistants to the continental counselors, the former were given permission from the Universal House of Justice in 1973 to have their own assistants whom they can appoint with the authorization of a counselor. Beyond generally helping auxiliary board members in the discharge of their duties, one of the main roles given to these assistants has been the guidance of new Baha'i communities in holding regular feasts, assembly meetings, and holy day celebrations.

The final piece of the Baha'i administrative structure is the International Teaching Center, which was created by the Universal House of Justice in June 1973. The general functions of the Center are to provide another communicative link between the Continental Boards of Counselors and Haifa and to assume some of the responsibilities formerly carried out by the Universal House of Justice. More specifically, the institution has been given the specific tasks of directing the activities of the continental boards, making reports on the state of Baha'i affairs throughout the world, submitting recommendations to the House regarding the need for literature and traveling teachers, and working out teaching plans at both the regional and global levels. Members of the International Teaching Committee include the one remaining member of the Hands of the Cause and a select group of individuals appointed by the House.

To gain a better understanding of the status that has been given to the appointed institutions in the Baha'i Administrative Order, it is important to realize that according to Shoghi Effendi, they comprise what Baha'u'llah referred to in his *Kitáb-i 'Ahd* (*the Book of the Covenant*) as "the learned," whereas the elected institutions comprise "the rulers." Although Baha'u'llah criticized the learned in past religions for being sources of division and contention because of their sense of intellectual and spiritual superiority, it is commonly believed that the Baha'i learned are protected from such false pride by their not being granted any legislative, administrative, or judicial authority. Moreover, the learned are not allowed to make authoritative scriptural interpretations. Such restrictions on the Baha'i learned have led the Universal House of Justice to claim that they have no parallel in past religions.[16]

SHOGHI EFFENDI'S VISION AND THE CURRENT
ADMINISTRATIVE ORDER

It is readily apparent from reading a series of letters written by Shoghi Effendi to the American Baha'i community between the years 1929 and 1936, which were later published under the title *The World Order of Baha'u'llah,* that there are several significant differences between the Guardian's vision of the Baha'i Administrative Order and the system as it currently exists. All of the variances revolve around Shoghi Effendi's assumption of an ongoing Guardianship. The Baha'i leader was so convinced of this reality that he could write: "Divorced from the institution of the Guardianship the World Order of Baha'u'llah would be mutilated and permanently deprived of that hereditary principle which, as 'Abdu'l-Baha has written, has been invariably upheld by the Law of God."[17]

The loss of the Guardianship has meant that the Baha'i Administrative Order lacks the functions originally designated to this institution. The most significant of these include: (1) the authority to officially interpret Baha'i scripture, (2) the power to appoint Hands of the Cause, (3) the right to require the Universal House of Justice to reconsider any of its enactments that are seen to be in conflict with the writings of Baha'u'llah or 'Abdu'l-Baha, and (4) the ability to dismiss any member of that body for grievous misconduct.

By far the most important of the above duties is the interpretive power (*tabyín*), which Baha'u'llah established in the *Kitáb-i Aqdas* when he commanded Baha'is to refer what they did not understand to his son, 'Abdu'l-Baha. In his own *Will and Testament,* 'Abdu'l-Baha transferred the interpretive responsibility to the office of the Guardian. Shoghi Effendi later elaborated on the distinction between the interpretive powers of the Guardian and the legislative powers of the Universal House of Justice: "The interpretation of the Guardian, functioning within his own sphere, is as authoritative and binding as the enactments of the International House of Justice, whose exclusive right and prerogative is to pronounce upon and deliver the final judgment on such laws and ordinances as Baha'u'llah has not expressly revealed."[18]

The implication of not having a living, authoritative interpreter of the sacred texts was not lost on a number of leading Baha'is when they came to know that the Guardianship had officially ended. Indeed, it was over this very issue that Mason Remey, a Hand of the Cause and close companion of Shoghi Effendi, later claimed to be the second Guardian of the Baha'i Faith. For Remey and those who followed him, it was unthinkable that a system that claimed the assurance of divine guidance as one of its essential features would be left without an individual or institution that could give official meaning to the sacred texts. The alternative of having each individual Baha'i interpret the scriptures for him or herself was seen to open up the possibility of doctrinal chaos.

Baha'i answers to the problem of the end of the Guardianship have ranged from the Shi'ite concept of *badá*—that God had changed his mind[19]—to the argument that while Shoghi Effendi passed away, the institution of the Guardianship still survives in the form of his writings. The former is now rarely expressed, while the latter seemingly fails to take into account that on several occasions Shoghi Effendi referred to future guardians. For example: "To the integrity of this cardinal principle of our Faith [that the Guardian does not hold a station coequal with those of Baha'u'llah or 'Abdu'l-Baha] the words, the deeds of its present and future Guardians must abundantly testify."[20]

In a letter to an individual believer dated December 12, 1969, the Universal House of Justice commented on this issue. While asserting that the Guardian had been made the interpreter of the word, the supreme institution also noted that it is the *Book* itself (the writings of Baha'u'llah and 'Abdu'l-Baha) that is the highest authority and that the writings of the Guardian and the advice given by him over the thirty-six years of his Guardianship demonstrate his interpretive understandings. The House also claimed that nowhere in the Baha'i writings is it stated that the lack of a living Guardian limits the infallibility of the Universal House of Justice in its own sphere. Moreover, it defined this sphere as extending beyond the enactment of legislation to include such additional functions as "protecting and administering the Faith, solving obscure questions, and deciding upon matters that have caused difference."[21] Finally, the letter observed that although future guardians are clearly referred to in the Baha'i writings, there is no promise that this institution would endure forever.

It seems obvious from the contents of the above letter that the Universal House of Justice was claiming that the lack of a living Guardian did not hamper it in carrying out its functions as the supreme administrative institution in the Baha'i world. What is more, the implied message of the subtext seemed to be that the writings of Baha'u'llah, 'Abdu'l-Baha, and Shoghi Effendi were not in need of official interpretation. It would then follow that individual Baha'is were free to interpret the writings for themselves with the proviso that their interpretations could not in any way be claimed as authoritative in nature.

At a later date (October, 1985), another House confirmed that the institution would not engage in the interpretation of the holy writings, but it also added that based on 'Abdu'l-Baha's *Will and Testament* and certain of Shoghi Effendi's letters, it had the right to "elucidate" upon obscure questions or problems that might cause division within the community.[22] It seems that elucidation in the manner that the House described it was meant to be similar to Islamic judicial reasoning (*ijtihád*) whereby the law in a specific case is derived from both the religious texts and reason. This is the method practiced by Shi'ite ayatollahs. Regardless of the term's exact technical meaning, it would appear that, again, the essential message that the House wanted to convey was that the lack of an official interpreter of the writings did not in any way undermine its institutional infallibility when it came to administering the affairs of the Baha'i community.

THE COVENANT

From the perspective of administrators and believers alike, the Baha'i Administrative Order is more than just a collection of elected and appointed institutions that manage the affairs of the Faith. At its heart, the system is seen to reflect a relationship between Baha'u'llah and his followers, a divine connection that is known as the Covenant.

There are actually two forms of the Baha'i Covenant. The Greater Covenant is between God and humanity through the person of the Manifestation. In this covenant, God promises to continue to send guidance to mankind, while humanity in turn promises to obey and follow the teachings of the Manifestation. As part of the Greater Covenant, the current Manifestation places upon his followers the obligation to accept the next Manifestation. The Lesser Covenant requires Baha'is to accept the leadership of Baha'u'llah's appointed successors and ordained institutions. As it is the Lesser Covenant that directly impinges upon the Baha'i Administrative Order, it is this element of Baha'u'llah's contract with the members of his community that will receive the main focus of attention.

Baha'is trace the Lesser Covenant to Baha'u'llah's *Kitáb-i 'Ahd*, in which the Baha'i leader appointed 'Abdu'l-Baha to be the legitimate leader of the Baha'i community after his death, but it is 'Abdu'l-Baha's *Will and Testament* that has become the most crucial of covenant-affirming documents. This is not only because of the emphatic language with which the *Will and Testament* demands that Baha'is give their allegiance to both the Guardian and the Universal House of Justice but also because of the reality that Shoghi Effendi did not leave a will of his own. As a consequence of this lapse, 'Abdu'l-Baha's *Will and Testament* became the last authoritative document to which Baha'is could turn when it came to an affirmation of the Lesser Covenant.

Baha'is see the ultimate purpose of the Lesser Covenant as the establishment of a unified world. Since this unity is understood to have been Baha'u'llah's specific historical mission, it would be impossible, the reasoning goes, for the Baha'i Faith to accomplish such a goal if it were itself disunited.[23] It is at this point that the Lesser Covenant and the Greater Covenant converge, for unity within the Baha'i community is understood as a guarantee that God's revealed guidance will become manifest for all mankind. In the words of Baha'u'llah: "It is evident that the axis of oneness of the world of humanity is the power of the Covenant and nothing else."[24]

For many Baha'is, the Covenant is mystical at its core. While the compact defines legitimate authority, provides a vision of the unity of mankind, and establishes a given moral order, it is the individual's "remembrance of God" as an irreducible commitment and ongoing relationship that forms its foundation.[25] This remembrance is then collectively expressed in the form of a commonwealth that in turn establishes the principles of a particular way of life that can be called Baha'i.

Since the Covenant plays such a central role in Baha'i life, it should not be surprising to find that the perceived failure to live up to that agreement, as demonstrated in the form of challenges to established leadership, is considered a grave matter. The term used to describe those who cause internal opposition and rebellion is "covenant-breaker." To be a recipient of this label, a Baha'i must willfully oppose the authorized leadership of the Baha'i Faith or be engaged in actively trying to split the Baha'i community by setting up an alternative center of power. Covenant-breakers are removed from the community at large, and Baha'is in good standing are not permitted to have any contact with them. Indeed, the failure to practice shunning can result in the offending believer also being declared a covenant-breaker.

During its short history, the Baha'i community has seen its leadership make use of the covenant-breaking charge on a number of occasions. Reference was made in Chapter 1 to the figures of Mírzá Muhammad-'Alí, who refused to follow his half brother, 'Abdu'l-Baha; Ruth White, who claimed 'Abdu'l-Baha's *Will and Testament* was a forgery; and Mason Remey, who challenged the legitimacy of the Universal House of Justice. In addition to these more well-known covenant-breakers, there have been numerous others including almost all of the family of Baha'u'llah, some of the family of the Bab, and several of Shoghi Effendi's relatives. Of greater interest to the contemporary American scene are those covenant-breakers who have sprung from the original followers of Remey. These include followers of a faction that split off under Donald Harvey and who now recognize as their leader Jacques Soghomonian, a resident of Marseilles, France. Another group of covenant-breakers, known as the Orthodox Baha'i Faith, is led by Joel Marangella, who declared that Remey had appointed him as the next Guardian. Then there is the Orthodox Baha'i Faith Under the Regency, led initially by Rex King and, after his death in 1977, by a council of his family members. This faction rejects all claimants to the Guardianship after Shoghi Effendi but expects the imminent appearance of a second Guardian. Finally, there are the Jensenites, led by Leland Jensen, who became known for their prediction that the world would come to a cataclysmic end in 1980. Total membership in the various Remeyite groups numbers only in the thousands.

The last three chapters have examined various Baha'i beliefs, principles, activities, and institutions from a basically normative perspective. It is now time to turn from the abstract to the concrete, from the largely ideal and theoretical to the historical, and in so doing trace the growth of the American Baha'i community from its late nineteenth-century origins to its current role as one of the world's most influential Baha'i communities.

Part II
The Baha'i Faith in America

5

Phase I (1892–1921)

The first known reference to Baha'u'llah at a public meeting in the United States took place at the World Parliament of Religions in Chicago in September 1893. The Reverend Henry H. Jessup, director of Presbyterian missionary operations in northern Syria, quoted E. G. Browne's description of the founder of the Baha'i Faith in a paper that was presented to the congress on his behalf titled "The Religious Mission of the English Speaking Nations." It is from this event that the American Baha'i community symbolically marks its beginning.[1]

IBRAHIM GEORGE KHEIRALLA AND THE FIRST AMERICAN BAHA'IS: 1892–1898

At the time of the presentation of Jessup's paper, there were two Baha'is living in the United States. Anton Haddad and Ibrahim George Kheiralla were Lebanese business partners who had arrived in New York in the summer and winter of 1892 respectively after converting to the Baha'i Faith in Egypt two years earlier. Of the two, it was Kheiralla who would initially carry forth the Baha'i missionary banner and thereby help establish the first Baha'i communities in the West.

Kheiralla came from a Christian family whose home village was some thirty miles from Beirut. He was educated in Protestant schools and eventually attended the Syrian Protestant College. After graduating, he emigrated to Egypt and became involved in a number of business ventures. It was there, through the person of his new brother-in-law, that he first came into contact with the Baha'i Faith.[2] After taking classes from the Baha'i teacher 'Abdu'l-Karím Tihrání, he converted. In 1890, Kheiralla wrote to Baha'u'llah announcing his decision, and he received in return a tablet from his new master that stated: "Verily we heard your supplications, and granted them to you, and remembered you with such remembrance whereby the hearts will be attracted to you."[3]

Shortly after Baha'u'llah's death and with the blessing of 'Abdu'l-Baha, the two men began their westward journeys. They eventually met in Chicago, where Haddad had made unsuccessful attempts to sell their "ticket book" invention (tickets that had space for advertising on them). After a year of further financial setbacks, Haddad returned to Syria, but Kheiralla remained in Chicago and attempted a succession of money-making ventures including the selling of oriental goods and the teaching and bestowing of healing practices. The latter brought him into contact with the Chicago spiritualist subculture and eventuated in 1895 in his offering a series of classes that contained such topics as spiritual healing, the nature of the mind and soul, reincarnation, and Biblical prophecy. Included in the last three classes of a given series were many of his own understandings of the Baha'i teachings that seem to have focused on Baha'u'llah and 'Abdu'l-Baha as seen from a Christian prophetic perspective.

Kheiralla had never met either Baha'u'llah or 'Abdu'l-Baha, and the only available literature to which he had access were several articles on the Babi movement by E. G. Browne. His grasp of Baha'i teachings, therefore, was limited to what he had learned from 'Abdu'l-Karím Tihrání, which he no doubt embellished with ideas from his own Christian background. Paramount among these was that Baha'u'llah was God the Father and that his son 'Abdu'l-Baha was the return of Jesus Christ. A passage from a letter to Professor Browne from a young woman who attended Kheiralla's classes exemplifies this approach: "According to this doctor, Behá [Baha'u'llah] was God Himself. He teaches that god did not manifest *through* the personality of Behá, as in the case of Jesus, but that He really was God, and that He will not come again during this cycle. We are all called upon to believe this, or else forever lose our chance of salvation."[4]

In the last class, Kheiralla would reveal the Greatest Name, *Alláh-u-Abhá*, which can be translated as "God is Most Glorious," but it was only given to those students who wrote a confession of faith addressed directly to 'Abdu'l-Baha. Kheiralla taught that knowledge and recitation of this form of Baha'u'llah's name, which he also claimed was prophesied in the Bible, was the most important element of Baha'i belief. This aspect of Kheiralla's teachings reflected the popular religious culture of the Middle East whereby dreams, magic, talismans, and divination played a significant role.[5]

The content of the classes was probably also influenced by discussions Kheiralla had with one or more of the four individuals who had become Baha'is at the end of 1894. These included William James, Marian Miller, Thornton Chase, and Edward Dennis. Of the four, Chase was the most influential. This is borne out by 'Abdu'l-Baha's future reference to him as the "first American believer" despite the reality that both James and Miller had declared their faith before him. In this connection, it would appear that Chase's fairly extensive knowledge about religion in general may have been important to the fledgling Chicago Baha'i community and possibly to Kheiralla as well.[6] Marian Miller was likewise significant. An English citizen residing in Chicago who had previously shown interest in theosophy, she became Kheiralla's first female convert, and in 1895, following his divorce from his third wife who was still in Egypt, she married her teacher.

By the beginning of 1896, Kheiralla had been able to enroll another six believers, thereby bringing the total number of Baha'is in the Chicago community to twelve, and by the fall of the same year, this figure had risen to thirty. He soon published *Za-ti-et Al-lah: The Identity and Personality of God*, in which many of his teachings about the Baha'i Faith were consolidated. The book emphasized that the religion was not just an attempt to reform Christianity but a new and independent expression of the divine will whose foundation for acceptance was reason and logic. The publication led to increased attendance in his classes and subsequent enrollments in the Baha'i community. In 1897 Baha'is other than Kheiralla began giving lessons, and consequently, by January 1898, there were 225 registered believers residing in Chicago. Among those who would later leave their mark on the early American Baha'i community were Dr. Edward and Louisa Getsinger, William Hoar, Henry Goodale, Charles Greenleaf, and Paul Dealy.

In the summer of 1897, Kheiralla took his classes on the road. Through his Chicago connections, he was invited to speak in Enterprise, Kansas, and Kenosha, Wisconsin. In both cases, a number of individuals received the Greatest Name, and Baha'i communities were established. Then in January 1898, Kheiralla set out for the East Coast, where he made presentations in Ithaca, New York, and New York City, which already had several resident Baha'is who had moved there from Chicago, the most prominent being Arthur Pillsbury Dodge. Dodge was a self-made man, an attorney, and founder of *New England Magazine*. Later he fashioned several inventions related to the railroad industry. Dodge was also intensely

interested in religion and had followed many different paths before becoming a Baha'i. For example, he had known Mary Baker Eddy, the founder
of Christian Science, and had been asked to be one of her lawyers.[7] It
was Dodge who provided Kheiralla with both lodging and meeting space
during his visit to New York City. After five months of teaching in the
metropolis, Kheiralla had brought another 141 people into the Baha'i
ranks.

By this time, Kheiralla's teachings had begun to spread as a result of the
efforts of other community members. In Chicago, classes were given by
several of the more prominent believers including Chase, Dealy, Greenleaf,
and Maude Lamson. A relatively new convert, Howard MacNutt, was
appointed by Kheiralla as the first Baha'i teacher in New York, and James
and Isabella Brittingham administered their teacher's classes in Hudson
County, New Jersey. Baha'i groups also began to form in Philadelphia,
Washington, D.C., and Baltimore. Simultaneously, individual Baha'is took
up residence in several locations throughout New England. Moreover,
because of the enthusiasm of the Getsingers, the missionary work spread
to California, and at a later date, Chase would introduce the Faith in
Cincinnati.

In Chicago there had been very little community organization since
Kheiralla had virtually complete control over the group. However, as the
Faith began to spread, rudimentary forms of leadership started to emerge.
In both Kenosha and New York, boards of counsel were elected by the
community members. Still, at this early period, it was the figure of Kheiralla
that dominated the American Baha'i community, as indicated by the
fact that he alone had the power of giving the Greatest Name to new
converts.

Looking at the statistics related to the social backgrounds of the members of the American Baha'i communities of Chicago, Kenosha, and New
York City at this stage in their history, several trends emerge. Although
the information is somewhat sketchy, it appears that except for the
Wisconsin communities, women were drawn to the Faith in much larger
members than men. In both Chicago and New York, female converts
outnumbered male converts by at least two to one. Up until 1897, nearly
all the believers were native-born Americans, but during the next few years,
individuals from immigrant backgrounds also joined, especially in Chicago,
Kenosha, and Racine, Wisconsin. The economic backgrounds of the new
Baha'is varied by community. Chicago was dominated by middle- and
lower-middle-class professions; Kenosha had a primarily blue-collar base;
and New York's membership contained a substantial number of upper-
middle-class business people. With the exception of a few Catholics and

unaffiliated individuals, all of the converts came from mainstream Protestant religious backgrounds, although members of the Kenosha community tended to have a more conservative approach to religious matters, while the New York Baha'is were significantly more liberal.[8]

What united nearly all of those who became Baha'is was dissatisfaction with traditional religion. The more conservative elements were likely attracted to the prophetic themes in Kheiralla's teachings as well as his emphasis on Biblical prophecy, whereas the more liberal-minded would have no doubt been drawn to the spiritualist aspects of his message or the claims of its scientific and rational foundation. Whether more conservative or liberal in their individual theologies, the new Baha'is had in common the fact that "the church" no longer provided for their spiritual needs.

PILGRIMAGE AND DISSENSION: 1898–1900

Two events acted as major catalysts for the first pilgrimage of American Baha'is to Akká. The first was the return in 1897 of Anton Haddad to the United States. During his absence, Kheiralla's former business partner had visited 'Abdu'l-Baha in the Holy Land, and the tremendous impression Baha'u'llah's son had made on him was soon relayed to those American believers with whom he came into contact. Given the fact that Kheiralla had taught that 'Abdu'l-Baha was the return of Christ, it should not be surprising that many of the American converts would desire to meet "the Master." The second significant event that led toward the actualization of this goal was the conversion of Phoebe Apperson Hearst by the Getsingers and her subsequent meeting with Kheiralla. In addition to being the widow of Senator George Hearst and one of California's most wealthy women, Phoebe Hearst was also well-known in the state's leading social and political circles. When she converted, she brought with her several wealthy friends and relatives as well as her butler, Robert Turner, who was the first African American to become a Baha'i. It appears that it was Hearst's idea for the first pilgrimage. She invited the Kheirallas and Getsingers to be her guests on an extensive trip that would include a visit to Akká.

The group departed New York in September 1898. They made stops in Paris and Egypt, where several additional members joined their party including two of Hearst's nieces, Agnes Lane and Anne Aperson, a Mrs. Thornburgh-Cropper, and May Bolles. In all, the assemblage totaled fifteen. In Egypt they divided into three groups for staggered arrivals in Akká. Kheiralla, who had earlier left the group to visit his former wife and children in Egypt, was the first to arrive, on November 11. For his achievements in the West,

'Abdu'l-Baha conferred upon him a number of titles including "Conqueror of America."[9] He was also given the honor of sharing with 'Abdu'l-Baha in the groundbreaking ceremony for the Shrine of the Bab on Mount Carmel. For his part, Kheiralla appears to have been overwhelmed by the experience, for he wrote that the Master "has shown me so much kindness and benevolence that it is beyond my power to express them either in writing or in speech."[10]

The pilgrims began arriving in December and continued through February. From their recorded accounts it is clear that they were enthralled by 'Abdu'l-Baha. Recalling her first encounter with the Baha'i leader, Thornburgh-Cropper wrote: "His white robe, and silver, flowing hair, and shining blue eyes gave the impression of a spirit, rather than of a human being."[11] Hearst concluded: "The Master I will not attempt to describe. I will only state that I believe with all my heart that he is the Master and my greatest blessing in this world is that I have been privileged to be in His presence and look upon His sanctified face. His life is truly the Christ life and His whole being radiates purity and holiness."[12]

Most of the pilgrims stayed in Akká for only short periods. However, both the Kheirallas and Getsingers remained in the Holy Land until March. During this time, fissures began to form in Kheiralla's relationship with 'Abdu'l-Baha, and these cracks would eventually open into a gaping divide. There were several causes for the increasing dissension. The first, it would seem, was the almost inevitable clash between two charismatic personalities. More specifically, there was a growing awareness among both pilgrims and the Persian Baha'is in Akká that some of Kheiralla's teachings, for example reincarnation and the idea that God had a personality, were not in accord with Baha'u'llah's pronouncements. This issue came to a head when Kheiralla submitted a manuscript of his next book on the Faith, *Behá'U'lláh*, for 'Abdu'l-Baha's approval and received only partial permission for publication. Then there was the question of Kheiralla's character, which centered around his relationship with his fourth wife, Marian. At some point during the pilgrimage, Marian had become aware of her husband's previous marriages and his children's lack of knowledge of his present marital situation. Kheiralla would later claim that 'Abdu'l-Baha had a hand in his wife's growing alienation, which would eventually lead to her separation from him.[13] Perhaps the most important factor in the estrangement was the rivalry that had developed between Kheiralla and Dr. Edward Getsinger over their relative prominence in the American Baha'i community. Kheiralla began to feel that he was not being given enough vocal support by 'Abdu'l-Baha, as exemplified when he complained to the Baha'i leader about Dr. Edward Getsinger's use of certain moneys obtained from Hearst for Baha'i promotional activities but 'Abdu'l-Baha had refused to intervene.[14] Thus, by the time the Conqueror of America was set to return to the United States, he may already have been reconsidering his proclaimed loyalty.

Kheiralla arrived in New York in early May 1899. During his absence, Baha'i membership figures had risen to more than 1,000, and the return of their teacher elevated the spirits of community members even further. Except for some disparaging remarks directed toward the Getsingers, there was initially little sign of the storm that was about to break. Kheiralla spoke warmly of 'Abdu'l-Baha and informed believers of his having obtained several of Baha'u'llah's manuscripts, which he would soon translate. Moreover, within months of his return, events in Kenosha would momentarily eclipse all other issues. In American Baha'i history, this episode is referred to as the Vatralsky Affair.

Stoyan Krstoff Vatralsky was a Bulgarian-born Protestant who had been educated at Harvard and was well-known as a writer and lecturer on philosophical, ethical, and religious subjects. In the latter months of 1899, his services were procured by several Christian churches in Kenosha to counter the teachings of the Baha'is (or Truth Knowers, as they were also known). Vatralsky held a meeting on October 29 at the Park Avenue Methodist Episcopal Church, during which he gave a talk to a packed house titled "The Kenosha Truth Knowers: the Few Truths They Know and the Many Errors They Teach." At the conclusion of his essentially anti-Islamic delivery, one of the local ministers announced that anyone who wanted to obtain the Truth Knowers' lessons could get them from Vatralsky. This is turn caused vehement reactions from some of the Baha'is present, including Thornton Chase. A minor commotion followed during which a Reverend Naylor claimed Kheiralla was a liar, while Baha'is or their supporters called Vatralsky an impostor.[15] For several weeks, the controversy was maintained in Kenosha newspapers only to eventually fizzle out when Vatralsky returned in December to counter a speech given in late November by Kheiralla himself. Only about fifty people attended Vatralksy's final diatribe, but the entire episode marked the first in what over the years would become a series of conservative Christian verbal attacks on the American Baha'i community.

By the time the Kenosha controversy had subsided, the conflict between Kheiralla and the Getsingers had begun to intensify. On several occasions, Kheiralla had made remarks in public to the effect that the couple did not understand the Baha'i teachings, while the Getsingers, in league with Hearst and Haddad, had decided that the latter should go to Akká and inform 'Abdu'l-Baha of Kheiralla's growing disloyalty. When Haddad returned from the Holy Land in December, he delivered a letter to Kheiralla in which 'Abdu'l-Baha stated that there could be no appointment of an American "leader" since Baha'u'llah had forbidden the existence of a Baha'i clergy. According to Haddad, Kheiralla responded by saying: "If there can be no chief of the Behaists in America, then there will be no chief of the Behaists in Acca, and I will show Abbas Effendi ['Abdu'l-Baha] that I mean what I say and He shall see what I am able to prove it."[16]

Soon the Getsingers and Haddad began touring the Baha'i communities and informing them of 'Abdu'l-Baha's response. As part of their program, they began introducing new organizational institutions. For example, in New Jersey a five-member Board of Council was appointed, and in Chicago a ten-member body was selected. For his part, Kheiralla refused to make a public statement of loyalty to 'Abdu'l-Baha and continued to paint the Getsingers and Haddad in a negative light. More significantly, he established his own House of Justice in Chicago. The result of the controversy was to effectively split the American Baha'i community into two hostile factions.

In a final attempt to heal the rift, 'Abdu'l-Baha sent 'Abdu'l-Karím Tihrání to the United States. This was the same teacher who years before had converted Kheiralla in Egypt, and now he was given the assignment of negotiating with his former student in the hope of bringing him back into the Baha'i fold. At first the talks seemed to go well, but then they broke down, and a slide toward the inevitable break began. By the time Tihrání addressed the Chicago Baha'is in May 1890, he would say within one of his prayers: "To obey our Master is a touch-stone to everyone. Therefore, I supplicate Thee, O my God, to remove from between Thee and Thy servants the black cloud which has intervened, that they may know Thy Command and that which is best for them."[17] Shortly thereafter Kheiralla would claim that Tihrání had first tried to bribe him and then kill him.[18]

Kheiralla later shifted his allegiance to 'Abdu'l-Baha's excommunicated half brother, Mírzá Muhammad-'Alí. However, he was never able to regain the type of support that he had experienced during his first years of teaching. He wrote several more treatises, including *Facts for Behaists* and *The Three Questions*, in which he robustly defended his position, and twice reorganized his small community, but his followers never numbered more than a few hundred. He died on March 8, 1929.

The battle over the question of leadership left the American Baha'i community severely damaged. Many left the Faith during this time, and teaching activities ground to a virtual halt. Still, a handful of the more prominent individuals whom Kheiralla had converted remained. It would be on the shoulders of such people as the Getsingers, the Brittinghams, Chase, MacNutt, Dealy, Hoar, Greenleaf, and Goodall that the community would begin to rebuild.

REBUILDING THE BAHA'I COMMUNITY: 1901–1912

The years between Kheiralla's disaffection and 'Abdu'l-Baha's visit were crucial ones for the American Baha'i community. An analysis of that period reveals six significant areas for investigation: (1) the leadership of 'Abdu'l-Baha, (2) communication with the Holy Land, (3) clarification of Baha'i teachings, (4) community organization, (5) teaching and expansion, and (6) spiritual practices.

Although Kheiralla had exalted 'Abdu'l-Baha and referred to him in terms of the return of Christ, Kheiralla's own charismatic personality and 'Abdu'l-Baha's lack of proximity meant that during the earliest years of American Baha'i history most believers had little more than an abstract conception of their master. This began to change with the first pilgrimage, yet the ensuing clash in which Kheiralla at first downplayed 'Abdu'l-Baha's leadership and then renounced it altogether left a significant number of those who remained in the community somewhat ambivalent to the whole question of charismatic authority. It thus became one of the primary tasks of those prominent American believers who had stayed the course to uphold and strengthen the image of 'Abdu'l-Baha.

One of the primary vehicles underlying this mission was the pilgrimage to Akká, which many well-to-do American Baha'is continued to practice throughout the decade. For example, in the fall of 1900, the Getsingers, Arthur and Elizabeth Dodge, and William and Anna Hoar all visited 'Abdu'l-Baha. Similar trips were made by Isabella Brittingham in 1902, Laura Clifford Barney in 1904, Thornton Chase in 1907, and Juliet Thompson in 1909, just to name a few. The pilgrims' experiences were later shared both orally and in writing with the believers at home, and like the first accounts, they inevitably gave the impression of an almost supernatural presence. For example, in her diary Thompson recorded: "Now I am conscious of a close communion with a heart consuming Spirit of Love, a Spirit more intensely real than the earth and all the stars put together, than the essence of all human love, even than mother-love."[19] For his part, 'Abdu'l-Baha had to begin insisting to the American believers that his position was only that of the servant of Bahá and not the return of Christ or the Son of God. Nevertheless, many American believers during this period continued to look upon the prisoner in Akká as their Lord.

Even with the solidification of 'Abdu'l-Baha's leadership, the question of communication remained. Not only were followers and the Head of the Faith geographically separated, the issue of language remained. 'Abdu'l-Baha knew little English, and, with the rare exception, Americans had no grasp of Persian or Arabic. Consequently, the flow of information was necessarily mediated through translators. Within this framework, three channels of communication emerged. As mentioned above, pilgrims provided a source of contact with 'Abdu'l-Baha. Many recorded in the form of "pilgrims' notes" both their personal impressions of the Master and the contents of their discussions with him. These documents, however, were unofficial, since they were not approved by 'Abdu'l-Baha. In an attempt to overcome this problem, the Baha'i leader sent several Persian teachers westward to convey his wishes. Mírzá Asadu'lláh and Hasan-i Khurásání had visited the United States as early as 1900, and shortly thereafter the renowned scholar of Islamic jurisprudence and former head of the Haskim Hashim Seminary in Teheran, Mírzá Abdu'l-Fadl, arrived in the country and remained until 1904. Although they had official translators with them, at times language still proved problematic. Nevertheless, these men were able to meet with Baha'i communities throughout the country and help clarify certain doctrinal matters as well as promote 'Abdu'l-Baha's designs for administrative organization.

The most lasting form of communication, however, proved to be 'Abdu'l-Baha's written correspondence with his American followers. Since the time of Kheiralla's first conversions, Baha'is had been in written contact with 'Abdu'l-Baha, and the volume of such correspondence expanded as the years passed. The importance attached to 'Abdu'l-Baha's tablets (*alwáh*) led to copies being circulated throughout various local communities, and soon collections of tablets were being assembled and distributed. By 1912, fifteen such works had been produced by the American Baha'is.[20]

As more American followers became aware of the discrepancies between some of Kheiralla's beliefs and those of 'Abdu'l-Baha, certain clarifications became necessary. While it appears that the Kheiralla's approach to doctrine was rather fluid and that he placed more importance upon loyalty than on correct belief, a number of his teachings, especially those related to traditional Christianity, were in need of correction. Consequently, we find Mírzá Asadu'lláh informing the American Baha'is that both the doctrine of Christ's atonement for original sin and the belief in his physical resurrection were not in accord with Baha'u'llah's teachings. Both of these explanations, it should be added, caused a number of converts to leave the community.

Further clarification on doctrine was provided by Mírzá Abdu'l-Fadl's *Baha'i Proofs*, which was published in 1902. Here the Baha'i scholar divided

Baha'u'llah's writings into four categories and then expounded on each. Included in his work were discussions concerning God and his messengers as well as illuminations on personal, social, and mystical guidance. Of great importance for American believers was Abdu'l-Fadl's emphasis on a religion's practical proof. In effect, Abdu'l-Fadl argued that because all the major religions had proved durable and they had also shown the ability to transform lives, this was testimony to their being divinely guided.[21] A similar approach was used as a proof of Baha'u'llah's prophetic claims: despite all worldly opposition, his religion had succeeded.

Access to several of Baha'u'llah's works also added to a better understanding of the teachings. In 1904 and 1906, the *Book of Certitude* (*Kitáb-i Íqán*) and the *Hidden Words* were translated into English, the former by Ali Kuli Khan and the latter by Dr. Amín Faríd. Shortly thereafter, Khan also translated a number of Baha'u'llah's tablets, including "Tablet of the World" and "The Glad Tidings."

Another step forward in the consolidation of Baha'i doctrine was the publication in 1908 of a series of table talks between 'Abdu'l-Baha and an American, Laura Clifford Barney, titled *Some Answered Questions*. The book covered a wide range of topics including proofs of God's existence, Progressive Revelation, and the nature of the soul. An entire section dealt with Biblical topics, such as prophecy and various aspects of Christology (Jesus' nature and mission). In his explanations, 'Abdu'l-Baha inevitably used metaphorical interpretations. For example, when speaking of Christ's resurrection he asserted: "Therefore we say that the meaning of Christ's resurrection is as follows ... The Cause of Christ was like a lifeless body; and when after three days the disciples became assured and steadfast, and began to serve the Cause of Christ, and resolved to spread the divine teachings, putting his counsels into practice, and arising to serve him, the Reality of Christ became resplendent and his bounty appeared."[22]

Even with the gradual clarification of the teachings, individual American Baha'is often maintained their own understandings. An examination of some of the introductory books and pamphlets produced in the United States during these years makes this apparent. For example, Dealy's *The Dawn of Knowledge and The Most Great Peace*, whose last edition was published in 1908, held to a position that today would be described as fundamentalist. The book claimed that Bible passages meant exactly what they state.[23] On the other hand, Isabella Brittingham's, *The Revelation of Baha-Ullah*, which went through nine editions through 1920, took a more liberal approach to Biblical interpretation. In MacNutt's *Unity Through Love*, influences of Hindu notions of God are plainly expressed. This variety of spiritual expression was another indication of 'Abdu'l-Baha's positive approach to his western flock. Their limited understandings did not produce in him any great need for doctrinal purity. The only case that was capable of raising his anger was an individual's claiming for himself a position of interpretive authority.

In terms of the ability to adapt to the official Baha'i teachings, research has indicated that before 1912 there were essentially two groupings in the American Baha'i community. The first contained individuals who were better educated and had a fairly well developed sense of their own worldviews, while the second consisted of people who were accustomed to believing in religious authority and scriptural literalism. The former group, which was more highly represented in the East Coast communities, especially in New York, had a much more difficult time giving up their prior beliefs.[24]

The Persian teachers likewise made attempts to help the American Baha'i communities develop local administrative institutions. The exemplary models were Chicago and New York, where bodies of nine men (the House of Spirituality in Chicago and the Board of Counsel in New York) were elected. The duties of the House of Spirituality included managing the community's treasury, sponsoring its worship meetings, planning its holy day observances, and handling its basic ministerial functions such as arranging funerals and comforting the bereaved.[25] A similar institution for women, The Women's Assembly of Teaching, was created in Chicago in 1902, and in 1910, New York established a Women's Board of Counsel. In both cities, the goal of cooperative consultation between men's and women's groups was seen as the ideal, although in reality conflict was not unusual. In Chicago, at least, this was partially a result of the more conservative male members of the House of Spirituality insisting on the primacy of their authority. For their part, the women felt that the House was overly cautious and lacking in initiative. Such gender conflict was to some degree a reflection of a growing feminist sentiment in the country, but in the eyes of one Baha'i historian it was primarily the result of the fierce individualism that characterized American Baha'is at this time, a temperament that tended to undermine formal authority and organization.[26] A natural consequence of this underlying mistrust of formal organizational authority was the emergence of a number of informal leaders, generally those who had received tablets from 'Abdu'l-Baha or who had proved themselves as teachers. As a result, a number of cliques developed in the larger communities, while the lack of numbers in the smaller communities made the leadership of dominant individuals almost inevitable.

One area of Baha'i institutional success was in the field of publishing. The New York, Washington, D.C., and Boston communities all published

Baha'i books, but it was the Baha'i Publishing Society in Chicago that became the foremost producer of Baha'i literature. In all, close to seventy books and pamphlets had been published by 1912 including volumes of Baha'i scripture, commentaries on the teachings, and pilgrimage accounts. Several periodicals were also produced during this period, the earliest being the New York Board of Counsel's *Baha'i Bulletin*. The most successful Baha'i periodical was *Star of the West*, published in Chicago starting in 1911. The magazine appeared nineteen times a year. In addition to recently received tablets from 'Abdu'l-Baha, it also contained accounts of local, national, and international Baha'i activities.

Despite the pull of individualism, over the latter part of the century's first decade, American local administrative institutions increased in both number and effectiveness, and by 1909 a new phase of organizational development began with the creation of the Baha'i Temple Unity. Inspired by the Baha'is in 'Ishqábád, Russia, who had already started the construction of the first temple (*Mashriqu'l-Adhkár*) in the Baha'i world, in 1903 the Baha'is of Chicago received permission from 'Abdu'l-Baha to erect a house of worship in the United States. For the next few years, the Chicago House of Spirituality amassed both administrative and financial support from a number of local communities, and on November 26, 1907, representatives convened in Chicago and appointed a nine-member committee to locate a suitable site for the proposed temple. By April 9, 1908, $2,000 had been raised for the purchase of two building lots situated near the shore of Lake Michigan. Then, in March 1909, a national convention was held in which thirty-nine delegates, representing thirty-six cities, established a permanent national organization known as the Baha'i Temple Unity. The new institution, which was registered as a religious corporation functioning under the laws of the state of Illinois, was invested with full authority to hold title to the property of the *Mashriqu'l-Adhkár* and to provide ways and means for its construction. At this time, a constitution was written, and an Executive Board of the Baha'i Temple Unity was elected and authorized by the delegates to complete the purchase of the land. Each year thereafter, a convention was called, and by the time of 'Abdu'l-Baha's visit in 1912, the Baha'i Temple Unity had already taken over the responsibility for national publications. Increasingly the Baha'i Temple Unity would change from an auxiliary administrative institution, whose sole concern was the construction of the *Mashriqu'l-Adhkár*, into a body whose members felt a general responsibility for the overall progress of the Faith in North America.[27]

With the creation of the Baha'i Temple Unity, the Chicago House of Spirituality began to flounder. Prior to this time, the body had tended to act as a de facto national institution, and with this function now having become virtually obsolete, some of its members became less than enthusiastic. Coupled with the departure for Los Angeles of Chase, who was one of its mainstays, and the somewhat bizarre claims of his replacement, Harry Thompson, to be the next prophet after Baha'u'llah, the institution's administrative integrity was called into question. In New York, the problem faced by the Board of Counsel was different but also destructive in nature. Vehement faction fighting within the community had resulted in some of the younger believers engineering a virtual coup by replacing the Board with their own leaders. Eventually, 'Abdu'l-Baha had the membership of the Board of Counsel expanded to twenty-seven to assure that members of all factions were elected.[28] Thus, on the eve of the Baha'i leader's visit to the United States, the country's two largest and most powerful local communities saw their administrative institutions struggling for both identity and respect.

In 1900 there were more than 2,000 Baha'is in the United States. Following Kheiralla's defection, that number dropped to probably no more than several hundred, but by 1906 membership had risen to close to 1,300. This growth spurt, though modest, was a clear sign that teaching activity had once again become a significant aspect of Baha'i life. Most teaching was accomplished through firesides, whereby small groups of Baha'is would invite friends and guests to hear about and discuss the claims and teachings of Baha'u'llah and 'Abdu'l-Baha. Many communities would hold such meetings on a weekly basis, and in some of the larger cities, several different weekly firesides were common.

Expansion also resulted from individual Baha'is either visiting or relocating to new localities. As a result of these early travel teaching and pioneering efforts, between 1900 and 1907, numerous new Baha'i groups were created. Among them were groups in Milwaukee, Wisconsin (opened by Charlotte and Henry Morton), Muskegon, Michigan (Charlotte Rosenhauer), Newark, New Jersey (Hooper Harris), Boston (Alice Breed), Oakland, California (Helen Goodall), Los Angeles (George and Rosa Winterburn), Tacoma, Washington (Nathan Ward Fitzgerald), and Portland, Oregon (Ella Cooper).

Two significant teaching-related situations that emerged during the decade deserve mention. The first was the Baha'i connection with the famed Green Acre Baha'I School in Eliot, Maine, where in 1894 Sarah Farmer had established a series of summer lectures on the arts and religion in which a number of well-known thinkers and spiritualists, including Swami Vivekananda of the Ramakrishna Mission, had taken part. In 1897 the site became the home of the Monsalvat School of the Comparative

Study of Religion under the direction of Dr. Lewis Janes. When Farmer became a Baha'i in 1900, Baha'i speakers began to frequent Green Acre. Their presentations not only established a credible forum for the explanation of Baha'i teachings, they also provided the Baha'is with contacts among the East Coast's intellectual elite.

The second circumstance developed in connection with the teaching activities of the Washington, D.C., community. Because of its talented membership, which included leaders such as Laura Barney, Mason Remey, and Pauline Hannen, Washington had become the third-most influential Baha'i community in the United States, behind Chicago and New York. Primarily as a result of the efforts of Hannen, the nation's capital became the first American Baha'i community to successfully take Baha'u'llah's message to African Americans, so that by 1908 fifteen blacks had joined its ranks. Then in 1909, a young African American lawyer educated at Washington's Howard University converted to the Faith. His name: Louis Gregory.

Gregory had been greatly influenced by W. E. B. Du Bois and the Niagara Movement, and while his decision to become a Baha'i meant that he had to give up the idea of political activism, he became convinced that the "path" of which Du Bois had spoken was to be found in the Baha'i Faith and its goal of global reconstruction. To this end, he began within the Baha'i community itself by leading the way toward the implementation of integrated public meetings.[29] In 1911 he was elected to Washington, D.C.'s Working Committee (the administrative equivalent of Chicago's House of Spirituality), and in 1912 he became the only African American elected to the Executive Board of Baha'i Temple Unity. In future years, Gregory would become a leading spokesman for racial unity both within and beyond the Baha'i community.

During these years, the teaching activities of the American Baha'is were not confined to the United States. In 1904 'Abdu'l-Baha sent the pilgrim Sydney Sprague on to India and Burma, where he visited Baha'i communities and spoke at numerous meetings. A similar trip was made in 1906–1907 by William Hooper Harris and Harlan Ober. In 1909 Dr. Susan Moody went to Iran and set up a medical practice in Tehran oriented around the health concerns of women. At a later date, she helped establish a school for girls under the auspices of the Tehran Baha'i community. Though not specifically a missionary effort, the formation in 1910 of the Persian-American Educational Society (which was, in essence, a social and economic development project designed to provide the Iranian Baha'i community with educational, medical, and technical assistance) was another step in giving American Baha'is a sense of international consciousness.

Baha'i spiritual practices at this time were a mixture of the new and the traditional. It would appear that most of the large communities celebrated some of the Baha'i holy days and that many believers were familiar with the fast, obligatory prayers, and marriage and burial rituals. More significantly, the first Nineteen Day Feast was celebrated in the United States on May 23, 1905, in New York City under the guidance of Howard MacNutt, who during his pilgrimage to Akká earlier in the year had been directed by 'Abdu'l-Baha to establish the institution in his homeland.[30] As a result of the travels of Isabella Brittingham, the Feast soon spread to numerous local communities, and by 1907 it had been established as far west as Oakland and San Francisco. These early feasts were comprised of only devotional and fellowship components; it would not be until the time of Shoghi Effendi's leadership that an administrative portion would be added.

Although Baha'i devotional practices were gradually becoming part of community life, much of the form and content of communal worship was still influenced by Protestant Christianity. Sunday worship services were popular, in which the use of music was common. The singing of Christian hymns such as "Joy to the World" and "Nearer My God to Thee" was customary. Gradually the hymns began to take on a specifically Baha'i flavor. A leading light in the development of a Baha'i hymnody was Louise Waite, who had converted in 1902 and had started writing Baha'i hymns almost immediately. In 1908 her *Baha'i Hymns of Peace and Praise* was published. While Waite's hymns had a distinct Baha'i orientation to them, many of the ideas expressed therein were still very Christian in orientation. For example, we find reference to the Christian theme of sacrificial atonement in the following words of her hymn "Alleluia Song."

> Alleluia! Alleluia!
> Christ our Lord has come again
> To fulfill His glorious promise
> Given through the Sacred Pen
> Once again He comes to save us,
> Once again our sins He bears,
> Tho' the Lord of all Creation
> Yet no diadem He wears.[31]

Waite's *Baha'i Hymns of Peace and Praise* quickly became popular, and by 1910 it had completely displaced the use of Christian hymns in Chicago. Thus, by the time of 'Abdu'l-Baha's travels west, Baha'is in the United States had begun to develop a distinctly American approach to both belief and devotion.

'ABDU'L-BAHA'S VISIT TO THE UNITED STATES: 1912

As far back as 1901, the Chicago House of Spirituality had approved a petition drafted by Chase and signed by 370 believers nationwide which asked 'Abdu'l-Baha to come and permanently reside in the United States. The Baha'i leader rejected the offer on the grounds that his status as a prisoner was a symbol of his servitude to Baha'u'llah. However, after the Young Turk Revolution and collapse of the Ottoman government, 'Abdu'l-Baha was released from captivity, and two years later he finally undertook a journey to the West. After touring Europe in the fall of 1911 and spending the winter and spring in Egypt, he left Alexandria by ship and landed in New York on April 11, 1912. In his party were a translator, a secretary, and personal attendants.

During his eight-month stay in the United States, 'Abdu'l-Baha traveled from coast to coast, visiting thirty-two cities and making close to two hundred addresses. From this perspective, his visit to the United States can be seen as one large teaching effort. His presentations can be divided roughly into two categories: those in which his emphasis was more strictly theological and others where he focused on Baha'i social principles. In both cases, 'Abdu'l-Baha's talks were adapted for the ears of Western listeners. For example, in a presentation on the Oneness of Religion delivered in the city of New York on May 29, he concentrated on the idea of the word of God. In expounding his thoughts, he turned to the New Testament:

> Consider the statement recorded in the first chapter of the book of John: 'In the beginning was the Word, and the Word was with God, and the Word was God.' This is a brief statement but replete with greatest meanings. Its applications are illimitable and beyond the power of books or words to contain or express. Heretofore the doctors of theology have not expounded it but have restricted it to Jesus as 'The Word Made Flesh'.... The reality of Jesus was the perfect meaning, the Christhood in Him which in the holy books is symbolized as the Word.... The Christhood means not the body of Jesus but the perfection of divine virtues manifest in him.... The reality of Christ was the embodiment of divine virtues and attributes of God.[32]

Here we find a perfect example of 'Abdu'l-Baha's approach to theological issues. Rather than directly denying the doctrine of the Incarnation, he presented it as one limited perspective of a greater divine mystery and then went on to expound the Baha'i understanding. This conciliatory rather than confrontational approach was also used to explain Baha'i interpretations of other orthodox Christian doctrines such as the Resurrection and the Ascension, which in 'Abdu'l-Baha's talks were commonly associated with human unity and the complimentary nature of science and religion.

On June 2 at New York's Church of the Ascension, he spoke of the characteristics of the man of God: "He must not consider divergence of races nor difference of nationalities; he must not view difference in denomination and creed nor should he take into account the differing degrees of thoughts."[33] In his addresses at both Columbia and Stanford universities, he extolled the work of scientists. On October 8 before a gathering of two thousand in Palo Alto, the Baha'i leader claimed: "The highest praise is due to men who devote their energies to science; and the noblest centre is a centre wherein the sciences and arts are taught and studied. Science ever tends to the illumination of the world of humanity. It is the cause of eternal honour to man, and its sovereignty is far greater than the sovereignty of kings."[34]

In addition to his public appearances, press coverage in the form of both newspaper and magazine articles helped increase public knowledge of the Baha'i Faith. In all of the major cities visited by 'Abdu'l-Baha, newspapers announced his arrival and commented upon his message. "Beginning in June nearly every major magazine in the country and scores of smaller ones wrote of 'Abdu'l-Baha, interviewed Him or editorialized about Him."[35] A short list of such newspapers and periodicals included: the *New York Times*, the *Chicago Daily News*, the *Boston Evening Herald*, the *San Francisco Examiner, The American Review of Reviews, The Fortnightly Review*, and *Current Literature*. All of his talks were also published in the Baha'i periodical *Star of the West*, and at a later date they were compiled into a single volume, thereby bringing them to an even wider audience.

While spreading the Baha'i message was an essential component of 'Abdu'l-Baha's visit, it was not his only goal. The Baha'i leader also expended a great deal of time and energy assisting in the process of unifying his American community. To help accomplish this task, he reorganized both the Chicago and New York consultative bodies and in the process allowed women to join their ranks. More significantly, he introduced what has become known in Baha'i circles as the Doctrine of the Covenant.

Although the number of Kheiralla's followers remained in the low hundreds, the ex-Baha'i missionary was still actively promoting his cause. 'Abdu'l-Baha responded by publicly reinforcing his own position as Center of the Covenant. In an emphatic gesture on June 19 before a Baha'i gathering in New York City, he named the metropolis the "City of the Covenant." When explaining the rationale for his authoritative position, 'Abdu'l-Baha made it clear that it was Baha'u'llah's means of preventing his community from splintering into rival sects and thereby following the path of former religions. In a stark statement, the Baha'i leader proclaimed: "Therefore whosoever obeys the Centre of the Covenant appointed by

Baha'u'llah has obeyed Baha'u'llah, and whosoever disobeys Him has disobeyed Baha'u'llah."[36] It was therefore no coincidence that during his American visit, 'Abdu'l-Baha expelled three individuals for covenant-breaking.

'Abdu'l-Baha also spent much time stressing to his followers the significance of living a spiritual life. He told them that words alone were not enough. Rather, they should manifest their faith in such acts of love and kindness as consoling the bereaved, feeding the hungry, and helping the needy. In their personal lives, Baha'is should do their utmost to avoid gossip and slander, and they should make every effort to work toward expressing those virtues that would lead in the direction of peace and social harmony.

Perhaps the most symbolic event of 'Abdu'l-Baha's visit to the United States took place on May 1 when he laid the foundation stone of the American House of Worship in Wilmette, Illinois. Though it would take several decades before the temple would finally be completed, his participation in the ceremonial occasion acted as a perpetual reminder to the American Baha'i community of its commitment to both the project and his leadership.

On December 5, 'Abdu'l-Baha departed the county. He had spent 239 days in North America, and the impression he made on a large number of his followers was similar to the feelings he elicited from the first American pilgrims to visit Akká in 1898–1899. The magnetism he seemed to display was amply expressed by Juliet Thompson when she wrote in her diary: "Suddenly I had a great glimpse. In the dim hall beyond the deck, striding to and fro near the door, was One with a step that shook you! Just that one stride, charged with power, the sweep of a robe, a majestic head, turban crowned—that was all I saw, but my heart stopped."[37]

CONSOLIDATION AND CRISIS: 1913–1921

The years immediately following 'Abdu'l-Baha's departure were productive ones for the American Baha'i community. The leader's visit created a heightened level of enthusiasm that in turn led to increased teaching activity. Taking their example from 'Abdu'l-Baha's addresses, Baha'i teachers began to shift their approach from an emphasis on Biblical prophetic fulfillment to the claim that their faith contained the universal principles necessary for the renewal of religion in the modern age. Their efforts were aided by numerous tablets sent from the Holy Land, which often referred to them as soldiers in the Cause of God. The communication culminated in 1916 with *The Tablets of the Divine Plan*, five separate letters in which

'Abdu'l-Baha outlined missionary activities for separate regions of the country. Individual teaching efforts were now supplemented by group-sponsored endeavors that included funding for part-time travel teachers. Special emphasis was given to delivering the message in those areas where there were few or no Baha'is. Consequently, by the end of 1916, the American Baha'i community was able to report a membership of 2,884.[38]

American Baha'is were also active on the international front. A number of individuals made overseas trips to help spread the message. For example, Mason Remey made a world tour during which he spoke at numerous Baha'i meetings, and Laura Dreyfus-Barney and her husband Hippolyte visited the newly found Baha'i community in Tokyo.

There was also a gradual movement during these years toward the idea of a national Baha'i community as opposed to separate and independent local communities. This new identity was assisted by the continual evolution of the Baha'i Temple Unity from a project-oriented body (the construction of the *Mashriqu'l-Adhkár*) to an institution that had numerous oversight powers and responsibilities. Its yearly national convention, which met in a number of different cities, became the symbol of this transformation, and its expanded activities in the fields of publishing and teaching added to its growing prestige. In 1917 the Temple Unity adopted new bylaws that gave its executive board the right to accept or reject membership applications from local Baha'i communities.

While there were advances in terms of both the expansion of teaching activities and the development of community organization, there was also an increasing tension between two dominant religious orientations that might be termed "liberal" and "authoritarian." To some degree, the conflict between liberal and authoritarian elements was a result of 'Abdu'l-Baha's ability to represent both strands within his own teachings. His conciliatory approach to many theological issues made it readily apparent that he encouraged individual spiritual search and was not overly concerned with correct doctrine. On the other hand, he also vigorously proclaimed the Doctrine of the Covenant, which placed emphasis on the infallible guidance given to the Center of that covenant. What initially allowed for an accommodation between these potentially conflicting positions was 'Abdu'l-Baha's charismatic personality, but as time passed and the impact of his personal presence gradually diminished, animosity between the liberal and authoritarian camps began to appear. This antagonism was heightened in 1914 when one of 'Abdu'l-Baha's interpreters, Dr. Amín Faríd, and several American believers who had close ties to him were declared covenant-breakers for refusing to follow 'Abdu'l-Baha's directives, but it was the so-called Chicago Reading Room Affair of 1917–1918 that developed into a nationwide community crisis.

The Chicago Reading Room was the name of a Baha'i study circle led by Luella Kirchner, which made liberal use of the teachings of the Boston spiritualist W. W. Harmon. Harmon mingled a number of occult ideas with those found in the Baha'i writings, but the dominant element in his approach was the claim that by grasping certain of Baha'u'llah's interpretations an individual could receive "divine illumination." To the Chicago House of Spirituality and many older and more conservative Baha'is, this proposition was unacceptable. The body voted to abolish the Reading Room and called upon representatives of the national community to investigate the situation. Following the 1917 convention, a national investigative committee chaired by Mason Remey decided in favor of the House of Spirituality and charged that members of the Reading Room "were violators, creating disunity and spreading false teachings, mingling human ideas with the Word of God."[39]

The expulsion of the Reading Room group marked a victory among American Baha'i leadership for those who placed emphasis on the authority of the Covenant. Chief among such individuals was Remey, who had developed his own interpretation of the doctrine that went beyond mere loyalty to 'Abdu'l-Baha as leader of the Faith and included the holding of correct doctrines. According to this interpretation, the spiritual poison of false belief that had been tolerated in the past now had to be removed from the community. With communications to the Holy Land cut because of World War I, contact with 'Abdu'l-Baha was virtually nonexistent, and despite the resultant alienation of a number of leading Baha'is, the ideal of firmness in the Covenant became the dominant theme within the American Baha'i community. Although it is difficult to measure the overall impact of this shift, the fact that Baha'i membership figures dropped from close to three thousand in 1916 to less than half that number by 1926 would seem to indicate that it had a purging effect. As the Baha'i sociologist Peter Smith, has noted: "At a time when the wider American society was increasingly turning in on itself, and suspected dissidents were being persecuted in the infamous Red Scare, the Baha'i community, in an act of parallel harshness, expunged what for the first time had been clearly identified as its own dissident element, and, also for the first time, began to establish mechanisms by which certain standards of doctrinal orthodoxy might be ensured."[40]

With the end of the war, contact with 'Abdu'l-Baha was once again reestablished. In 1919 all fourteen of the Baha'i leader's letters comprising *The Tablets of the Divine Plan* were presented at the National Convention, and with the arrival of 'Abdu'l-Baha's personal envoy, Mírzá Asadu'lláh Fádil-i Mázandaráni, a new teaching campaign was inaugurated. The convention also focused on reconciling the divisions caused by the Reading Room episode, and its deliberations helped create a new feeling of community purpose. The following year, the architectural design produced by Louis Bourgeois was selected for the Wilmette temple. Thus, as the decade came to an end a more streamlined and reinvigorated Baha'i community set out to meet the new challenges of postwar America.

THE BAHA'I FAITH AND THE AMERICAN CULTURAL MILIEU

Any attempt to understand the "hows" and "whys" related to the establishment and development of the Baha'i community in the United States must include a brief analysis of certain features of American cultural and social life during both the late nineteenth century and the early decades of the twentieth century. While there was a significant Catholic and Jewish presence in the country, the dominant religious orientation was Evangelical Protestantism. However, there were signs of dissatisfaction within the Protestant denominations. This estrangement took on essentially two forms: religious liberalism and millennialism, or belief in the Second Coming of Christ. Moreover, on the cultural fringes, there was a growing interest in spiritualism and the occult, both of which were influenced by the rivulets of Eastern ideas that were gradually entering the mainstream. Together these diverse elements formed what might be termed "nineteenth-century American counterculture."

The flexibility of Baha'i religious ideas during this stage of its history made the movement capable of relating to unorthodox thinking. Kheiralla's emphasis on Biblical prophecy and the fulfillment of scriptural interpretation through the appearance of a new Manifestation spoke to certain currents within American millennialism. More substantial was the attraction Baha'i teachings had to those who had chosen the path of theological liberalism. Principles like the Oneness of Humanity, the primacy of morality over dogma, the disregard for priestly functionaries, the sanctity of the individual search for truth, and the claim of the compatibility of science with religion, many of which became even more openly emphasized after Kheiralla's departure, fit very nicely into the liberal Protestant approach, and thus, "there seems every indication that the Baha'i expression of such religious concerns was a major factor in its appeal."[41]

The Baha'i message likewise found fertile soil among people with spiritualist leanings. Again, this was partly a result of Kheiralla's approach, which contained his own notions of spiritual healing and reincarnation. Up until the Remey-led purge of 1917, it was not unusual to find such ideas and practices as astrology, cosmic consciousness, psychic communication, and spiritual healing mixed together with Baha'i beliefs and practices, and even after the expulsions, sympathies for many of these ideas remained common. One reason for the existence of spiritualist and occult elements was the lack of any formal enrollment procedure or clearly defined set of beliefs to which all American Baha'is had to submit. Also, as indicated on several previous occasions, 'Abdu'l-Baha's leadership style was not one that placed great emphasis on correct belief, focusing instead on "living the Baha'i life" and loyalty to the Covenant.

The Baha'i principles related to political, social, and economic reform, especially those advocated by 'Abdu'l-Baha in numerous speeches during his 1912 visit, were also a factor in bringing a number of people into the Baha'i fold, but perhaps more significantly, they spoke to a number of receptive groups whose membership spread beyond the inner core of proclaimed believers. Educational establishments, women's circles, peace groups, and institutions supporting racial integration were examples of the breadth of the sympathetic audience. In subsequent years, this social activism approach to the Baha'i Faith would become one of its important teaching themes.

Theoretically, at least, the Baha'is were somewhat ahead of the contemporary social curve when it came to the questions of racial integration and women's rights. Baha'u'llah had written on both subjects, and during his time in the United States, 'Abdu'l-Baha had addressed them in several of his presentations. In terms of social action, Louis Gregory helped integrate a number of Baha'i meetings in Washington, D.C., and Corrine True worked for the establishment and promotion of a woman's administrative institution in Chicago. However, in both arenas, Baha'is often proved to be less inclined to fully live out their proclaimed principles.

In Washington, D.C., Gregory soon ran into opposition regarding complete integration of Baha'i meetings. Under 'Abdu'l-Baha's instructions, nineteen day unity feasts had become open to all members of the community, but firesides and public talks remained largely segregated, and by 1914 the community was divided into three different camps: one that desired a community facility where only white Baha'is would be welcome; another that desired complete integration; and a third that opted for not having such a facility. This split eventually led to three separate community meetings: a white meeting took place on Sundays at the Pythian Temple; a "colored" meeting was held on Wednesdays at the Washington Conservatory of Music; and on Fridays there was a mixed meeting held in individual Baha'i homes away from the public limelight. After World War I, when contact with 'Abdu'l-Baha was eventually reestablished, a compromise was reached whereby publicly advertised meetings would be open to all races, while attendance at domestic gatherings would be left up to individual discretion. Even more problematic was Gregory's marriage to a white woman, Louisa Mathew. Although 'Abdu'l-Baha had praised, even encouraged, mixed marriages, most Baha'is—blacks included—found it difficult to accept the Gregorys' marriage or to imagine its survival in a segregated society.[42]

Despite the facts that women could vote in Baha'i elections and females were often in the forefront of teaching and outreach activities, when it came to political decision making, the pre-1912 American Baha'i community reflected many of the gender biases of the time. Both the original Chicago House of Spirituality and the New York Board of Counsel were restricted to male membership, and when women were allowed administrative power, it was through their own separate institutions (The Women's Assembly of Teaching in Chicago and The Women's Board of Counsel in New York). The division of power was not without controversy, as numerous Baha'i women were openly opposed to this form of gender segregation. The leader in the struggle for female administrative equality was Corrine True, who wrote two letters to 'Abdu'l-Baha, one in 1902 and another in 1909, in which she addressed the situation. 'Abdu'l-Baha's 1902 response maintained the status quo, but in his 1909 letter he appeared to have changed his mind:

> According to the ordinances of the Faith of God, women are the equals of men in all rights save only that of membership on the Universal House of Justice [bayt al-'adl 'umumi], for, as hath been stated in the text of the Book, both the head and the members of the House of Justice are men. However, in all other bodies, such as the Temple Construction Committee, the Teaching Committee, the Spiritual Assembly, and in charitable and scientific associations, women share equally in all rights with men.[43]

The Chicago House of Spirituality consulted on the new tablet at its meetings on August 31, 1909, and September 7, 1909, but the practice of excluding women from its membership did not change. The Chicago House assumed that 'Abdu'l-Baha's reference to a male-only Universal House of Justice was intended for the local Chicago institution, and as a consequence, it was not until 'Abdu'l-Baha's visit to America in 1912, when he sent word to the Baha'is of Chicago that the House of Spirituality should be reorganized to include women, that the change was finally made.

In the early hours of November 28, 1921, 'Abdu'l-Baha passed away. He had been in ill health, and his death was not totally unexpected. Nevertheless, word of his passing was traumatic for Baha'is around the world. The man who for the last three decades had been their leader and "perfect exemplar" was no longer with them. Waiting in the wings was his twenty-four-year-old grandson, Shoghi Effendi Rabbání, who would soon find out that 'Abdu'l-Baha had appointed him Guardian of the Cause of God. The American Baha'i community was about to enter a new phase of its history.

6

Phase II (1922–1957)

As noted in Part I, the initial years of the Guardianship were tumultuous ones for Shoghi Effendi. In 1922, and again in 1923 and 1924, he was forced to take extended leaves of absence in Europe, and on one occasion, he removed himself completely from his leadership role by leaving Baha'i affairs in the charge of 'Abdu'l-Baha's sister, Bahiyyih Khánum. However, when the new Guardian finally committed himself to the task that had so dramatically been thrust upon him, he began to exhibit a work ethic that knew no boundaries. From his headquarters in Haifa, Shoghi Effendi saw that his essential goal was one of guiding the Baha'i Faith into a new phase of its historical development. Moreover, he came to understand the significant role the American Baha'i community would play in this process. As his future wife would later explain: "Whereas Persia cradled this new world religion in the 19th Century, North America was to cradle the Administrative Order which in turn would be the precursor of the new World Commonwealth."[1]

CLARIFYING WHAT IT MEANT TO BE A BAHA'I

Shoghi Effendi inherited an American community whose membership standards were at best vague. Since the time of Ibrahim Kheiralla's departure, there had been no formal procedure that marked an individual's entrance into the Baha'i community. Unlike many other religions, there was no fixed creed to which new Baha'is had to pledge their allegiance, nor was there a requirement that new members leave their former religious communities. Consequently, even after the 1917 purge, the situation was one that allowed for a great deal of flexibility in terms of both individual belief and commitment. What had actually developed over the first two decades of the twentieth century was a multileveled membership system whose basic distinction was between "enrolled" and "unenrolled" Baha'is. Among the latter, one could find men and women who considered themselves Baha'is merely on the basis of their agreement with certain Baha'i principles or their personal attraction to either Baha'u'llah or 'Abdu'l-Baha. From the perspective of the unenrolled Baha'i, the Faith was not necessarily a new and independent religion but rather a "spiritual force" that had the ability to reinvigorate the world's great religious traditions.

Although Shoghi Effendi was not overly doctrinaire in his approach to the Baha'i teachings, he did realize that there were certain key components that a declared Baha'i had to accept and that these beliefs went beyond the scope of social principle or personal feeling. Foremost was belief in the sacred figure of Baha'u'llah, "transcendental in His majesty, serene, awe-inspiring, unapproachably glorious."[2] Second was the acceptance of 'Abdu'l-Baha as the Center of the Covenant and the perfect exemplar of Baha'i life. Finally, there was the acknowledgment of Shoghi Effendi's own position as Guardian of the Cause of God and the acceptance of his powers to interpret scripture and provide community leadership.

In setting out these three dimensions of Baha'i belief, Shoghi Effendi was very careful not to allow them to cross over or merge into one another. Thus, the Guardian frequently reminded the Baha'is that despite his immense spiritual power, 'Abdu'l-Baha was not to be put into the same category as his father. He was not the "return of Christ" but the "servant of Baha." Likewise, throughout his own period of leadership, Shoghi Effendi often stated that in no way whatsoever should the believers confuse his station with that of 'Abdu'l-Baha's. To this end, he forbade his followers to display his picture in Baha'i buildings and to celebrate his birthday publicly.

In connection with the new guidelines, in the late 1920s more specific enrollment procedures were established in local communities nationwide. These generally included a letter of application and an interview with the local administrative body. By the 1930s, it had become customary in most local communities in North America for persons to attend study classes for as long as a year before being allowed to enroll.[3] Upon acceptance into the community, the new Baha'i would be required to sign an enrollment card that declared his or her belief in Baha'u'llah as the Manifestation of God for this day. The signature also affirmed the Bab as Baha'u'llah's forerunner, 'Abdu'l-Baha as the Center of his Covenant, and the existence of specific Baha'i laws and institutions to which a believer must submit.

Another significant factor affecting Baha'i identity in the United States in the post–'Abdu'l-Baha period was Shoghi Effendi's determination that the Baha'i Faith should be seen as an independent world religion and that its members should therefore sever themselves from their former religious affiliations. Like many other aspects of his thinking, Shoghi Effendi saw the identity question in terms of stages. He viewed the world Baha'i community over which he had been given charge as a loosely organized society in its initial phase of historical development. Its members were to a great extent still clinging to their former traditions "like children to their mothers." There were Protestant Baha'is, Catholic Baha'is, and Jewish Baha'is. "They believed in the Baha'i Faith but were intimately connected with their former churches. Like fruit on a tree, they were a new crop but still stuck to the old branch."[4] The Guardian saw it as his responsibility to harvest the crop. Consequently, by the mid-1930s he had made it a requirement for all American Baha'is to officially give up their memberships in other religious organizations.

STRENGTHENING THE BAHA'I ADMINISTRATION: 1922–1936

It was Shoghi Effendi's conviction that the foundation needed for developing a mature and independent Baha'i Faith was a strong and viable administrative system. One of his first actions as Guardian was to meet with leading European and American Baha'is in Haifa and explain his plans for creating such an entity, one that would contain the foundation blocks for a future world order. The focal point of his message was that the Universal House of Justice, which would be the supreme Baha'i legislative institution and forerunner of a world parliamentary system, could not be created until Baha'i local and national institutions had both been strengthened in numbers and become more mature in operation. Toward this end, he instructed the Executive Board of the Baha'i Temple Unity that it was to change from an administrative arm of the National Convention into a legislative body that would guide all national Baha'i affairs in the United States. As part of this process, the Board would eventually evolve into the National Spiritual Assembly of the Baha'is of the United States and Canada.

By means of constant communiqués from Haifa, Shoghi Effendi relayed his instructions for the creation of the new system. In any locality where there resided nine or more Baha'is, a local spiritual assembly was to be elected that would be in charge of all local Baha'i affairs.

Similarly, delegates to the National Convention were to elect members of the National Spiritual Assembly, who would have control over all questions of national significance. In their modes of operation, these assemblies were to employ Baha'i methods of consultation whereby all opinions were to be voiced in an open and detached manner. Where there were areas of special need, the assemblies should appoint committees that would investigate and then report back their findings to the elected bodies for further consultation and decision making. It was extremely important, however, that local and national issues be distinguished from one another and that the appropriate assembly be given jurisdiction.

In his letters, the Guardian made very clear the degree of power he was handing over to the assemblies. In this regard he wrote: "The Baha'is must obey and be submissive to the decisions made by the Spiritual Assembly and not engage in any activity related to the Baha'i Faith without having consulted the Spiritual Assembly."[5] Though he still requested that minutes of all local assembly meetings be sent to Haifa as well as to the National Spiritual Assembly, Shoghi Effendi's goal was to create both local and national institutions that were capable of independent functioning within their own spheres of reference.

By 1925, the first stage of the administrative transition was virtually complete. The loosely organized Baha'i communities of the pre-Guardian period had, for the most part, transformed themselves into viable functioning units. It was in this year that Shoghi Effendi instructed the National Spiritual Assembly that the term "assembly" should only be used to refer to an elected Baha'i institution and not, as in previous years, to individual Baha'i communities as a whole.[6]

For the remainder of the decade, emphasis was placed on developing positive methods of communication between the various Baha'i administrative institutions. Special attention was given to the proper relationship between local and national assemblies as well as the desired manner of interaction between the National Convention and National Spiritual Assembly. This effort was assisted by the national publication of *Baha'i News* beginning in 1924, which provided all Baha'is access to the Guardian's correspondence. What is more, the adoption of a Baha'i National Constitution in 1927 officially set down the powers, duties, and functions of the National Spiritual Assembly and thereby gave it a firm legal foundation. Consequently, despite the fact that there were difficulties along the way, by 1927 there were forty-seven functioning local spiritual assemblies in North America, and by 1929 enough institutional maturity had taken place that Shoghi Effendi could publish the first in a series of letters in which he would detail the evolution of what he referred to as "The World

Order of Baha'u'llah." In these epistles to the believers, written between the years 1929 and 1936, the Guardian spoke of the current Baha'i administrative institutions as the building blocks for a future world civilization and the Baha'is as their craftsmen. In his own words:

> I cannot refrain from appealing to them who stand identified with the Faith to disregard the prevailing notions and the fleeting fashions of the day, and to realize as never before, that the exploded theories and the tottering institutions of present day civilization must needs appear in sharp contrast with those God-given institutions which are destined to arise upon their ruin. I pray that they may realize with all their heart and soul the ineffable glory of their calling the overwhelming responsibility of their mission, and the astounding immensity of their task.[7]

During the years that Shoghi Effendi was penning his World Order letters, the National Spiritual Assembly was struggling to find the correct balance between centralized and localized modes of authority. As the Guardian's official correspondence indicates, the national body often had the tendency to be overly officious, and he had to periodically remind its members that proper administrative form should not be allowed to kill the spirit of the Faith. For its part, the Assembly introduced several innovations designed to lessen its authoritarian image, including visits by its members throughout 1933 to numerous local communities and the convening in the following year of a series of conferences that were intended to better acquaint representatives from local assemblies with the national institution's methods of operation. The success of these ventures helped Shoghi Effendi conclude in 1936 that both the national and local American Baha'i administrative institutions were strong enough to take the lead in an international campaign of expansion.

OPPOSITION AND RESPONSE

Shoghi Effendi's Guardianship and the move toward institutionalized authority that it embodied were not free from opposition. Those who felt that the Baha'i movement was more of a spiritual attitude than a formalized religion found the new leader's approach difficult to accept. Harrison Gray Dyar, an eminent entomologist and editor of the magazine *Reality*, whose articles from the time of its inception in 1919 had been influenced by Baha'i themes, was highly critical of the new order. Though never an official member of the community, Dyar became a spokesman for some of those believers who felt that 'Abdu'l-Baha had portrayed the Baha'i Cause as one that could never be organized. From his original criticisms, Dyar went on to advocate an extreme individualism in which all forms of religious authority were rejected. His approach eventually led him to deny that the Baha'i movement had any social program at all.[8] Since the magazine was not under Baha'i ownership, there was little besides steering its members away from contributing or subscribing that American Baha'i leadership could do to counter Dyar's offensive. Eventually *Reality* shifted away from Baha'i content and became almost thoroughly oriented toward the occult and the "new thought" movement. By 1929, the magazine was out of production.

A significant contributor to *Reality* during this period was Mírzá Ahmad Sohrab, one of 'Abdu'l-Baha's former secretaries and translators. Though not as bombastic in expression as Dyar, Sohrab shared the editor's belief that the Baha'i Faith was not meant to be highly organized, and his former close relationship with 'Abdu'l-Baha gave his opinions a degree of authority that Dyar's lacked. In 1927, Sohrab moved to New York, where he soon found himself at odds with the city's local spiritual assembly for not requesting their permission before speaking publicly on Baha'i themes. Sohrab had earlier come into conflict with leading Baha'is such as Mason Remey and Horace Holley, whom he had identified with "the dark ages of blind authority,"[9] and this renewed antagonism only confirmed for him his belief that the American Baha'i community was heading in the wrong direction. In 1929, in cooperation with several other Baha'is including Mr. and Mrs. Lewis Stuyvesant Chanler, Sohrab formed the New History Society, whose aim was to spread his vision of the Baha'i Faith. The Society became engaged in sponsoring public lectures and the publication of Baha'i books, and from its ranks, a youth section emerged known as The Caravan of East and West.[10]

In response to the activities of the New History Society, the National Spiritual Assembly made efforts to bring the group under its administrative control, and when these attempts failed, with Shoghi Effendi's consent, the national body expelled Sohrab and the Chanlers from the Baha'i Faith. In addition, the Assembly advised American Baha'is not to cooperate in any way with the Society or its members. Conflict between the two communities would erupt once again in 1939 when the New History Society opened a Baha'i bookshop in New York and the National Spiritual Assembly sued in an attempt to disallow Sohrab the use of the name Baha'i. The legal challenge failed, and Sohrab responded in 1942 by writing *Broken Silence*, in which he now freely expressed his negative feelings toward Shoghi Effendi. Ironically, while for some years the New History Society continued to have a liberal appeal, its overall impact on the American Baha'i community was to make its members even more vocal in defense of the Covenant.[11]

Another anti-organization spokesperson who raised her voice against Shoghi Effendi was Ruth White. White believed that 'Abdu'l-Baha had conclusively stated that the Baha'i Faith could not be organized because it was "the spirit of the age." Specifically, she held that the function of spiritual assemblies was not that of governing the Baha'i community but spreading the Faith and promoting international good will.[12] In her opposition to Shoghi Effendi's leadership, she went as far as to question the validity of 'Abdu'l-Baha's will. To this end, she found a British handwriting expert who, based on his examination of photographs of the document, claimed that it was a forgery. White was subsequently declared a covenant-breaker, and in 1930 she went on to form the Baha'i World Union. The new movement found little support in the United States and eventually fizzled out. In the 1940s, White became a follower of the Indian mystic, Meher Baba.

While the arguments put forth by the likes of Dyar, Sohrab, and White caused a number of disruptive waves within the American Baha'i community, the more significant issue regarding the question of organization was not whether authoritative institutions were required but the degree and extent to which authority would be distributed on the national level. Here, reference is made to the power struggle that took place during the late 1920s and early 1930s between the National Convention and the National Spiritual Assembly.

From the time that the Baha'i Temple Unity came into existence (1909), the National Convention had become an important Baha'i institution, and in 1925, Shoghi Effendi increased its status by raising its functions beyond a mere elective body to one with limited consultative powers. At the 1927 Convention, the delegates broke with tradition and presented their own agenda in place of the National Spiritual Assembly's program. For several years afterward, efforts were made by prominent Baha'is to make the National Convention an independent administrative institution with which the National Spiritual Assembly would be required to consult on a regular basis. In 1930, the National Spiritual Assembly officially opposed this development, but certain elements within the community continued to push for the change. Such antagonisms have led one Baha'i scholar to conclude that "the convention was the last stronghold for individuals who could not quite accept the authority of the National Spiritual Assembly over them."[13] The situation was aggravated by the fact that one of the members of the National Spiritual Assembly, Alfred Lunt, was at odds with other members of that body and attempted to use the 1933 and 1934 conventions to promote his own agenda. This led the National Spiritual Assembly to expel him from its membership, and it appeared that the crisis might permanently split the American Baha'i community. Only Shoghi Effendi's intervention, which came in the form of a telegram warning of the dire consequences that would follow if the situation was not resolved, prevented a breakdown. The Guardian called for Lunt's reinstatement and a commitment by all parties to the undivided authority of the National Spiritual Assembly. The warning from Haifa brought about a fragile peace between the two factions, but in time the supporters of the National Convention lost their impetus, and the institution took a permanent back seat to the National Spiritual Assembly.

PLANNED EXPANSION: 1937–1963

In April 1938, one year after his marriage to the Canadian-born Mary Maxwell (later known as Amatu'l-Bahá Rúhíyyih Khánum), Shoghi Effendi launched an American Seven Year Plan designed to systematically expand and enlarge the American Baha'i community. The plan was built on the foundation of two earlier and less ambitious teaching projects known as the Plans of Unified Action, which the National Spiritual Assembly had initiated with limited success between the years 1926 and 1934. In addition to increasing the number of believers, the Seven Year Plan called for Baha'is to find permanent residences in all American states and Canadian and Latin American provinces. The scope that Shoghi Effendi gave to the plan can be seen in the following message, which he sent to the American believers upon its release: "Viewed in the perspective of Baha'i history, the Seven Year Plan, associated with the closing years of the First Baha'i Century, will come to be regarded as the mightiest instrument yet forged, designed to enable the trustees of a firmly established, steadily evolving Administrative Order to complete the initial stage in the prosecution of the world mission confidently entrusted by the Center of the Covenant to His chosen disciples."[14]

On the eve of the American Baha'i community's "historic mission," the 1936 religious census conducted by the federal government revealed that there were 2,584 Baha'is residing in the United States. This meant that the number of American believers had doubled over the previous ten years. The Baha'is were fairly evenly spread across the country, with the largest communities being found in Illinois, New York, Michigan, Wisconsin, and California. The number of local spiritual assemblies totaled sixty-four.

A more thorough sociological glimpse of the American Baha'i community during this period can be gleaned from the contents of another 1936 survey, this one carried out by the National Spiritual Assembly.[15] The internal census showed that roughly two-thirds of the current membership had joined the movement after 1919, and that the large preponderance of all believers (76 percent) were of northwest European background (and among these, British and German ancestry predominated). There were virtually no members whose ethnic identity was either eastern European or Irish, but 6 percent of the membership was African American. Given the social status of African Americans as expressed in both official and less overt practices of segregation, this was a remarkably high number.

The religious backgrounds of the Baha'is were reflective of this ethnic profile. Nearly one-third reported mainstream Protestant denominations (Episcopalian, Methodist, Presbyterian, Congregationalist, Baptist) as their prior affiliations, and another 37 percent cited other Protestant identities. Those claiming Catholic associations amounted to 4 percent. The community was now old enough to report a 14 percent Baha'i identity (second generation). Those claiming no prior religious association amounted to less than 1 percent of Baha'i membership. In addition, there were several believers who came from either Jewish, Muslim, or Mormon backgrounds. Among the large Protestant contingent, more liberal persuasions were predominant, while extreme fundamentalist affiliations were completely lacking.

The one statistic in the 1936 survey that proves somewhat puzzling given other sources of information concerning the early growth of the Faith in the United States is the small number of individuals (4 percent) claiming metaphysical or spiritualist links. One suggestion has been made that the low percentage may have been a result of the fact that those who had such connections were also members of Protestant denominations, and only the latter association showed up on the survey.[16] It also may reflect the long-term impact that the 1917 "housecleaning" had on the more marginal religious positions within the American Baha'i community.

The survey revealed one particular in the American Baha'i community that had remained a constant since its founding years, namely the high percentage of female followers. Women comprised a full two-thirds of the 1936 membership. At the moment, there is not enough information available to come to any firm conclusions as to why this was the case, although it does fit the general picture of the feminization of religion that was taking place in the United States during the late nineteenth and early twentieth centuries, whereby religious affairs within families were increasingly becoming the domain of females. One might also speculate that the charismatic presence of figures such as Ibrahim Kheiralla and 'Abdu'l-Baha may have been particularly attractive to females. All in all, the findings of the National Spiritual Assembly's 1936 survey can be summed up as follows: "The typical Baha'i of that time was elderly, female, Anglo-Saxon, and had been Protestant."[17]

The First Seven Year Plan was a reflection of 'Abdu'l-Baha's strategy (as laid out in his *Tablets of the Divine Plan*) of targeting North America as the continent where the Baha'i Faith would have to become numerically and administratively strong enough to support the movement's worldwide expansion. To this end, the dispersion of existing believers throughout the Americas was given just as much priority as the enrollment of new members. Even though the plan was launched at a time when the country was still feeling the impact of the Great Depression and World War II would later overshadow its crucial years, the goals related to the strategic movement of Baha'is were successfully met. By 1945, there were 134 local spiritual assemblies in North America (compared to sixty-nine in 1937), and in Latin America, the Faith expanded from one isolated believer to forty functioning localities. What is more, twenty-three of these new "southern" communities contained local spiritual assemblies. The scheme was also successful in terms of North American conversions. By 1947, the Baha'i population had risen to more than 5,000. In addition to the 134 local spiritual assemblies, Baha'is now resided in more than 900 localities.

In his 1946 message to the American Baha'i National Convention, Shoghi Effendi announced the commencement of the Second Seven Year Plan by asking the followers of Baha'u'llah "to arise and simultaneously bring to fruition the tasks already undertaken and launch fresh enterprises beyond the borders of the Western Hemisphere."[18] The first objective of the new plan was the consolidation of those goals already accomplished throughout the Americas by increasing the scale of teaching efforts. In addition, the Guardian called for the formation of three new national spiritual assemblies: one for the Dominion of Canada, another for Central America, and a third for South America. In terms of international expansion, systematic teaching activity was to be initiated on the European continent that aimed at the establishment of assemblies in the Iberian Peninsula, the low countries, the Scandinavian states, and Italy. Shoghi Effendi reminded the American community that in order to fulfill these goals it would have to rise to new levels of commitment in response to its divine mission.[19] Like its predecessor, the Second Seven Year Plan met with a number of successes. In 1948, the National Spiritual Assembly of the Baha'is of Canada was created, followed in 1951 by the establishment of the National Spiritual Assembly of Central America. On the teaching front, by 1953, American pioneers were actively involved in the European phase of the plan. While some American members were lost to the new Canadian community, there was a modest increase in the number of followers in the United States, so that by the early 1950s, there were approximately 6,000 Baha'is residing in the country.

Both Seven Year Plans contained specific objectives related to the completion of the House of Worship in Wilmette, Illinois. The cornerstone of the *Mashriqu'l-Adhkár* had been laid in 1912 during 'Abdu'l-Baha's visit to Chicago, but financial problems had delayed and then slowed its construction. By 1938, the superstructure had been raised, and the first plan saw the finishing of the exterior ornamentation. The second plan had as one of its main objectives the completion of the interior ornamentation. This final construction goal was accomplished on time, and the "Mother Temple of the West" was publicly dedicated on May 1, 1953.

The American Baha'is began their most ambitious program of expansion in 1953. A multination conference held that year in Wilmette kicked off the community's participation in Shoghi Effendi's Ten Year Global Crusade. The new scheme assigned each national Baha'i community its own international teaching and consolidation agendas. In comparison to the two previous plans, the American component of the Ten Year Global Crusade placed more emphasis on consolidation and internal growth than geographical diffusion. As a result, even in the face of Shoghi Effendi's sudden and community-jarring death in 1957, by the end of the Crusade in 1963, the Baha'i population in the United States had risen to more than 9,600.[20]

AMERICAN LIEUTENANTS

There were a number of individuals who came to the forefront of American Baha'i leadership during the period of the Guardianship. None, however, eclipsed the prominence attained by Mason Remey, Horace Holley, Louis Gregory, and Dorothy Baker.

Remey, who was an Episcopalian from a prominent Washington, D.C., naval family, first heard of the Baha'i Faith in Paris in 1899, where he was studying architecture. Along with his roommate, Herbert Hopper, he converted after taking lessons from May Bolles. Upon his return to the United States, Remey threw himself into Baha'i activities. For example, in 1907, he helped organize Washington, D.C.'s first Baha'i consultative body, known as the Working Committee. In 1908, he received permission from 'Abdu'l-Baha to travel for the Faith in Iran and Russia, and by 1909, he had become sufficiently well-known in the American Baha'i community to be elected to the Executive Board of the Baha'i Temple Unity, on which he played a leading role in the organization of the temple project. From November 1909 to June 1910, he and his traveling companion, Howard Struven, made a world-encircling teaching trip that took them to Hawaii, Japan, Burma, India, and Akká. As already mentioned, after

'Abdu'l-Baha's visit to America, Remey became the leading spokesman of those who favored centralized authority, and during World War I, when contact with Akká was broken, he vigorously opposed what he considered marginal elements within the community. His loyalty to 'Abdu'l-Baha and Shoghi Effendi brought him praise from both Baha'i leaders. In one of his tablets to the American believers 'Abdu'l-Baha spoke of his infinite love for Remey,[21] and the Guardian often mentioned him as one of America's most eminent Baha'is.

In June 1923, Remey was elected a member of the National Spiritual Assembly of the Baha'is of the United States and Canada, and for the next thirty-four years, he continued to fill important administrative positions on both the national and international levels. In addition to his administrative roles, Remey also made numerous international teaching trips and penned several popular Baha'i pamphlets. When Shoghi Effendi established the first International Baha'i Council in March 1951, he appointed Remey as its president, and later that year the Guardian named his American lieutenant a Hand of the Cause of God.

Like Remey, Horace Holley first heard of the Baha'i Faith in Europe. In 1911, at the age of twenty-four, he went with his wife to Thonon-les-Bains, France, to hear 'Abdu'l-Baha, and the couple met the Baha'i leader again the following year when they moved to Paris. While living in the French capital, Holley published his first work on the Baha'i Faith, *Bahaism: The Modern Social Religion*. Holley returned to New York after the outbreak of war in Europe, and by the early 1920s, he had become active enough within the Baha'i community to be known nationally. In 1923, he was elected to the National Spiritual Assembly of the Baha'is of the United States and Canada, and he would continue to be elected annually to this body until 1959. He would serve as the institution's secretary from 1924 to 1930 and again from 1932 to 1959 (see Table 3). It was during his first term that the position was made full-time, and Holley gave up an established career in advertising to fulfill its requirements.[22] In addition to serving on the National Assembly, Holley acted as editor of *World Unity Magazine* and also and helped with the publication *Star of the West*. When in the late 1930s the national administrative headquarters was moved from the East Coast to the vicinity of the *Mashriqu'l-Adhkár*, Holley took up permanent residence in Wilmette, from where he came to be known for his top-down approach to administration, a style he shared with Remey.

Despite a heart attack suffered in 1944, Holley refused to retire and even expanded his Baha'i role by taking part in many international events. For example, in 1948, he represented the National Spiritual Assembly of

Table 3 Significant National Spiritual Assembly Secretaries

Name	Years of Service
Horace Holley	1924–1930 & 1932–1959
Charles Wolcott	1961–1963
David Ruhe	1963–1968
Glenford Mitchell	1968–1982
Robert Henderson	1983–present

the United States at the election of the first National Assembly in Canada, and after being appointed a Hand of the Cause by Shoghi Effendi in 1951 he participated in several overseas conclaves as Shoghi Effendi's personal representative. Of the international conferences held in 1953, Holley attended those in Kampala, Stockholm, New Delhi, and Chicago.[23]

Louis Gregory was the first prominent African American to become a Baha'i. It was noted previously that he converted in 1909 after graduating from Howard University with a degree in law and that he was elected to both Washington, D.C.'s Working Committee (1911) and the Executive Board of the Baha'i Temple Unity (1912). In the spring of 1911, Gregory went on pilgrimage to meet 'Abdu'l-Baha and received the Baha'i leader's support for both integrating Baha'i meetings and actively teaching the Faith to African Americans. According to Gregory's biographer, Gayle Morrison, 'Abdu'l-Baha also envisaged and encouraged Gregory's future interracial marriage to a fellow pilgrim, Louisa Mathew.[24]

In 1922, Gregory was elected to the National Spiritual Assembly, and he served as a member of the national institution for extended periods in the 1920s, 1930s, and 1940s. His gifts, however, were not primarily those of an administrator but of a teacher and social activist.

From his earliest days as a Baha'i, when he gave up his law practice to direct all of his energies into his religious activities, until the latter years of his life, Gregory made numerous teaching trips throughout the country, focusing his efforts on the southern states. For a period of time in the 1920s and 1930s, he was paid by the National Spiritual Assembly for his service, and when this monetary support ended, he continued his teaching endeavors despite the financial hardships they brought him. His primary pursuit within the American Baha'i community focused on racial harmony. He was a leading light in promoting the earliest Baha'i Race Amity Conventions of the 1920s and 1930s (see below), and in the 1940s, he served on the National Spiritual Assembly's Race Unity Committee. As subsequent pages will reveal, his work in this arena often brought him heartbreak, but it was never enough to dampen his faith. Shortly after his death in

July 1951, Shoghi Effendi posthumously awarded Gregory the position of Hand of the Cause. The Guardian's cablegram of August 6 contained the following: "Profoundly deplore grievous loss of dearly beloved, noble-minded, golden-hearted Louis Gregory, pride and example to the Negro adherents of the Faith.... Deserves rank of first Hand of the Cause of his race. Rising Baha'i generation in African continent will glory in his memory and emulate his example.[25]

Dorothy Baker's paternal grandmother was Ellen Beecher, who had become a Baha'i before 1900. As a child, Dorothy was taken by her grandmother to meet 'Abdu'l-Baha, but she did not really become committed to teaching her religion until 1929, when she had a mystical experience while attending the National Convention in Chicago. Following her return home, she and her husband began to participate more actively in the affairs of their local Baha'i community of Lima, Ohio. At this time, she started corresponding with Shoghi Effendi, and in 1934, with the Guardian's encouragement, she began to expand her activities by both speaking to groups outside of Lima and teaching at Baha'i summer schools.

Baker soon began to attain national recognition and was asked to participate on several national committees, including the Race Unity Committee. Meanwhile, she continued her travel teaching efforts. In 1937, she was elected to the National Spiritual Assembly, and she would remain a member of this body for fifteen years, serving as its chairman between 1945 and 1949. By the 1940s, her lecture schedule had increased dramatically, yet she continued to serve on her local and national spiritual assemblies as well as participate in the work of the Inter-America Committee, the Race Unity Committee, and the Regional Teaching Committee for Ohio and Indiana. From 1943 on, her teaching activities were split between the United States and international goal areas. Over the next ten years, she periodically visited fifteen countries in Latin and South America and fourteen nations in Europe.

In December 1951, Shoghi Effendi appointed Dorothy Baker to the rank of Hand of the Cause. After making a pilgrimage to Haifa in 1953, she attended all four international teaching conferences that were part of the opening of the Ten Year Global Crusade. Following her participation in the New Delhi conference, during which she was able to speak to Indian Prime Minister Jawaharlal Nehru, Shoghi Effendi instructed Baker to remain in the subcontinent another month to make an extensive teaching tour. Her itinerary took her not only to the large metropolitan centers of Delhi, Varanasi, and Bombay, but also to a number of smaller cities and towns. Her popularity and success led the Guardian to extend her stay an extra six weeks. As fate would have it, the plane on which she eventually departed from Karachi later crashed on the final leg of its journey from Rome to London, killing all on board. A month after her death, Shoghi Effendi was quoted as saying: "Now the Mediterranean has the blessing of the pearl that was Dorothy."[26]

RACE RELATIONS: "THE MOST CHALLENGING ISSUE"

To understand where the American Baha'i community stood in relationship to the existing social norms governing race relations in the United States during the first half of the twentieth century, two avenues of investigation must be pursued. On the one hand, Baha'i teachings regarding race will be examined from a theoretical perspective. This approach will include an examination of what Baha'is claimed to believe as well as an assessment of the degree to which such teachings were attractive to specific elements within the African American community. The second aspect will examine to what extent American Baha'is both emphasized and implemented these teachings.

Baha'u'llah taught that the time was ripe for humanity's coming of age and that part of this maturity was the conscious awareness of its fundamental unity. To achieve this goal, he urged the abolition of racial and religious prejudice. While 'Abdu'l-Baha shared some of the racial stereotypes that were characteristic his time and place,[27] he was also a champion of racial equality, as indicated by his claim that "God maketh no distinction between the white and the black.... God is no respecter of persons on account of either colour or race. All colours are acceptable unto Him, be they white, black, or yellow."[28]

It would appear that Ibrahim Kheiralla did not focus on social issues and that the early Baha'i communities followed suit. It was not until 1907 in the Washington, D.C., community that any real effort to teach the Faith to African Americans was made. The leaders in this endeavor were Joseph and Pauline Hannen, who began inviting blacks to their home to attend Baha'i meetings. It was the Hannens who introduced Louis Gregory to the Baha'i teachings, and after his conversion, the young lawyer began actively spreading his new beliefs among local African American groups. In 1910, Gregory made his first teaching trip to the South, where he spoke at a number of black churches in Richmond, Virginia, Durham, North Carolina, and Charleston, South Carolina. During his visit to the United States, 'Abdu'l-Baha followed in Gregory's footsteps by addressing several black gatherings, including a group at Howard University and the Fourth Annual Convention of the National Association for the Advancement of Colored People (NAACP).

As a result primarily of the work of Gregory and a few leading Baha'i pioneers in the field of interracial relations, by the 1920s, a number of African American intellectual and cultural leaders had heard of and investigated the Baha'i Faith. Chief among these was Alain Locke, who graduated in philosophy from Harvard University in 1907 and was the first black Rhodes scholar, studying at Oxford (1907–1910) and the University of Berlin (1910–1911). He subsequently received his PhD in philosophy from Harvard in 1918, the same year in which he declared himself a Baha'i.

Locke would subsequently become the intellectual source behind the artistic movement of black culture known as the Harlem Renaissance. As editor of the anthology *The New Negro*, Locke contributed the title essay, which served as the movement's manifesto.[29] Although Locke's Baha'i activities were intense but irregular, there is little doubt that his ideas related to cultural pluralism and tolerance were influenced by the Baha'i ideal of unity in diversity. While there is no available evidence at this time as to the extent to which Locke shared his religious convictions with other leading lights in the Renaissance, it would be hard to imagine that a certain degree of personal interchange did not take place. Along with his involvement in several of the Baha'i-sponsored Race Amity Conventions spoken of below, the outstanding events in Locke's Baha'i life included his pilgrimage to Haifa in 1924 in which he met Shoghi Effendi, and the Guardian's later request, which Locke fulfilled, that the American scholar make suggestions related to his translation of Baha'u'llah's major doctrinal work, the *Kitáb-i Íqán*.[30]

W. E. B. Du Bois was also aware of the Baha'i movement. As the acting editor of the journal of the NAACP (*The Crisis*), Du Bois printed a version of 'Abdu'l-Baha's address to the group's fourth annual convenion and affirmingly noted the universalism inherent in the Baha'i leader's message. He also lectured one summer at the Baha'i Green Acre Baha'i School in Maine. Later, especially after his views became more separatist in orientation, Du Bois harshly criticized the Baha'is, primarily for their failure to live up to the standards that 'Abdu'l-Baha had set. It is an interesting historical footnote, however, that in 1936 Du Bois' wife, Nina, enrolled in the New York Baha'i community, only to resign shortly thereafter as a result of her husband's negative response.[31]

The story of the American Baha'i community's promotion and implementation of its principles relating to race relations during this time is characterized by alternating periods of enthusiasm and restraint. Endorsement from the Holy Land was usually followed by increased activity that would subside over time only to be revived by further encouragement from

Haifa. Several factors contributed to those periods when interracial activity and policy implementation were not given priority. These included financial restrictions, subtle racist sentiment within the community, and fear that an emphasis on racial questions would either lead to internal disunity or alienate the non-Baha'i public to such a degree that the overall growth of the Faith in the United States would be hampered.

In his *Tablets of the Divine Plan*, 'Abdu'l-Baha had emphasized the need for teaching the Faith in the southern section of the country. Louis Gregory had previously made teaching contacts in the South, and he once again took the lead in this endeavor so that by the early 1920s, there were many scattered believers in the region. The next major step was a Baha'i-sponsored race amity convention held in Washington, D.C., in May 1921. At the time, the United States had just experienced one of the greatest periods of interracial strife in its history, and the amity convention was designed to bring whites and blacks together to encourage the implementation of the Baha'i principle of unity in diversity. Baha'is served as chairmen of the sessions and also gave a number of talks. Included among the African American Baha'is to address the convention were Gregory, Coralie Cook (the wife of a Howard University professor), and Alexander Martin, an attorney who had been one of the first black Phi Beta Kappas. One session was chaired by Alain Locke. Gregory later claimed that it was "the first convention for amity between the white and colored races in America, and so far as we know, the world."[32]

A second amity convention followed later in the year. Held in early December in Springfield, Massachusetts, the conclave brought together more than 1,000 people from both races and of varying creeds for two days of addresses and discussions. As with the first convention, the program avoided political innuendo and focused instead on constructive means for fostering interracial harmony. One result of this approach was that several Christian churches decided to form their own interracial committees.

Despite the accomplishments of the first two amity conventions, it was another two years before the next convention took place. 'Abdu'l-Baha's death and the adjustment to Shoghi Effendi's leadership seemed to sap much of the American Baha'i community's teaching energy. The Guardian, however, continued to praise the events, and when the New York Race Amity Convention was finally held in March 1924, it proved to be even more successful than the first two gatherings primarily because the organizers made the decision to invite representatives from such groups as the NAACP and the National Urban League in addition to leaders of religiously based organizations. Besides Baha'i speakers, the audience was able to hear from such prominent individuals as writer and Acting Secretary of the

NAACP James Weldon Johnson, and Franz Boas, professor of anthropology at Columbia University, both of whom made appeals for cross-cultural understanding.

After another convention was held in October 1924, there was a two-year respite. This was possibly a result of the fact that Gregory was not reelected to the National Spiritual Assembly in 1924. By 1927, however, the national body seemed once again committed to the question of race relations, as seen by its formation of the National Committee on Racial Amity, of which Gregory was a leading member. The committee proceeded to draft a statement of purpose that was subsequently sent to Shoghi Effendi. The Guardian responded by describing the document as admirable in its purpose and then went on to say that "it served as a potent reminder of these challenging issues which still confront in a peculiar manner the American believers."[33] Following the committee's formation and Shoghi Effendi's positive reply to its efforts, a series of interracial meetings were held, with major gatherings taking place in Washington, D.C., New York, and Boston. A similar level of activity followed in 1928, and in 1929, amity conferences took place in Detroit, Michgan; Dayton and Columbus, Ohio; and Buffalo and Rochester, New York. Indeed, these three years marked the apex of Baha'i-sponsored interracial activities.

In 1931, the National Spiritual Assembly introduced an amity project in the South that involved sending two interracial teams of traveling teachers to the region. Gregory and his white companion, Willard McKay, toured the states of Georgia, Tennessee, and Alabama. They spoke at Tuskegee Institute, where both George Washington Carver and Booker Washington's son praised Baha'i social principles.

In 1932, the number of amity activities again began to fall off so that by 1935, Alain Locke would describe the situation as one of stagnation. Fallout from the Great Depression was certainly part of the reason for the decline, but it was more likely the growing heedlessness toward the race question by the American Baha'i community as a whole that was the major cause.[34] Inevitably, it was Shoghi Effendi who stimulated a reversal of attitude with the publication of his *The Advent of Divine Justice*, in which he referred to the racial situation in the United States as "The Most Challenging Issue" and quoted 'Abdu'l-Baha: "If this matter remaineth without change enmity will be increased day by day, and the final result will be hardship and may end in bloodshed."[35] In 1939, the National Spiritual Assembly responded by forming a new five-member Race Unity Committee, which during the next few years initiated a number of projects including a 1940 teaching campaign in the South. As part of the campaign, the

National Spiritual Assembly held one of its meetings in Atlanta, Georgia, where the national administrative body criticized the local community for not following the Baha'i teachings concerning racial unity. In the eyes of one contemporary author this event was "a watershed in American Baha'i history."[36]

The Race Unity Committee also introduced special courses on race and racism in several Baha'i summer schools, and in 1942, it helped the Chicago Baha'i community hold a race unity banquet. On its own initiative, the Miami community created a local Race Unity Committee, the first such body to be established in a southern state. As momentum increased, the National Spiritual Assembly made race unity a major proclamation theme for the final months of the First Seven Year Plan. As a result, fifty-seven race unity meetings were held in local Baha'i communities nationwide. Then in 1944, the National Spiritual Assembly addressed a letter to President Franklin D. Roosevelt in which it supported the chief executive's efforts to prohibit racial discrimination in American defense industries.

At the 1947 Baha'i National Convention, the feeling that race unity activities were accenting racial distinctions rather than group unity again raised its head. The new National Spiritual Assembly responded by placing the Race Unity Committee under the control of the National Teaching Committee. The move was based partially on the fear of general public criticism and partially on the fact that the Race Unity Committee's efforts had resulted in minimal conversions. Once again, it took a virtual rebuke from Shoghi Effendi to reverse national policy. At the 1953 All-America Conference in Chicago, Hand of the Cause Dorothy Baker relayed what the Guardian had told her during her recent pilgrimage to Haifa, namely, that unless top priority was given to taking Baha'u'llah's message to Negroes, disaster would befall the American community. Soon thereafter, the National Spiritual Assembly appointed an Interracial Teaching Committee, but the act was more symbolic than substantive, and by the year of his death, Shoghi Effendi was again admonishing the American Baha'i community for their failure to meet head-on "The Most Challenging Issue":

> The attitude toward teaching the Faith in the southern states of the United States should be entirely changed. For years, in the hope of attracting the white people, in order to "go easy" with them and not offend their sensibilities, a compromise has been made in the teaching work throughout the South. The results have been practically nil. The white people have not responded worth mentioning, to the Faith, and the colored people have been hurt and also have not responded.... Your committee should devote the major part of its effort towards attaining these goals in the South, and it would also as part of its work, urge the Baha'is, wherever they may be, to devote more attention to minorities.[37]

LOCAL BAHA'I COMMUNITIES

As might be expected of a study that has as its focus the American Baha'i community as a whole, emphasis in the current work has been placed on national events and trends. It is important to remember, however, that for the great majority of believers, Baha'i identity was largely reflected in the activities of their local communities. Consequently, in bringing this chapter to a close, a few examples of Baha'i devotional and administrative life will be examined as they were experienced in four local communities: Kenosha, Wisconsin; Baltimore, Maryland; Sacramento, California; and Atlanta, Georgia.

Along with Chicago, Kenosha was one of the oldest Baha'i communities in the United States. Its membership had suffered during the dispute between Ibrahim Kheiralla and 'Abdu'l-Baha, so that by 1923, there were only eighteen believers in the city. In that same year, following a personal letter to the community from Shoghi Effendi in which he urged its members to discharge their sacred duties,[38] the Kenosha Local Spiritual Assembly was elected.

Like many other local communities, the level of Baha'i activity in Kenosha was cyclical in expression. For example, in addition to the holding of monthly nineteen day feasts and weekly local spiritual assembly meetings, between 1922 and 1925, there were on the average four gatherings of various types being sponsored in the city each week, including teaching, study, and children's meetings, but by 1926, only the Sunday meeting, the Feast, and administrative sessions were scheduled. Then during the 1930s, activities again picked up with the establishment of a special lecture series and the visits of a number of well-known Baha'i teachers such as Ruth Moffett. At the same time, there was considerable organizational development. For example, the Nineteen Day Feast became more structured with the establishment of a formal order of operation and the introduction of a period of administrative consultation. The result of the increased activity and organization was a rising membership that in 1938 reached fifty.

The major conflict in Kenosha during this time seems to have been one of class rather than race or religious background. The original community had been mainly blue-collar in composition, but during the 1930s, new converts came primarily from the middle class. A seemingly minor example but one that was probably symbolic of deeper attitudes was a disagreement in the early 1940s over the singing of a benediction at the end of Sunday public meetings.[39] The working-class desire for congregational singing was contested by elements of the middle class, who felt that the poor level of performance would leave a bad impression with non-Baha'i guests.

Apparently this group felt that Baha'i-related presentations should reflect higher cultural standards.

The 1940s saw a continuation of activity despite jurisdictional changes that limited the local spiritual assembly's powers to the city proper. Numerous new committees were appointed to direct such activities as teaching, welfare, children's education, and devotional music. A local Baha'i Center was maintained, and special prayer campaigns were introduced whereby groups of believers would rotate the saying of prayers over nineteen-day periods.[40] Yet, throughout the decade and continuing into the 1950s, community membership gradually declined, so that by the time of Shoghi Effendi's passing, there were only twenty-one registered believers in Kenosha. Natural death, pioneering, and local economic conditions led to a reduction in numbers for which there were no substantial replacements, and this trend would continue throughout the following decades. Kenosha is thus a good example of the category of Baha'i local community that reached a certain level of membership and then, lacking any subsequent growth, fell into a state of relative stagnation.

The Baltimore Baha'i community also traced its origins back to the end of the nineteenth century, and like the Kenosha community, was adversely affected by Kheiralla's break with 'Abdu'l-Baha. Consequently, by 1926, there were only thirteen adult Baha'is residing in the city, but the lack of numbers did not diminish community spirit. Educational, administrative, and public meetings were held regularly, and they were guided by fixed procedures that were similar to the order of church services.[41] Because of its proximity to the Washington, D.C., Baha'i community, Baltimore often hosted prominent Baha'i teachers such as Louis Gregory, Albert Vail, and Howard Colby Ives. Thus in 1927, Gregory spoke to a group of black ministers at Morgan College, and in 1930, Vail addressed close to 200 people at the First Unitarian Church. Ives conducted educational sessions for the Baltimore Baha'is during February 1931 that resulted in the establishment of regular deepening classes held biweekly throughout the next two years.

In a manner similar to that in Kenosha, the Baltimore Local Spiritual Assembly began to follow tighter administrative procedures and appoint specific committees to monitor such events as the Nineteen Day Feast and public proclamations. Following suggestions from the National Spiritual Assembly, in 1932, the Baltimore Assembly began to require that new believers study 'Abdu'l-Baha's *Will and Testament*. The local body's decision reflects the fact that emphasis on the Covenant, which national Baha'i leadership had made such a dominant theme during this period, was filtering down to local communities.

Baltimore was a city of Jim Crow laws that made it difficult for Baha'is to openly express their Faith's race unity ideals. Nonetheless, public meetings and firesides were made open to African Americans, and in 1937, Albert James became the city's first black Baha'i.[42] The hurdles that the community faced in regards to race relations are reflected in the fact that it would not be until the 1950s that the next African Americans would join the community. Several black women declared in the early 1950s, and shortly after Shoghi Effendi's death, a black dentist, Eugene Byrd, and his wife began attending Friday night firesides. Some eighteen months later, they also declared their faith. Other efforts to expand the community's ethnic base were seen in the conversions of two individuals from Jewish backgrounds, one of whom, Faith Amberg, would leave her sizable estate to the Baha'i Faith. With the arrival of several Persian Baha'is who came to study at Johns Hopkins University, Baltimore could soon boast of a small but diversified group of believers. Unlike Kenosha, the constant level of community activities and emphasis on minority teaching prepared the way for the future expansion that would take place in the city during the post-Guardian period.

The first Baha'i to reside in Sacramento was 'Alí M. Yazdí, who had immigrated to the United States from Iran in 1923. He departed the city shortly thereafter, but as a result of the efforts of Orcella Rexford, who used a Kheiralla-type approach to her presentations, a Baha'i group of more than twenty people was formed in 1924. However, this group was not administratively affiliated with the American Baha'i community, and the National Spiritual Assembly refused to recognize it. Two years later, Henry and Francis Kuphal moved to Sacramento from Boise, Idaho, and along with Yazdí (who had recently returned to the city), they established the state capital's first official Baha'i group.

During the next few years, the group gradually added new members, and by the early 1930s, there was a small but active community composed mainly of educated, middle- or upper-middle-class, white women. Feasts and study meetings were held regularly, and a local spiritual assembly was established in 1937. In 1939, the Sacramento Baha'is hosted a regional teaching conference at the Hotel Sacramento.

In the 1940s and 1950s, the Sacramento community seemed to become bogged down in concerns over matters of administration. "The Baha'is of Sacramento were coming to see their religion as governed by a set of prescribed procedures. Functioning in accordance with these procedures was given the highest importance."[43] With the addition of several new and younger members, conflict over this orientation began to emerge. In 1952, one man and his wife found themselves brought before the Assembly and chastised for not having received the body's consent to present a Baha'i display booth at the State Fair.[44] The couple later left the Faith.

Further administrative disputes and conflicts between Assembly members resulted in a certain degree of community paralysis that would not be overcome until the 1960s. Consequently, the state of Baha'i affairs in Sacramento during the 1950s presents us with a good example of that type of small Baha'i community, of which there were no doubt many, in which the attention given to administrative correctness in the wake of Shoghi Effendi's efforts to furnish the American Baha'is some degree of procedural unity went beyond proper limits and thereby minimized the spirit of the Baha'i message.

The first Baha'i pioneer to settle in Atlanta was Dr. James Charles Oakshette, who moved to the city in 1909. In 1927, Dr. Oakshette organized the Liberal Catholic Church of St. Michael the Archangel, and during church services, he would teach the Baha'i message and make liberal use of Baha'i prayers.[45] Shortly before his death in 1937, Dr. Oakshette was joined by two other pioneers, Olga Fink from New York and Doris Ebbert from Illinois. Within two years of the women's arrival, the number of Baha'is in Atlanta had grown to more than nine. Included in this group were three African Americans. The small community held integrated feasts and holy day celebrations, but teaching meetings, where nonbelievers might be present, were segregated by race so as to insulate Baha'is from the resentment and outrage of supporters of the Jim Crow system.[46] It was this dualistic policy for Baha'i meetings in the South, which had been established at the 1937 Baha'i National Convention, which led W. E. B. Du Bois to harshly criticize the American Baha'i community in a column in the *Pittsburgh Courier* (October 30, 1937). He claimed that the Baha'is had finally surrendered their ideals to the reality of American racism. The fact that Atlanta's first local spiritual assembly (elected in 1939) was not integrated added fuel to Du Bois' attack, and it was only after the previously mentioned 1940 meeting of the National Spiritual Assembly in Atlanta, when it was made very clear to the white Baha'is that restrictions within a Baha'i community based on color were unacceptable, that an African American was finally elected to the local administrative body. However, Essie Robertson's selection to the assembly took place only after a number of whites had left the Faith. Between Robertson's election and the end of the Guardianship, Baha'i community meetings and programs in Atlanta began to reflect a more positive approach to race unity.

Integrated feasts and other internal meetings became the norm, and when possible, public meetings were also integrated. When public facilities would not allow for integrated gatherings, a second meeting with the same speaker would be held at a facility open to both races.[47] At times, integrated meetings became a source of conflict between the Baha'is and a few Atlanta racists. The most extreme example of this phenomenon took place in April 1947, when the Ku Klux Klan broke up a feast held in a Baha'i home. Such confrontations finally led the Atlanta Baha'is to purchase a building in a nonresidential area of the city where integrated meetings could be peacefully conducted. Despite the difficulties facing the Atlanta Baha'i community during these years, membership doubled from thirteen to twenty-five, and the continuing willingness of many believers to face the racial issue head-on would serve as a springboard for future growth.

On November 9, 1957, Shoghi Effendi was laid to rest at the Great Northern London Cemetery. During his Guardianship, the American Baha'i community had been transformed from a group of relatively independent localities into an administratively cohesive national unit. Growth during this period was measured. Membership increased from close to 2,000 believers to just fewer than 8,000. Opportunities for more rapid expansion were certainly missed, especially in terms of bringing more African Americans into the Faith. Moreover, the emphasis on procedural uniformity likely caused some Baha'is to fall away. Nonetheless, the emergence of a coordinated and unified administrative system along with an increasingly "deepened" membership would allow the American community to enter the socially turbulent 1960s a much stronger and more self-confident religious organization, one that would shortly experience the largest growth spurt in its short history.

7

Phase III (1958–2000)

Shoghi Effendi's death occurred during the middle of the Ten Year Global Crusade and produced dismay and disbelief throughout the American Baha'i community. As recounted in Chapter 1, since the Baha'i leader did not leave a will or appoint a successor, the Hands of the Cause quickly gathered in Haifa and soon thereafter issued a statement to the Baha'i world that for the immediate future a group of nine of their own members would guide the affairs of the Faith. The transition of authority appeared smooth until Shoghi Effendi's chief American lieutenant, Hand of the Cause Mason Remey, declared that the Guardianship had to continue and that because of his position as president of the International Baha'i Council he should be the new Guardian. The Hands reacted by declaring him a covenant-breaker, after which he went on to establish the Orthodox Baha'i Faith.

THE BAHA'I FAITH AND THE CIVIL RIGHTS MOVEMENT

When the shock of not having a Guardian had begun to subside, the American Baha'i community again turned its attention to the goals of the Ten Year Global Crusade. At the time, American society was beginning to experience the effects of the Supreme Court's landmark decision in *Brown v. the Board of Education, Topeka, Kansas* (May 17, 1954), when the justices declared that separate educational facilities were inherently unequal and therefore unconstitutional. This historic determination stimulated many blacks as well as white sympathizers to try to end the segregationist practices and racial inequalities that were firmly entrenched across the nation, particularly in the South. The crystallizing events took place in December 1955, when Rosa Parks was arrested for refusing to move to the Negro section of a bus in Montgomery, Alabama, and local blacks responded by staging a boycott of the bus system. Fusing immediate feelings of injustice with the historic force of the African American churches, Rev. Dr. Martin Luther King Jr. succeeded in transforming a spontaneous racial protest into a massive resistance movement, which after 1957 was led by his Southern Christian Leadership Conference.

Because of the Faith's previous involvement with the NAACP and the Fellowship of Reconciliation, a number of Baha'is had established connections with important individuals within the civil rights movement. Despite their religious obligation to avoid partisan political involvement, many of these believers were deeply committed to racial equality and harmony. Moreover, the members of a small but influential corps of African American Baha'is were anxious to publicly express their views and move beyond the gradualist approach of ending segregation. One such group was centered in Nashville, Tennessee, where Sarah Pereira had been appointed chair of the Department of Romance Languages at Tennessee Agricultural and Industrial State University and had recently converted the son of the university president. Also at Tennessee A & I was a twenty-year-old African American student named Cal Rollins, who had become a Baha'i at the University of Arizona in Tucson. The black Baha'i poet Robert Hayden, who had not yet become a major figure in American letters, was at nearby Fisk University.[1]

In the summer of 1959, Rollins and some other Baha'i friends organized a large interracial meeting at Fisk under the banner of The Oneness of Mankind, which was attended by more than 300 people.[2] The meeting had no explicit protest or activist civil rights content, but given the tense racial atmosphere in the city at this time, the gathering's theme of interracial unity was easily misread. Thus, the activities of the African American Baha'is and their white allies soon came to the attention of the National Baha'i Center, whose policy toward racial integration was still dominated by a gradualist and nonconfrontational approach. The question of Baha'i participation in such events only became more controversial when two African American Baha'i youth were arrested during the Nashville lunch counter sit-in known as Big Saturday (February 27, 1960). Consequently, by the time the 1960 National Baha'i Convention took place (April 28 through May 1), the issues of the nature and degree of Baha'i participation in the civil rights movement were ready to take center stage.

Consultation among the 1,100 Baha'is present at the Convention was heated. Conservatives argued for restraint, while the more activist elements wished the Baha'i Faith to be publicly and officially associated with civil rights demonstrations. Even the National Assembly was divided, and at one point African American member Ellsworth Blackwell was ruled out of order for his fiery speech.[3] Moderates advocated a tolerance for individual Baha'is who became involved in demonstrations as long as they did not explicitly bring the Baha'i Faith into their actions. In the end, no clear policy regarding individual Baha'i activity emerged from the gathering. However, the National Spiritual Assembly declined to openly support the civil rights movement.

One of the arguments conservatives used to defend their position was that Shoghi Effendi forbade involvement in civil rights issues. This, however, was not the case. For example, in 1948, Ellsworth Blackwell wrote to the Guardian asking him if it was wrong for Baha'i students at the University of Chicago to have protested against racial prejudice by joining a demonstration in which they carried a placard with the word "Baha'i" on it. Shoghi Effendi replied through his secretary (January 1948) as follows: "He does not see any objection to Baha'i students taking part as Baha'is in protest such as that mentioned in the clipping. On the contrary, he does not see how they could remain indifferent when fellow students were voicing our own Baha'i attitude on such a vital issue and one we feel so strongly about."[4]

By 1963, those at the 1960 Convention who had desired to keep Baha'is out of the civil rights marches altogether began to lose influence. The mood in much of the country was rapidly turning, and this shift could not be kept apart from the Baha'i community. What is more, there was significant change of membership on the National Spiritual Assembly. Sarah Pereira had been voted a member of the institution in 1961, and when the first Universal House of Justice was elected in 1963, several men among its all-male membership came from the American national body. This opened up new positions in Wilmette for younger members. Elected to the National Spiritual Assembly that year were Firuz Kazemzadeh, a Yale historian, and Daniel Jordan, a professor of education. Like Pereira, both were openly liberal on the race question.

A major issue facing the new National Assembly was the composition of Baha'i meetings in the South. Many white believers in that region were still following the 1937 policy of allowing segregated meetings in those Baha'i communities where it was believed that open integration would result in white disinterest in conversion. Young Baha'i idealists were perplexed that Baha'is should be allowed to segregate when the practice was both contrary to their most cherished ideals of human unity and in opposition to the goals of civil rights activists. The Assembly made its intentions clear by voting to take away the administrative rights (that is, Baha'i voting rights) of a southern restaurant owner who had refused to desegregate his establishment.[5] As a consequence of the intervention, by the late-1960s, most Baha'i communities in the South were holding integrated meetings.

The National Spiritual Assembly also had to come to terms with an increasing demand by many Baha'is that they be allowed to openly take part in various civil rights demonstrations and other nonviolent activities. The fact that Assembly-member Daniel Jordan and his wife had close personal relations with Dr. and Mrs. Martin Luther King Jr. was probably significant in helping stimulate a change of attitude on the national level. This shift can be marked from a decision made at the 1963 National Baha'i Convention when a prominent black couple from Baltimore, Mr. and Mrs. Eugene Byrd, approached the National Spiritual Assembly and asked for the body's approval of their participation in King's upcoming march in Selma, Alabama. At the last minute, the body gave its blessing to the request, whereafter the Byrds and a number of other Baha'is took part in the march.[6] Although the National Spiritual Assembly would not openly endorse the civil rights movement or allow Baha'is to march with Baha'i placards, the granting of permission for individual Baha'is to participate in civil rights marches was an advance on the conclusions of the 1960 National Convention. Tellingly, the 1948 letter of Shoghi Effendi to Ellsworth Blackwell authorizing Baha'is to participate as Baha'is in demonstrations against racism was republished in the June 1964 issue of *Baha'i News*. In this context, while most Baha'i administrators never did come to terms with civil disobedience as a concept, current research has indicated that Baha'is were present at every major event in the civil rights movement from the Montgomery boycott to the freedom rides and from the Albany movement to the founding of the Student Nonviolent Coordinating Committee.[7]

THE UNIVERSAL HOUSE OF JUSTICE'S NINE YEAR PLAN: 1964–1972

The first Universal House of Justice was elected in April 1963, and a year later, the supreme Baha'i administrative institution issued its Nine Year Plan. The scheme adopted an approach and tactics similar to Shoghi Effendi's designs for expansion, but whereas the Guardian's strategy had emphasized dispersion, the central focus of the Nine Year Plan was a global increase in conversions. In the United States, the number of local spiritual assemblies was to be expanded from 334 to 600, and the number of localities where Baha'is resided was to be raised from 1,650 to 3,000. In the message that signaled the commencement of the Plan, the Universal House of Justice once again reminded the followers that the desired expansion also needed to be accompanied "by the dedicated effort of every believer in teaching, in living the Baha'i life, in contributing to the Fund, and particularly in the persistent effort to understand more and more the significance of Baha'u'llah's Revelation."[8]

The timing of the Nine Year Plan in the United States proved opportune, as it coincided with the emergence of significant changes within the American social and religious landscapes. The social idealism related to the civil rights movement, the gradual disillusionment with the Vietnam War, the eventual rise of militant black power, and a general rejection by large numbers of students and social activists of many traditional social institutions and values became the signatures of the 1960s counterculture. In terms of religion, conservative theologies and codes of morality were openly challenged and often found wanting. "The New Morality" and "the Death of God" became popular slogans.[9] Some attempted to fill the spiritual gap by turning to a medley of different religious, philosophical or psychological systems, a large number of which were non-Christian in orientation.

In such a convulsive social environment, the principles of the Baha'i Faith, combined with its universalist religious claims and spiritual practices, found a significant number of sympathetic ears. Moreover, the new approach to Baha'i teaching that had been so successful in India during the opening years of the decade was now being used more extensively in the United States. As a result, many conversion-oriented activities were shifting from primarily firesides and other public meeting formats into more spontaneous forms. Potential converts were now frequently approached anonymously and in the streets. Incorporated with the more open teaching style was a changing attitude toward conversion that placed the heart above the head. To some extent, the spirit of this approach can be seen in a 1964 message from the Universal House of Justice. When speaking about qualifications for enrollment the institution proclaimed: "The prime motive should always be the response of man to God's message, and the recognition of His Messenger. Those who declare themselves as Baha'is should become enchanted with the beauty of the Teachings; and touched by the love of Baha'u'llah. The declarants need not know all the proofs, history, laws, and principles of the Faith."[10]

At the beginning of the Nine Year Plan, the Baha'i population in the United States was somewhat more than 10,000. By 1968, this number had risen to 17,765, and just two years later, it had reached 23,994. The main social characteristic that stands out during these years of rapid growth was the youthfulness of the new converts. Some indication of this phenomenon can be ascertained from a statistical compilation derived from questionnaires given to new Baha'is between January 8 and February 5, 1969. Of the 160 individuals who returned the survey (193 were distributed), 112, or a full 70 percent, were under the age of 24.[11] Even though the survey was not a perfect measure of the age characteristics of all the Baha'is who were enrolled during this period, it was probably a reasonable indicator.[12] The American Baha'i historian Robert Stockman described the situation in a somewhat more colorful manner when he wrote: "Older Baha'is became used to a community filled with persons with long hair, dirty clothing, and youthful enthusiasm."[13]

The consequences of the jump in enrollments were numerous. Monetary donations rose dramatically, and income from the accelerated sale of Baha'i books was so substantial that the Baha'i Publishing Trust was able to purchase a new building. The staff at the Baha'i National Center in Wilmette increased tenfold, and the number of youth-related activities, especially youth conferences, multiplied. The new wave of enthusiasm to which Stockman referred was altering the face of the American Baha'i community. The following paragraphs offer a brief look at the conversion stories of five individuals who would seem representative of this new influx of youthful believers.

Kathy was twenty-one and recently married when, along with her husband, she became a Baha'i in 1968.[14] She came from an upper-middle-class white family in the San Fernando Valley area of Los Angeles County and was a senior at the University of California at Los Angeles. Her religious background was liberal Methodist. During the 1965 Watts riots, her church had opened its doors to temporarily house a number of African American families. Kathy's Christianity was primarily of the social gospel variety. As she stated: "I never really accepted the idea that one had to believe in Jesus to be saved. What was important to me was the example of Jesus' life and his concern for the less fortunate members of society."[15] During the spring of 1967, Kathy attended a UCLA-sponsored retreat whose title was "Religion—Institution or Inspiration?" At the conference, Kathy made the acquaintance of two African American Baha'is who, during the course of the next few days, introduced her to their beliefs. She was impressed by the ideas that all of the world's religions contained certain spiritual truths and that mankind was one. When she returned home, she and her husband made contact with the Baha'i club at UCLA and began reading more about the history and teachings of the Faith. Approximately one year later, they both signed declaration cards.

Andrew was only seventeen when he became a Baha'i in 1970 in Corvallis, Oregon. His lower-middle-class white parents were agnostic, although much importance was placed in the home on ethical values. During his junior year in high school, Andrew began what he termed "a spiritual search." He read a great deal and was particularly moved by the novels of Herman Hesse, most notably *Siddhartha*. During a special week at school when alternative courses were offered, he enrolled in a class on the Baha'i Faith. He was especially impressed by the teacher's high regard for other religions. During the following months, Andrew read several books on the Baha'i Faith, including *Baha'u'llah and the New Era*, which he found in the public library. What he remembered most from that time was the image of 'Abdu'l-Baha. As he recalled: "'Abdu'l-Baha seemed to me to be the very embodiment of spirituality."[16] In the spring of 1970, Andrew heard about a Baha'i fireside that was being held on the campus of Oregon State University, and he decided to attend. On the way to the meeting, he experienced a strong intuition that he had found what he was looking for. When the speaker had completed his presentation and asked if anyone wanted to become a Baha'i, Andrew signed a declaration card and affirmed his belief.

John was of working-class, Irish-Catholic background and in the Navy when he heard of the Baha'i Faith in 1974.[17] He was twenty-one years old and deeply religious; on one memorable occasion he had experienced a vision of the Virgin Mary while saying the rosary and for a short time thereafter had considered becoming a priest. John was at sea when one of his shipmates told him about the Baha'i Faith. The two men subsequently staged a religious debate in front of a crowd of sailors. At one point, John asked: "If the Kingdom of God has arrived, then what am I doing aboard a war ship?" His friend replied with the question: "Where is the Kingdom of God?" This response resulted in John's having the intense spiritual experience of floating over the ocean during which time he heard the answer: "The Kingdom of God is within you." At that point John became a Baha'i, and he continued in his newfound faith after he was discharged from the navy. His wife, Clare, who was likewise Catholic, also converted. The change of religion caused a great deal of tension within both John's and Clare's strong Catholic families, but they remained committed Baha'is.

Carl was a junior at a small college in northern Michigan in 1967 when he first heard about the Baha'i Faith. He was a middle-class son of an American father and English mother who had met during the war. As a religious studies major who was engaged in the study of Hinduism and Buddhism, Carl was impressed that the Baha'is accepted the spiritual validity of traditions other than Judaism or Christianity. He was also attracted to what he understood as Baha'i historiography—that human history displayed certain patterns based on the rise and fall of religiously inspired civilizations. His major stumbling block in becoming a Baha'i was his hesitation to claim that he believed in divine revelation. After numerous discussions on this topic with his Baha'i friends, he finally stated his position as follows: "If such a reality as a Manifestation of God exists, then Baha'u'llah would be that Manifestation."[18] The Baha'is responded that this was enough. That evening Carl signed a declaration card.

Merie and her husband were holiness preachers in Hartsville, South Carolina, who had started their own church. Merie was prone to having religious dreams and visions, and on one occasion, she experienced Jesus in the spirit telling her that he had already returned to the world.[19] She began a religious search that lasted several years. She heard about the Baha'i Faith at a fireside in Florence and soon thereafter began reading Baha'i books. "Merie felt torn because she was preaching one thing and beginning to believe another."[20] To resolve her dilemma, in 1970 she went to Edisto Island, where she pitched a tent and for three weeks prayed and read her Baha'i books. At the end of her stay on the island, Merie had found her answer. When she returned to the mainland, she declared herself a Baha'i and shortly thereafter went to the Baha'i National Headquarters in Wilmette to attend a deepening institute. At a later date, she informed her congregation of her decision, which resulted in the collapse of her church. Nevertheless, Merie did not renounce her belief in Baha'u'llah.

In her 1985 study of the Washington, D.C., Baha'i community, June R. Wyman noted that the declaration stories she encountered contained two essential categories, which she labeled "through the heart" and "through the mind."[21] Those who became Baha'is through the mind were primarily directed by a rational, intellectual approach, while those who accepted through the heart were more apt to have been inspired by some event, either an intuitive experience, dream or vision, that made them feel that they were being called to conversion. The two categories were not necessarily mutually exclusive, although most individuals tended to lean strongly in one direction or the other. In looking at the conversion stories cited above, these two categories are visibly evident. John and Merie are the best examples of conversion through the heart; in the process of investigating the Baha'i Faith, both had overt religious experiences that might well be termed mystical. Carl's declaration, on the other hand, was a prime example of conversion through the mind. He was impressed by the Faith's truth claims as expressed in its explanations related to his study of religion and history. Kathy and Andrew had more balanced approaches, although

Andrew did experience a powerful wave of intuition just prior to his declaration. What all of our conversion stories have in common is what Wyman referred to as "subjectivizing the process of becoming a Baha'i." In other words, they all reflect an American model in which a private search containing unique obstacles forms the basic pattern.[22] This can be contrasted with conversion stories from other parts of the world where either group mission or family identity often play a prominent role.

During the latter years of the Nine Year Plan, a series of events took place that would result in another massive increase in Baha'i declarations. The focal points for these events were the rural districts of South Carolina. By the final years of the decade, there were a handful of Baha'is scattered around the state. Two of the more active communities were Florence and Charleston, and when the National Spiritual Assembly appointed the Deep South Teaching Committee in 1969, one of the results was a marked increase in public exposure in these localities, an example of which was the regular holding of "unity picnics." At about the same time that Florence and Charleston were sponsoring an increased number of Baha'i events, a black believer named Alberta Williford returned from Indiana to her home in Adam's Run, South Carolina. There she began hosting firesides, and by early January 1970, nineteen people had signed declaration cards. "Between January first and January nineteenth, forty-seven people, both black and white, became Baha'is. The snowball had begun to move."[23]

Concurrent with the Adam's Run firesides were a series of youth conferences held in South Carolina, Alabama, Tennessee, and Georgia. One of the speakers was Poovah Murday, a Mauritanian Baha'i who had experienced the mass teaching techniques used in India and the Indian Ocean islands. Murday suggested that such an approach was appropriate for the rural South, and "he called the Baha'is to go out on the highways and byways to tell the masses the good news that Baha'u'llah had come."[24]

In the winter of 1969–1970, the Deep South Teaching Committee organized a large-scale teaching project in and around Dillon, South Carolina. Two chiropractor couples, Jordan and Annette Young and Roger and Sandy Roff, helped take the organizational lead. More than 200 Baha'i teachers, many of them youth, arrived and began to carry out their assignments. Organized in teams of three or four, they would walk the streets and roads of country towns and make conversation with people on their porches and in the fields. After sharing their message, the Baha'is would ask their listeners if they wanted to proclaim their belief in Baha'u'llah. Thousands of people, a large percentage of them black, accepted by signing declaration cards. Following the successes in Dillon, mass teaching was extended to various areas throughout the rural South.

As an example, one Baha'i who participated in the mass teaching projects in the South was David Langness, a twenty-year-old draftee from Arizona who in 1970 was stationed at Fort Rucker Army Air Command in Dothan, Alabama, where he was being trained as an air traffic controller. During many of his weekends, David would travel to different areas throughout Alabama and southern Mississippi to join other Baha'i teachers. As part of an interracial teaching team, he would begin each day by taking part in prayer sessions and organizational meetings. Then he and his fellow Baha'is would go on foot to the targeted areas of a specific town or hamlet. Besides declaration cards, all they had with them were copies of a small pamphlet titled *The Baha'i Faith* and a reprint of an article on the religion that had appeared in *Ebony* magazine. Individuals were approached on the street or on their front porches and given the Baha'i message, which emphasized the appearance of Baha'u'llah as the "return of Christ" and the theme of racial unity. If people accepted Baha'u'llah, they were signed up on the spot. Moreover, according to Langness, new believers were not told that they had to leave their churches.[25] As a result, on some days his team collected more than twenty-five declaration cards.

Mass teaching in the South continued throughout 1970 and 1971, and in early 1972, a special teaching project known as Operation Gabriel was launched from Charleston, South Carolina. Thirty volunteer teachers who were mostly younger than thirty years of age assembled in the city and were divided into various teams. Some teams were responsible for initial teaching, while others were assigned follow-up or consolidation roles. The target area was North Augusta. Among the participants was an auxiliary board member, Thelma Thomas Kilgani.

Operation Gabriel's teachers expanded on earlier mass teaching approaches by giving new believers prayer books and inviting them to nightly firesides. The consolidators also sought out people who had earlier signed declaration cards but had not made further contact with Baha'is.[26] The project lasted six months, during which Baha'i teachers obtained more than 20,000 declarations.

While there was much enthusiasm in the American Baha'i community for mass teaching, the approach also had its critics. Many older and more conservative Baha'is felt that the method did not provide enough time for individuals to know what they were agreeing to when they signed declaration cards. Some Baha'i administrators feared that the large influx of new believers would create problems that were beyond the ability of Baha'i institutions to control. In contrast to earlier periods of growth, the Southern mass teaching projects brought a new economic and social class to the

American Baha'i community—the rural poor. Many of these new Baha'is came from extremely impoverished families and were generally under-educated, while the bulk of the Baha'i population came from middle- or upper-class families and were relatively well-educated. These major economic and cultural differences led some conservative Baha'is to express what Langness described as class prejudice. On several occasions he heard comments to the effect that the Baha'i Faith did not need such elements.[27] In any case, by mid-1972, the mass teaching movement began to lose momentum. Many teachers returned home, and logistical problems mounted. Although deepening programs continued and a new teaching institute named after Louis Gregory was established in Hemingway, South Carolina, limited manpower restricted their effectiveness. Thus, of the 20,000 initial declarations, after major teaching activity ceased, only 1,000 new Baha'is remained officially on the rolls.[28]

A more violent form of opposition came from white hate groups. Between 1970 and 1972, there were a number of instances of harassment from members of the Ku Klux Klan as well as angry individuals. In 1970 in Dillon, South Carolina, anonymous threats against the Baha'is resulted in the cancellation of a public function. Two years later in Greenwood, South Carolina, Klansmen attempted to interrupt a Baha'i meeting but were dissuaded by the local police chief. In Alabama, shots were fired at the Baha'i Center in Montgomery.[29] To the Klan, the Baha'i Faith not only represented an attack on their racial theories, but its concept of world unity also connoted a form of communism. In addition to these more overt examples of opposition, on more than one occasion there was an attitude of mistrust voiced toward Baha'i activities by white authorities, including civic officials and members of local police forces.

Such public criticism no doubt fueled the arguments of those critics within the Baha'i community who believed that mass teaching tactics were causing social disunity and were therefore opposed to Baha'i principles. What is more, as the Nine Year Plan entered its last phase, a more conservative mood began to appear in Wilmette. This attitude applied not only to mass teaching in the South but also to youth-centered activities in general. For example, in 1971, the National Spiritual Assembly dissolved all of the nation's youth committees and put them under the jurisdiction of district teaching committees. According to Anthony Lee, who at the time was serving at the Youth Office for the National Teaching Committee in Wilmette, the National Youth Committees were closed down for purely ideological reasons. There had always been great tension in the community between those who wanted all activities to be homogenous and unified and those who argued for specialized activities to reflect the diversity of the community. "Any specialized activities always came under suspicion, including advanced deepening classes, women's activities, youth activities, meetings just for men, meetings for blacks, meetings for former addicts, and so on. Some people thought (and still think) that such things are against the spirit of the Faith. From their point of view, all Baha'is should have the same activities."[30]

Subsequently, the Youth Office was also closed down, and a year and a half later, Lee returned to Los Angeles. Eventually, he came to see the new policy as the biggest single mistake that the National Spiritual Assembly had ever made with regard to the development of youth activities in the United States: "It simply stopped the youth movement in its tracks, and there have never been as many Baha'i youth again as there were then."[31]

The end of the decade also witnessed the beginning of a retreat from community-engendered self-criticism. A good example can be seen in the history of the Baha'i periodical, *The American Baha'i*. The national Baha'i newspaper was the brainchild of Dick Betts, chairman of the National Teaching Committee. Betts contacted Bob Ballenger, who was enrolled in journalism school at UCLA, and asked him to take on the editorship of the paper. The young Baha'i agreed and left for Wilmette. Almost immediately, Ballenger began to run into trouble. As a trained journalist, he had envisioned a "real newspaper."[32] A number of articles that raised certain problems within the American Baha'i community, such as one about the growing number of inactive believers, were nixed. After exactly four issues (January–April, 1969) the National Spiritual Assembly shut down the publication. Ballenger was told by a leading member of the National Spiritual Assembly that certain things needed to be adjusted and that the Assembly wanted to rethink the direction of the paper.[33] After a year of working in the public relations office, Ballenger returned to California. Shortly thereafter, *The American Baha'i* resumed publication, and the paper has been continually printed since that time, although its approach has become primarily promotional in nature with little room in its pages for critical analysis.

When the Nine Year Plan was completed, both membership and local spiritual assembly goals had been more than met. Whereas the blueprint had called for the existence of 597 local assemblies by 1973, there were in that year 867 such functioning bodies, and the number of Baha'is residing in the United States had ballooned from 10,000 to 60,000. The large influx of new converts had a dramatic impact on community demographics. The 1969 survey of new believers indicated that they were drawn in overwhelming numbers from youthful, unmarried, student, and educated sectors of the American population.[34] In terms of religious background, the former Protestant bias was beginning to shift toward a more representative mix of religious experience, and while the racial balance between Caucasian and African American Baha'is remained essentially the same, this would be offset in the next few years by the influx of African Americans resulting from the mass teaching in the South. The major significance of these demographic shifts was not so much in the lifestyle changes that they brought to the American Baha'i community, although these did occur, but rather that they indicated that the Baha'i Faith was a religion whose appeal was not confined to a single age group, religious tradition, or racial or ethnic identity.

THREE CONSECUTIVE PLANS: 1974–1992

Between 1974 and 1992, the Universal House of Justice initiated another three international teaching plans. Compared to the Nine Year Plan, the eighteen-year period covered by the projects saw relatively slow membership growth in the United States. American society in the late 1970s and 1980s took a more conservative turn, and fewer Americans seemed interested in a non-Christian religion.[35]

A major emphasis during these years was given to community consolidation. A fair number of the youth who had enrolled during the late 1960s and early 1970s either left the Faith or became inactive, but many of those who remained completed their education, married, and started families. The new generation of believers revitalized many local communities and helped lay the foundation for future American Baha'i leadership.

Diversification of community membership continued. As will shortly be seen, to a great extent this was the result of the 1979 Iranian Revolution and the large number of Persian refugees who came to the United States in the early 1980s, but the process was also reinforced by Southeast Asian refugees who began to enter the United States following the conclusion of the Vietnam War. Some of the immigrants had been Baha'is in Vietnam and Cambodia, and others had converted in refugee camps. Teaching efforts on Native American reservations added a new ethnic mix to the American community. The establishment of the Native American Baha'i Institute on the Navajo Reservation in Arizona in 1982 was a milestone in terms of Native American teaching and consolidation efforts.

In 1985, the Universal House of Justice published its *Promise of World Peace*. The document stated that for the first time in history, conditions existed that could lead to world peace. The House proclaimed that the goal was inevitable, but it also warned that this peace would be reached either through acts of cooperation or only after unimaginable horrors and that the actions of the world's leaders could determine this process. The message went on to say that it was out of a deep sense of spiritual and moral duty that "we are impelled at this opportune moment to invite your attention to the penetrating insights first communicated to the rulers of mankind more than a century ago by Baha'u'llah, Founder of the Baha'i Faith, of which we are the Trustees."[36]

Promise of World Peace was widely distributed throughout American Baha'i communities, and local spiritual assemblies were advised to make presentations of the document to civic and religious leaders. In Washington, a senator agreed to submit a resolution based on the document to the state legislature. On the national level, copies of the peace message were given to numerous congressmen and to President Ronald Reagan.

One of the most significant developments during this period was the gradual curtailment of organized mass teaching. There was a short revival of the technique in South Carolina in the summer of 1976 in the form of Project Outreach. On this occasion, the dean of the Louis Gregory Institute presented a proposal to the Regional Teaching Committee that set as its goal contacting everyone who lived within a thirty-mile radius of the Institute to let them know about the Baha'i Faith and be given the opportunity to investigate it.[37] However, disagreements among participants concerning the proper teaching approach as well as fluctuating manpower undermined the effort. Eventually, greater emphasis was placed on consolidating the gains of the earlier mass teaching period. Here the Louis Gregory Institute came to play a significant role. The Institute was opened all year and maintained both a permanent and volunteer staff of teachers. It provided many of the new believers (sometimes up to 10,000 per year) with five-day intensive training sessions in all aspects of Baha'i life. In 1984, the radio station *Radio Baha'i* was built on Institute grounds and has been a major tool in teaching and consolidation efforts ever since.

The demise of organized mass teaching was a victory for those believers who could not come to terms with the idea that a person might become a Baha'i after only a brief five-to-ten minute presentation. The accepted American Baha'i model for conversion once again became the one that favored prolonged reflective choice. This can be contrasted with the situation in India, where the National Spiritual Assembly allowed the mass teaching process to continue for decades, with the result that hundreds of thousands of individuals from a primarily Hindu background declared belief in Baha'u'llah. For American Baha'i leadership, the possibility of having to deal with such large numbers of unschooled and poor Baha'is was apparently too disconcerting.

The outstanding event of the period in terms of the impact it would have on the ethnic makeup of the American Baha'i community was the 1979 Iranian Revolution. By February of that year, the shah's government had completely disintegrated, and with the return of the Ayatollah Khomeini from his exile in Paris, the battle was effectively over. Gaining the support of numerous army officers, Khomeini was able to establish an Islamic Republic in which supporters of the traditional Shi'ite religious hierarchy became intrenched. The hostility that many of the religious leaders held toward the Iranian Baha'is produced widespread persecution of the 300,000-member community. Attacks took the form of economic and political sanctions, the closing down of many of the religion's institutions, and, in some cases, arrests and executions. Such actions resulted in large numbers of Persian Baha'is leaving the country. Of these, some 12,000–15,000 came to the United States.

The contents of a 1980 letter sent from the Universal House of Justice to all Iranian refugees makes it apparent that the supreme Baha'i institution was aware of the potential problems that the sudden influx of Persians might have on Western Baha'i communities. In addition to reminding the Iranian believers of their duties and responsibilities as Baha'is, the House added:

> Therefore there is no need for the Iránian friends to congregate in one place. Often such a congregation creates problems. For example, should the number of Iránians exceed the number of native believers in a community, they would inadvertently bring about such difficulties as might hamper the progress of the Cause of God, and the world-conquering religion of the Abhá Beauty might appear to others as a religion which is limited and peculiar to Iránians. This could but lead to a waste of time and the disenchantment of both Baha'is and non-Baha'is. Under such circumstances the dear Iránian friends would neither enjoy their stay in that place nor would they be able to serve the Faith in a befitting manner. It is our ardent hope that, wherever possible, the Iránian friends may settle in those towns or villages which are pioneering goals, so that through their stay the foundation of the Cause may be strengthened.[38]

A large number of the refugees settled in Southern California, and their impact on local Baha'i communities was profound. Local spiritual assemblies suddenly found themselves providing the refugees with financial, cultural, and bureaucratic assistance (dealing with the Immigration and Naturalization Service). Confirmation of identity was also an issue, since many of the refugees were unable to document their Baha'i membership. Eventually, a system was adopted whereby two other Baha'is could confirm the legitimacy of a third.

One of the immediate issues facing Baha'i life within these communities was the language barrier. Many of the immigrants did not speak English, and this presented problems related to community meetings, especially the

Nineteen Day Feast. In order that the communities would not be split into Persian and non-Persian groups, the National Spiritual Assembly demanded that Baha'i meetings be conducted in English. This required that translation from English to Persian be made available, a process that often made meetings slow and cumbersome. Over time, as many of the newcomers started to learn English, this problem began to subside.

As might be expected, cultural misunderstandings between the new immigrants and American Baha'is often occurred. According to Payam Afsharian, an American businessman of Persian ancestry who was serving on the Santa Monica Local Spiritual Assembly, the Persians tended to view the Americans as lacking in proper religious reverence. Such American practices as using the names of Baha'i holy figures without a preceding title of respect or handling prayer books in a less-than-dignified manner were considered unacceptable.[39] For their part, American Baha'is often viewed certain Persian cultural idiosyncrasies, such as disregard for exactness of time or formal modes of politeness (*tarof*), as indications of laziness or phoniness. Certain stereotypes concerning Persians also began to emerge; for example, the notion that since the refugees came from "the cradle of the Faith," they were somehow more "spiritual" than their American counterparts.[40] Added to this was the common belief that the Persians were more knowledgeable about their religion than their hosts.[41]

Of a potentially more serious nature was the strong sense of class identity common among many of the Persians. According to a document published by the U.S. Baha'i Refugee Office: "Iranians will go to great lengths, sacrificing their own interests, to help their friends and family members. However, outsiders, strangers and those who do not belong to their social class or group will not usually receive such consideration."[42] Such practices resulted in what some American Baha'is considered social prejudice. "Although few would charge the newcomers with racism, they were sometimes accused of slighting others, particularly the African-American members of the broader Baha'i community in Los Angeles."[43]

On the national level, representatives of the National Spiritual Assembly were able to get the U.S. Congress to introduce several resolutions (in 1982, 1984, 1988, 1990, 1992, and 1994) that condemned the actions of the Iranian government against the Baha'i community. In addition, extensive contacts with the media and government agencies resulted in the creation of a Baha'i Office of External Affairs in Washington, D.C. The management of internal issues was handled by the Baha'i Refugee Office, which was established in Wilmette in 1984.

At about the same time that certain local Baha'i communities were experiencing the impact of the influx of the Persian refugees, American

Baha'i leadership was beginning to confront another issue. As the converts from the baby boomer generation matured, a small number had become interested in Baha'i history, Islamic studies, comparative religion, and other fields in the humanities and social sciences. One result of these intellectual endeavors was that the field of Baha'i studies began to develop. In 1979, the Association for Baha'i Studies was established, and in 1982, Kalimat Press, an independent Baha'i publishing house, offered the first of its Baha'i studies volumes.

However, the emergence of a small cadre of American Baha'i scholars and intellectuals began to create certain problems for Baha'i administrators. As early as 1976, a study group of about a dozen believers had been formed in Los Angeles for the purpose of interacting with one another on the level of ideas.[44] The group produced a newsletter that at the height of its circulation was being sent to roughly 120 individuals. No topic was considered beyond discussion at the meetings, and inevitably, a number of sensitive issues came up, such as the nature of the Universal House of Justice's infallibility, that began to ruffle feathers in Wilmette. In 1979, a member of the National Spiritual Assembly visited one of the classes and cautioned its members about the tone of their discussions. He implied that the discussions and newsletter were causing dissent within the community and that such activities were contrary to Baha'i practice. The National Assembly subsequently demanded the right to censor the newsletter through a local spiritual assembly review.[45] There was virtually universal agreement among members of the group that the review process would be impractical, and a decision was finally made that it would be best not to have a newsletter.

In the mid-1980s, the question of intellectual freedom became a more significant issue. In 1986, a group of California believers published the first issue of the Baha'i magazine *Dialogue*. According to the magazine's chief editor, Steven Scholl, "the quarterly's aim was to foster Baha'i engagement with contemporary social and intellectual issues, including disarmament and peace, human rights, inter-faith dialogue, sexual equality, third world development and the environment."[46] As with all publications that make reference to the Faith, *Dialogue*'s articles were required to be submitted for administrative review. In the first issue, the Office of the Secretary of the National Spiritual Assembly denied permission for one article to be given the title "War and Peace: A Baha'i Perspective," since it claimed that such a title implied an official Baha'i statement. What is more, an extended dispute between the editors and the review board took place over another article, which was titled "Disinvestment: Is it a Baha'i issue?" The piece was rejected twice for containing phrases such as: "The anti-apartheid movement is in step with Baha'i principles, and it behooves us to wholeheartedly support it," as the reviewers felt the statement suggested not only criticism of the South African government, but also active Baha'i engagement against a sovereign state. After several revisions, the article was finally accepted.

Despite *Dialogue*'s success (at its height there were some 2,000 subscriptions), over time a feeling of distrust toward the magazine's editorial line developed in Wilmette. In the spring of 1988, the editors proposed the publication of a nine-point administrative reform program, "A Modest Proposal," which included arguments against academic and editorial review as well as a proposal that there should be term limits for National Spiritual Assembly members. In response, the editorial staff members were required to meet individually with national representatives at a hotel near the Los Angeles airport, during which their motives were questioned. Subsequently, the editors were denounced on the floor of the 1988 National Convention in Wilmette and accused of engaging in negative campaigning. Worried that *Dialogue* could not survive such official condemnation, the editors closed down the magazine.

While the *Dialogue* affair was a minor event in terms of the number of people involved, it still sent a widespread message that the National Spiritual Assembly was not to be challenged regarding its publication policies, nor was public critique of its actions to be allowed. In this sense, the episode appears to have been another example in a long history of tension in the American Baha'i community over questions of individual freedom and administrative authority. Moreover, it was an indicator of future disagreements that would arise between the community's more liberal intellectuals and academics and representatives of the Administrative Order.

THE 1990s AND BEYOND

During the final decade of the twentieth century, several major Baha'i events took place in the United States. These years also saw the creation of new administrative institutions and educational programs, the expansion of Baha'i literature, and the continued alienation of some of the movement's leading intellectuals and academics.

In 1991, the National Spiritual Assembly issued *The Vision of Race Unity*, a public statement of the Baha'i understanding of the racial issues facing American society. This was followed by an active distribution campaign during which hundreds of copies of the document were given to government officials and leaders of thought. One result of the Baha'i Faith's increased involvement in the area of race relations was the appointment in 1992 of a representative of the National Spiritual Assembly to the Martin Luther King Federal Holiday Commission. At the behest of Coretta King, the Universal House of Justice instructed all Baha'i communities to officially observe Martin Luther King Day. Consequently, the Baha'is became visibly prominent in helping the holiday become nationally recognized.

In November 1992, the Second Baha'i World Congress was held at the Jacob Javits Center in New York City. It was the largest gathering of Baha'is ever, and it brought together some 30,000 believers from 180 countries to commemorate the 100th anniversary of Baha'u'llah's death. One of the Congress' primary goals was to proclaim to the world the aims and purpose of Baha'u'llah's Covenant. The four-day event, which contained musical and artistic performances as well as public addresses, brought the Baha'is extensive media coverage and introduced the religion to many of the city's inhabitants and visitors. The Congress culminated with the Universal House of Justice's outline of the challenges facing the international Baha'i community during the century's remaining years. One sign that the American Baha'i community was coming of age was the arrival at the Congress of a letter from President George Herbert Walker Bush, in which he sent his greetings on the occasion of the anniversary. The president went on to add: "Baha'i teachings on religious tolerance, the unity of mankind, the elimination of prejudice, equality of the sexes, and universal peace embody principles that all people of good will admire and support."[47]

The holy year also witnessed the publication of the first official translation of Baha'u'llah's book of laws, the *Kitáb-i Aqdas*. It was expected that the book would stimulate American Baha'is to proclaim to their fellow citizens the significance of Baha'u'llah's teachings, especially as they related to a variety of contemporary social problems. Shortly thereafter, the Universal House of Justice made applicable for the first time outside the Middle East the Baha'i ordinance of *huququ'llah*, which calls for a voluntary contribution to the World Center of 19 percent of a believer's net profits for the year (see Chapter 3).

In an attempt to decentralize some of the administrative responsibilities related to teaching and educational planning, in 1997, the Universal House of Justice directed the American Baha'i community to create four regional Baha'i councils. In November of that year, nine-member councils were elected for the northeast, southern, central, and western districts. According to the National Spiritual Assembly: "Their main tasks will be to devise and execute teaching and consolidation plans derived from those developed by the National Spiritual Assembly, and to create strong local Spiritual

Assemblies."[48] In their formulation of teaching and consolidation projects, the councils were directed to consult with specific continental counselors who would help guide them within the framework of Haifa's international expansion plans.

The driving force behind the creation of the regional councils was the desire to find the proper balance between centralized and decentralized administrative control, since the complaint of overly centralized authority had been a virtual constant throughout American Baha'i history. The new councils were viewed as providing for a degree of decision making at a level both below the National Spiritual Assembly and above the local assemblies. It was anticipated that this intermediary level of administrative institution would allow for greater popular participation in the formulation and enactment of teaching and consolidation plans without creating an atmosphere of disunity to which an overly decentralized system might potentially fall prey.

The shift to a more regional approach to administration was augmented in 2001 with the introduction of the Cluster System. In that year, Baha'i institutions began the task of mapping the country and sectioning it into clusters. The various Baha'i institutions within each cluster were to work together to achieve goals related to both consolidation and expansion. It was also intended that the clusters would have a dimension of community action and social service associated with them.

One of the problems that the American Baha'i community had faced during its period of rapid membership growth was a relatively high withdrawal rate; perhaps one-third to one-half of the new believers did not remain Baha'is.[49] Other new converts ceased active participation in community life but never notified the Baha'i National Center of their status. In an effort to prevent future losses of this magnitude, a new emphasis was placed on providing a more systematic approach to deepening the believers. One example of this trend was the introduction on a national level of training institutes and study circles at which a standardized curriculum known as the Ruhi method was used. The deepening course was originally developed at the Ruhi Institute in Colombia and was later adopted by Baha'i communities all over the world. It contained units such as "Reflections on the Life of the Spirit," "Twin Manifestations," and "Teaching the Cause." The Ruhi curriculum focused on the spiritual essentials taught by Baha'u'llah and used a step-by-step workbook method of imparting the desired information. Special study circle leaders were trained to lead participants through a series of seven books. The two main goals of the process were to assist believers in their understanding of the Baha'i Writings and to investigate ways that the spiritual principles contained in the texts could become manifest in their daily lives. The frequency and duration of each study circle was set by the group, and the facilitator served to maintain the focus and pace. Every participant in the group also made a commitment to some form of social service.

The Ruhi study circles have not been unanimously supported. Some in the community have suggested that the courses are reminiscent of Jehovah's Witness study methods and feared that indoctrination would replace dialog and critical discussion as the accepted approach to Baha'i education. Those who defend the method have responded that good group leaders will lessen the catechism-type style, but they have also noted that those Baha'is who are not university educated can benefit from the more straightforward presentation of material as offered by Ruhi. In any case, by the late 1990s, the study circles had become the educational method of choice for American Baha'i leadership, and they were seen as a vital element of the new Cluster System.

The 1980s had seen a modest increase in the number of Baha'i publishing endeavors, and by the 1990s, there was a virtual explosion of Baha'i-oriented books on to the market. Not only the official Baha'i Publishing Trusts but also smaller independent presses such as Kalimat Press and the London-based George Ronald were now providing believers with a wide variety of books whose range and scope went beyond the traditional scriptural compilation or more scholarly treatises to include social commentary, novels, self-help, popular histories, biographies, and more. This publishing boom greatly increased the depth and texture of Baha'i cultural life.

By the mid-1990s, a significant number of Baha'is had turned to e-mail lists to talk over matters related to their religion. One such list was Talisman, created in October 1994 by Indiana University professor John Walbridge for the scholarly discussion of Baha'i history, doctrines, and current affairs. After the first year of its existence, Talisman's membership had risen to more than 100, and the list was becoming known for its open and frank exchange of ideas that included such topics as the interpretation of Baha'i scripture, the potential limits of infallibility, the question of women's future service on the Universal House of Justice, and the prospects for the elimination of official literature review.[50] At times, criticisms were also voiced about past and current administrative policies.

In April 1996, Baha'i counselors made charges against several posters to the Talisman list alleging that they were making statements that were contrary to the Covenant.[51] Some of these individuals were questioned in person or over the telephone, sometimes late at night. Perhaps the most prominent of the group was Juan R. I. Cole, a professor of Middle Eastern

studies at the University of Michigan who had become a Baha'i in the
early 1970s and later pioneered in Lebanon. Cole responded by denying
that he had ever challenged the Baha'i Covenant and withdrawing his membership.[52] Several other scholars soon followed suit. A Universal House of
Justice letter was later published in *The American Baha'i* in which Talisman
was referred to in connection with the earlier *Dialogue* affair. The letter
went on to describe the Talisman scholars as a "dissident group of Baha'is
who were attempting to arouse widespread dissatisfaction in the community
and to thereby bring about changes in the structure and principles of Baha'i
administration, making it accord more closely with their personal notions."[53]
A similar view was subsequently stated by a Baha'i writer as follows:

> It is worth repeating at this point that the Counselor's involvement is primarily for
> reasons of conduct not personal understanding; the Counselor's involvement is *a call
> to proper conduct* rather than an imposition of orthodoxy. The Counselor may, indeed,
> discuss a person's views and try to show where errors of understanding have occurred;
> however, in the last analysis a Baha'i may stick to his/her understanding so long as
> they do not hector others in the community or misinform seekers.[54]

Both statements seemed to imply that some scholars on Talisman were
not just expressing their opinions but also engaging in behavior that was
designed to undermine the Baha'i administrative system. Those who were
accused responded by claiming that in denying public discourse, the institutions were going beyond the boundaries set for them by Baha'u'llah and
'Abdu'l-Baha and that the defining of intellectual expression as a mode of
conduct was a form of Baha'i doublespeak. As in the case of the Church
of Jesus Christ of Later Day Saints, liberal scholars and more conservative
administrators found themselves locked in an ideological tug-of-war in
which the former believed that they were being given a choice between
falling silent or being declared covenant-breakers.

Walbridge closed Talisman in May 1996. Soon thereafter, Cole created
a new Talisman list and subsequently helped establish the H-Bahai list,
part of the H-Net Discussion Network administered at Michigan State
University. The latter has become known as the premier electronic academic
forum for the discussion of topics related to Shaykhí, Babi, and Baha'i
Studies. At a later date, both Walbridge and his wife, Linda (an anthro-
pologist and professor at Indiana University), withdrew from the Faith.

THE BAHA'IS AND 9/11

Like most communities in the United States, the Baha'is were shocked
by the events of September 11, 2001. In the days immediately following

the tragedies, Baha'i communities across the nation joined with Christians, Jews, Muslims, Mormons, Sikhs, Hindus, and others in prayer sessions designed to bring healing and comfort to those whose lives were so suddenly devastated.

For example, on September 12, Baha'is in Atlanta organized a prayer vigil at the Baha'i Unity Center, and several days later in Dayton, Ohio, Baha'is joined sixty local religious and community leaders in signing an antiviolence message that ended with the pledge: "With the goal of building better race relations, I pledge to do everything I can to make our community a place where equality, justice, freedom and peace will grow and flourish. I commit myself to achieving this goal by loving, not hating, showing understanding, not anger, making peace, not war."[55] Many Baha'i communities were also active in the effort to remind Americans that the religion of Islam should not be judged by the actions of extremists.

On Sunday, December 23, 2001, a statement from the U.S. Baha'i community titled "The Destiny of America and the Promise of World Peace," was published in the *New York Times*. The piece spoke of the tests and trials that would cause the United States to become a land of distinction and a champion of justice. Included in the pronouncement was the following:

> During this hour of crisis, we affirm our abiding faith in the destiny of America. We know that the road to its destiny is long, thorny and tortuous, but we are confident that America will emerge from her trials undivided and undefeatable.[56]

Certain segments of the Baha'i community tended to see 9/11 in mildly apocalyptic terms since the events seemed to mirror some of Shoghi Effendi's earlier statements concerning the planetary crisis that would result from the world's leaders failing to heed Baha'u'llah's warnings. Such an interpretation by contemporary Baha'is was not historically unique, however, as similar ideas had appeared within the community during both world wars. In more general terms, there seemed to be a common acceptance within the American Baha'i community (as exemplified in the *New York Times* statement noted above) that part of God's plan for mankind involved a necessary tearing down of the old world order before a new foundation could be established.

Although it did not directly address the events of 9/11, the Universal House of Justice's "Letter to the World's Religious Leaders, April 2002" made reference to some of the factors that helped produced the tragedy. Prominent among these was the failure of the world's religious leaders to accept the principle that all of the world's great religions are equally valid in nature and origin. The document went on to claim that "organized religion stands paralyzed at the threshold of the future, gripped in those very dogmas and claims of privileged access to truth that have been responsible for creating some of the most bitter conflicts dividing the earth's inhabitants."[57] The House concluded its statement by calling on religious leadership to break with the past regarding this bias and then warning that "with every day that passes, danger grows that the rising fires of religious prejudice will ignite a worldwide conflagration the consequences of which are unthinkable."[58]

LOCAL COMMUNITIES (CONTINUED)

Returning to the local communities surveyed in the last chapter, in 1960, the Area Teaching Committee for the Central United States spoke of Kenosha as an aging community that was in need of outside assistance. A traveling teacher was sent to the community to get firesides and study classes reestablished, but after an initial upswing of enthusiasm, the situation returned to one of stagnation. While many Baha'i localities experienced growth spurts in the late 1960s and early 1970s, Kenosha struggled to maintain a viable community. By 1970, the number of believers was down to fifteen, with only ten exhibiting any degree of active involvement, and in 1979, the Baha'i Center had to be given up. There was a small recovery during the 1980s, but the momentum could not be sustained. Thus, having contributed richly to Baha'i history, the Kenosha Baha'i community became virtually indistinguishable from those other Baha'i communities in the United States that struggled to keep their heads above water.[59]

While the Kenosha community stagnated, in Baltimore, the Faith attained a new level of civic awareness as a consequence of various community-sponsored proclamation events. For example, on September 5, 1963, the Baltimore Baha'is commemorated World Peace Day by holding a well-publicized public celebration. A racially mixed audience of nearly 900 people attended the occasion. As a result of such efforts, declarations of faith increased at a slow but steady rate throughout the early and mid-1960s.

Following the riots that occurred in Baltimore after the 1968 assassination of Dr. Martin Luther King Jr., the hub of Baha'i activity moved from the inner city to the county districts. As in numerous other Baha'i communities across the nation during these socially turbulent years, large numbers of youth began to attend Baltimore firesides, with the result that county communities began to experience a significant increase in declarations. As one Baha'i writer has put it: "Young people began to enroll in the Faith so regularly that the Baha'is would consider the fireside a failure if there were no enrollments in one week."[60]

In the aftermath of the 1979 Iranian Revolution, a significant number of Persians came to the Baltimore metropolitan area. Their arrival added to the growing ethnic diversity found within the area's Baha'i communities, which at the beginning of the 1990s numbered four: Baltimore city and three county localities. Despite instances of misunderstanding that resulted from the new ethnic mix, in 1992, the claim could still be made that the Baha'i communities stood as examples of racial and cultural unity that was unusual in Baltimore.[61]

Between the mid-1960s and the early 1990s, the Sacramento Baha'i community experienced extreme fluctuations both in the number of public activities it sponsored and the size of its active membership. The arrival in 1965 of several new and enthusiastic believers resulted in the holding of regular firesides that began to attract as many as fifty people each evening. By 1967, the community had added thirty-five new individuals to its roles and membership totaled fifty-five. Conflict soon developed, however, between the newcomers and the established Baha'is over the questions of acceptable teaching techniques and lifestyles. These disagreements were partially generational and partially differences of race and social class.[62] The problems became so severe that the National Spiritual Assembly was invited to help resolve them. As a byproduct of the confusion, by the end of 1968, Baha'i activities in Sacramento had virtually ground to a halt.

As the 1970s approached, Sacramento began to experience the effects of the youth movement. Notwithstanding the issues assailing the local Baha'is, within the next few years a group of approximately twenty young believers joined the Faith and began to reshape community life. A rented building in downtown Sacramento acted as the Baha'i Center, where firesides, study classes, and administrative meetings took place just about every night of the week. The Center operated in a "come-and-go" counterculture style. Apparently, it was not unusual to find "a number of young people there in various costumes and hairstyles, sitting cross-legged on the floor and praying, with incense burning."[63]

Ironically, it was a common feature of the youth culture that eventually led to a decline in community membership and returned Sacramento to another period of relative inactivity. The same itinerant life style that had brought many of the young people to the city was by the mid-1970s causing them to leave. Some filled Baha'i pioneering goals, while others just moved on to new destinations. Those who remained seemed burned out from the frantic pace of the preceding years. The symbolic end of the short-lived state of affairs came in 1974, when the Baha'i Center had to be abandoned. In addition, over the years, the inner city had slowly given way to urban blight. This condition would gradually result in the

Sacramento suburbs becoming the homes for larger and more independent Baha'i communities.

During most of the 1980s, the Sacramento Baha'i community lay virtually dormant. Although there were upward of sixty members on the books, it was not uncommon to find only five or six attending the Nineteen Day Feast.[64] In the latter part of the decade, the situation began to improve once again with the emergence of new community leadership and the arrival of a sizable number of Baha'i immigrants from Southeast Asia as well as the enrollment of several local Hispanic believers. The reinvigorated community sponsored various public events, including a 1987 commemoration on the capitol steps of 'Abdu'l-Baha's visit to Sacramento. Subsequently, some of the inactive believers began to once again participate in Baha'i functions, and by the early 1990s, the average number of adults attending the Feast had risen to approximately thirty. Consequently, while the level of enthusiasm that marked Sacramento Baha'i life in the 1960s and early 1970s has not been repeated, recent years have seen the emergence of a more stable and less conflict-ridden community.

Like many local communities during this phase of American Baha'i history, Atlanta experienced a growth spurt in the late 1960s and early 1970s followed by a leveling off of membership figures in the 1980s. The city also experienced the process of "suburbanization" that characterized so many American urban centers at this time, so that by 1992 there were seventeen separate local spiritual assemblies in the Atlanta metropolitan area. Total membership for all Atlanta Baha'i communities was close to 500.

In one of the ironies of American Baha'i history, during the 1990s, the once-segregated Atlanta community became a leading example of the principle of race unity. Weekly interracial meetings known as Pupil of the Eye were held throughout the metropolitan area, where issues related to the National Spiritual Assembly's *Vision of Race Unity* were openly discussed. While the deliberations were sometimes tense, the principle of unity allowed for open and honest expression of the participants' various views.[65] On the national level, Atlanta led the way in celebrating the Martin Luther King Jr. national holiday. In 1993, the secretary general of the National Spiritual Assembly, Robert Henderson, who also happens to be an Atlantan and an African American, was selected as co-grand marshall of the nationally televised March of Celebration, and the following year, he gave a prominent speech at the King Center for Nonviolent Social Change. The Atlanta Baha'i Gospel Choir was also a regular participant in a number of musical events related to Martin Luther King Jr. Week. Later in the decade, Atlanta was selected by the National Spiritual Assembly as the test site for a nationwide media campaign entitled "The Vision of Race Unity."

In contrast to some Southern California Baha'i communities, and more in accord with the Baltimore experience, Atlanta appears to have had few problems when it came to integrating Persian and American believers. While the previously discussed difficulties were not absent, expressions of cultural superiority on the one hand and resentment on the other appear to have been the exception rather than the rule. Consequently, the general feeling of the American Baha'is in Atlanta was that the Persian influx had enriched their global perspective.[66]

As the American Baha'i community enters the new millennium, it can look back upon the previous century as one of significant development and change. From a handful of essentially Protestant-influenced seekers, many of whom had metaphysical or spiritualist leanings, the community has expanded to include a wide range of people from diverse religious and ethnic backgrounds. According to official Baha'i statistics, as of July 2000, the total number of Baha'is in the United States was 142,245,[67] and of these, it has been estimated that approximately 10–15 percent were of African American background and 8 percent of Southeast Asian background. In the last three decades, two or three of the nine seats on the National Spiritual Assembly have consistently been held by black Baha'is, and there have been two black executive secretaries: Glenford Mitchell and Robert Henderson (currently serving). In addition, the community contained somewhere between 12,000 and 15,000 Persian Baha'is. Like members of other religious communities in the United States, the Baha'is are having to come to terms with a variety of contemporary issues, some of which are related to internal strains and others to the more general social consequences of modernity. The next chapter will take a closer look at some of these vital questions.

8

Priorities and Issues
in the Modern American
Baha'i Community

In his article on the American Baha'i community in the 1990s, Baha'i
historian Robert Stockman wrote:

> But such a discussion must begin with the recognition that the Baha'is, within their
> own community, do not think in terms of "issues." Their primary concern is with
> community priorities, which are largely set by their institutions, not by the Baha'is
> individually. Furthermore, the American Baha'i community has been heavily, but by
> no means completely, insulated from the intellectual trends in American society by
> the consistent focus of the Baha'i on their scriptures and their obedience to their
> elected Baha'i institutions. Finally, the Baha'i religion has elaborate rules of discourse
> that strongly direct and sharply limit the nature of discourse among Baha'is.[1]

While it is relatively easy to identify the major priorities that the American
Baha'i community has set for itself during the last two decades, the above
passage reflects the difficulties involved in discussing some of its more
controversial issues. First, the emphasis on unity that is continually stressed
by Baha'i leadership and in Baha'i publications tends to undermine the
discussion of controversial topics in open forums. Also, the idealized views
of both community and consultation create an atmosphere in which individual outspokenness, especially if it is seen to be negative in tone, is
discouraged. Yet, as our historical survey has shown, controversy and conflict have been ever-present realities in the American community, and the
thought that contemporary Baha'is do not think in terms of issues would
seem to defy common sense. If anything, we can most likely assume that

controversial subjects are discussed by Baha'is in contexts that are not open to institutional censure or group pressure. One example, though statistically limited, would be the relatively high number of Baha'i-related discussion lists on the Internet. The fact that the Universal House of Justice has written letters on many of the issues that will be discussed below would seem to indicate that at least some American Baha'is are not comfortable with the limitations placed on them by official Baha'i consultation. Before turning to these questions, however, a brief survey of the priorities that recent Baha'i leadership has established for the American community is necessary.

CURRENT PRIORITIES

A meaningful understanding of the priorities adopted by contemporary Baha'i leadership must be seen in terms of the historical situation in which the community currently finds itself. As stated several times before, there is an element of orthodox Baha'i thinking that views the chaos of the modern world as a consequence of humanity's failure to respond to Baha'u'llah's message. In this vein, comparisons are often made to the decline of the Roman Empire, when the small but expanding Christian communities were gradually able to strengthen themselves to the point that when civilization collapsed, their religion's institutions were able to provide new spiritual leadership. Hence, as recently as April 2004 in a speech given in Raleigh, North Carolina, a member of the Universal House of Justice was recorded as saying:

> The Roman Civilization collapsed over a long slow process. People gradually gave up. They stopped paying taxes, stopped sending kids to school. While this was happening an alternative force arose. It did the housekeeping and ultimately the whole of Europe fell into the lap of Christ. Now, we are doing the house cleaning and will be increasingly doing it and the world will fall into Baha'u'llah's lap. But we have to stay the course and not be distracted.[2]

Translated into strategic priorities, the meaning of the above passage would seem clear: Baha'i communities must energetically prepare themselves, both numerically and organizationally, for the future role God has ordained for them.

At the moment, the number of American Baha'is is claimed to be in the vicinity of 150,000. However, as noted by several observers, approximately one half of the names on current enrollment lists do not have accurate addresses. This statistic can be taken to mean that a large number of people who originally signed declaration cards are no longer participating in Baha'i community activities. In addition, the community's growth rate during the 1990s was around 4 percent, and given the loss of believers from withdrawal (both official and unofficial) and natural causes, to use an apt metaphor, the American Baha'i community is basically treading water. When this fact is put into the context of Baha'i leadership having spoken for a number of years in terms of imminent large-scale enrollments, the need for numerical expansion has begun to take on a psychological as well as a practical significance. Thus, when the Universal House of Justice announced in its 2003 Ridván Letter: "While the world continues on its tumultuous course, the Five Year Plan has reached the operational capacity to enable our community to make giant strides towards its major aim of advancing the process of entry by troops,"[3] the American Baha'i community was once again being reminded of its critical role in initiating the mass conversion process.

With entry by troops as a major objective, recent American Baha'i leadership has been concentrating on another series of goals that are seen as necessary for such expansion. As indicated in Chapter 7, the introduction of regional Baha'i councils, the development of a more universal form of community education (the Ruhi method), and the establishment of the Cluster System have all been recent developments in the United States that point in the direction of a more rationalized approach to spreading the Faith. Rather than relying on individual and/or local community initiative, Wilmette has given priority to centrally planned deepening courses and geographically oriented teaching strategies. At the core of the new cluster approach are the teaching institutes, whose courses are designed to create a multitude of regional and local study circles, devotional meetings, and children's classes. These activities, in turn, are geared to attract seekers who, it is hoped, will attend firesides and subsequently go on to declare their faith in Baha'u'llah.

In addition to these major goals, there are a number of secondary priorities that the American Baha'i community continues to pursue. These include addressing the problem of religious prejudice by supporting different interfaith activities, encouraging local social and economic development projects, making efforts to encourage interracial unity and gender equality, and working with various United Nations agencies to help promote the principle of the Oneness of Mankind.

CONTEMPORARY ISSUES

The issues that will be discussed here fall roughly into two categories: those that are unique to the Baha'i community and those that Baha'is share with society at large. The strictly Baha'i issues will be covered first. These will then be followed by short examinations of how the American Baha'i community is attempting to come to terms with some of the more controversial social issues of the time. In both cases, the author makes no claim to statistical assessment; that is, he is not suggesting that these questions are problematic for anyone other than those Baha'is who have either written about such matters, expressed their views over the Internet, or shared their feelings through direct conversation. While these individuals amount to a fairly sizable number and could undoubtedly be statistically projected out to a much larger figure, it is not the purpose of this section to establish the existence of Baha'i factions but rather to indicate that differences of opinion do exist and are likely to remain part of the fabric of future American Baha'i discourse.

Women and the Universal House of Justice

Several times in previous chapters, it has been stated that although the Baha'i Faith holds the equality of men and women as one of its primary principles, females are not allowed to serve on its supreme administrative institution, the Universal House of Justice. The reason given for the ban is that in his *Kitáb-i Aqdas*, Baha'u'llah spoke of the men (*rijál*) of the House of Justice, and when later questioned, 'Abdu'l-Baha replied: "According to the ordinances of the Faith of God, women are the equals of men in all rights save only that of membership on the Universal House of Justice, for, as hath been stated in the text of the Book, both the Head and the members of the House of Justice are men."[4] Later, in a letter written on his behalf to an individual believer, Shoghi Effendi stated: "There is a Tablet from 'Abdu'l-Baha in which he definitely states that the membership of the Universal House of Justice is confined to men, and that the wisdom of it will be fully revealed and appreciated in the future."[5]

In 1988, a group of eight Baha'i scholars collaborated to produce a paper titled "The Service of Women on the Institutions of the Baha'i Faith." One of the article's main arguments was that the exclusion of women from membership on the Universal House of Justice was not necessarily permanent. In taking this position, the authors relied on two essential lines of thought. The first related to language usage. While admitting that the Arabic term *rijál* was indeed masculine, they also noted that in other contexts Baha'u'llah had employed *rijál* in such a manner as to include females. For example, they quoted the following from the religion's founder: "Today the Baha'i women must guide the handmaidens of the earth to the Lofty Horizon with the utmost purity and sanctity. Today the handmaidens of God are regarded as gentlemen [*rijál*]. Blessed are they! Blessed are they!"[6] Second, the authors claimed that on several occasions in Baha'i history, laws had changed over time. More specifically, they traced the record of women's service on Baha'i institutions in the United States, and in the process pointed out that at one time, females were not allowed to serve on local assemblies (houses of justice as they were then known). Until 'Abdu'l-Baha reinterpreted the law in 1912, it was common belief that Baha'u'llah's ban on women's service included local assemblies as well as the future national and international houses of justice. Developing the implications of the Master's change of mind, the paper concluded that the way was open for a future Universal House of Justice to reinterpret previously understood gender requirements for service on the supreme institution.

Defenders of the current prohibition maintain that both 'Abdu'l-Baha and Shoghi Effendi made it sufficiently clear that women's service was restricted when it came to the Universal House of Justice, and since that body does not have the power to interpret the sacred text (and without a living Guardian, no such power exists), no future change is possible. This position was confirmed by the Universal House of Justice in 1988 when the body wrote: "As mentioned earlier, the law regarding the membership of the Universal House of Justice is embedded in the Text and has been merely restated by the divinely appointed interpreters. It is therefore neither amenable to change nor subject to speculation about some possible future condition."[7]

The House and its supporters are quick to point out, however, that female ineligibility for membership on the supreme body does not constitute evidence of male superiority, and that women are not excluded from serving on other international institutions (for example, continental boards of counselors). Moreover, believers are reminded of 'Abdu'l-Baha's promise that clarity of understanding regarding this issue will be achieved in due course and that for the moment, it must be accepted on faith.

Those who suggest the possibility of future change claim that the Universal House of Justice can use its legislative powers to amend the law. They also note the inherent contradiction between the isolated legal restriction and the Baha'i principle of the equality of men and women. They conclude that the assertion that the ban does not indicate inequality is spurious. Perhaps more significantly, they also advance the argument that in Western countries, at least, the ineligibility of women to serve on the Universal House of Justice creates a major obstacle to the Faith's future growth.

Individual and Institutional Infallibility

Since the notion of infallibility is part and parcel of standard Baha'i belief, it can be assumed that for most American Baha'is the idea per se is not considered questionable. The problem begins when it comes to sorting out just what infallibility means. As a Manifestation of God, Baha'u'llah's writings are considered divine in origin, and 'Abdu'l-Baha and Shoghi Effendi's written interpretations of those writings are also believed to be divinely inspired. Setting aside certain theological subtleties between "divine in origin" and "divinely inspired," the areas of dispute, when they have arisen, have concerned the question of whether the infallibility of the holy figures extends beyond theological and ethical domains to include such categories as science and history. Regarding Shoghi Effendi, the Universal House of Justice clarified matters when they wrote: "The infallibility of the Guardian is confined to matters which are related strictly to the Cause and interpretations of the Teachings; he is not an infallible authority on other subjects, such as economics, science, etc."[8]

As for Baha'u'llah and 'Abdu'l-Baha, no definitive pronouncement has appeared, although the House did write in 1982 that Baha'u'llah had warned that his own statements should not be judged against the inaccurate standard of the acquired knowledge of mankind. The supreme body also noted that there was nothing in the holy texts that would lead to the conclusion that what Shoghi Effendi had said about his own statements on subjects not directly related to the Faith (that is, his fallibility) also applied to 'Abdu'l-Baha.[9]

The House's comments in this regard may partially explain the wide range of understanding current among American Baha'is, which stretches from the belief that anything the two men penned was literally true to a more modest notion that while their spiritual and ethical guidance is to be considered infallible, neither man was a historian or scientist. A case in point is Baha'u'llah's references in his *Lawh-i-Hikmat* (*Tablet of Wisdom*) to the Greek philosopher Pythagoras being a contemporary of King Solomon and Empedocles living at the time of King David. Baha'u'llah was echoing a view held by traditional Muslim historians with whose works he would have been familiar. Neither claim, however, is supported by contemporary scholarship. In a similar vein, disagreement has appeared regarding several of 'Abdu'l-Baha's writings concerning evolution, in which he made references to human beings as "having always existed." Some Baha'is have taken these to be a confirmation of what might be called a traditional creationist stance, while others point out that the pronouncements were not intended to be taken literally but rather meant to emphasize, by way of metaphor, the moral significance of the human species in creation as a whole.

At times, certain believers have been chastised for not accepting the infallible nature of the Baha'i scriptures, as when a Baha'i publisher was notified in writing by a counselor that his Internet post, in which he stated that he did not expect all Baha'is to agree on everything that Baha'u'llah or 'Abdu'l-Baha had said, was either a misunderstanding of Baha'i teachings or a lack of acceptance of fundamental beliefs.[10]

At the institutional level, the concept of infallibility appears to be understood in a variety of ways within the American Baha'i community. To some degree, this has been a consequence of the end of the Guardianship. 'Abdu'l-Baha's *Will and Testament* makes it clear that when engaged in the act of legislation, the Universal House of Justice should be considered as being free from all error. However, the supreme institution is not to be regarded as infallible in certain other spheres (such as the interpretation of Baha'i scripture), which were to be solely the functions of a living Guardian. The inherent ambiguity between the categories of legislation and interpretation has led many Baha'is to consider every pronouncement made by the Universal House of Justice as being unquestionably correct. In this context, it has lately been noted that "an unreflected, even magical vision of the unerring guidance which has been conferred on the House of Justice currently prevails in the community."[11]

The sense of confusion may well have been added to by an earlier House's claim that while it could not interpret the sacred texts, it could elucidate upon their meaning. Concerning this distinction, a later House wrote: "The elucidations of the Universal House of Justice stem from its legislative function, while the interpretations of the Guardian represent the true intent inherent in the Sacred Texts. The major distinction between the two functions is that legislation ... is susceptible of amendment by the House of Justice itself, whereas the Guardian's interpretation is a statement of truth which cannot be varied."[12] Furthermore, elucidation has been identified with such additional House powers as: (1) the deliberation upon all problems that have caused difference within the community, (2) the clarification of obscure questions, and (3) the handling of matters that are not expressly recorded in scripture. Thus, while in theory a difference is made between interpretation and elucidation, in practice it becomes somewhat difficult to distinguish between the two. For most American Baha'is, however, these distinctions would appear to be irrelevant, as the Universal House of Justice is seen as the final point of authority on all matters Baha'i.

Fundamentalism, Liberalism, and Baha'i Scholarship

In 1992, Moojan Momen's "Fundamentalism and Liberalism: Towards an Understanding of the Dichotomy" was published in the *Baha'i Studies Review*. While the paper was essentially an overview of the underlying differences between the two approaches to religion in general, it ended with a short section related to the Baha'i Faith. The author noted that both perspectives were represented in the Baha'i community and that ideally the Faith was capable of providing for the coexistence of the different styles that each represented. Ten years later, a more scathing piece by University of Michigan Professor Juan R. I. Cole titled "Fundamentalism in the Contemporary U.S. Baha'i Community" was published. The article made use of the paradigm adopted in the University of Chicago's Fundamentalism Project, which included within its definition of fundamentalism such characteristics as moral dualism, inerrancy of scripture, and authoritarian organization. Although the two articles were very different in tone and purpose, both recognized the existence of a fundamentalist/liberal clash within the Baha'i Faith, which they believed to be harmful to the religion's advancement. Thus, Momen's publication claimed that despite various protections, the presence of fundamentalists and liberals had caused a certain amount of tension within the Baha'i community: "There have been numerous episodes and situations known to the author of this article, and no doubt to any other person who has been a Baha'i for any length of time, where this tension has caused problems and even damage to the Baha'i Faith."[13] Cole's article went much further. It argued not only that Baha'i fundamentalism contradicted key emphases found within Baha'i scriptures but also that Baha'i leadership on both the national and international levels had become essentially fundamentalist in orientation.[14]

Fundamentalist and liberal interaction took place on several Baha'i Internet lists that sprang up in the 1990s. When interchange became heated, fundamentalists often blamed liberals for holding suspect ideas and doctrines drawn from the secular world. Another criticism frequently leveled by fundamentalists was that liberals arbitrarily selected what they claimed to be essential scriptural passages on the one hand and culturally determined (and therefore dispensable) selections on the other. At times, liberals were challenged as to the sincerity of their faith, and on occasion, it was even suggested that some might be covenant-breakers. For their part, liberals asserted that the intolerant attitude of the fundamentalists was opposed to the true spirit of religion as seen in the person of 'Abdu'l-Baha. Moreover, they repeatedly maintained that Baha'u'llah had forbidden blind obedience (*taqlid*) in his religion.

A related issue to the liberal/fundamentalist divide is the question of appropriate methodologies for Baha'i scholarship. Over the past two decades, debates surrounding this subject have periodically become heated, especially on the Internet. The problem first surfaced in England, where in the early and mid-1970s, a group of young Baha'i intellectuals had begun meeting to discuss issues of Babi-Baha'i history and subsequently held scholarly seminars at the University of Lancaster. One of these intellectuals was Denis MacEoin, who had become a Baha'i in Northern Ireland in the mid-1960s and later entered graduate school in Middle East studies at the University of Edinburgh. He went on to Cambridge University, where he produced a PhD dissertation titled "Shaykhism to Babism: A Study in Charismatic Renewal in Shi'ih Islam," thereby becoming the first Western Baha'i to study the Babi movement with the tools and methods of modern scholarship. Some of his approaches to Babi history, such as challenging the authority of the standard Baha'i version of Babi history, *Nabil's Narrative*, brought him into conflict with Baha'i authorities, and he was eventually called to a meeting with two members of the Universal House of Justice. Not long thereafter, MacEoin withdrew from the Faith.

The methodology question was raised in the United States during the 1980s and 1990s in relationship to the proposed publication by some Baha'i scholars of *Baha'i Encyclopedia*, for which they initially gained the backing of the National Spiritual Assembly. Many of the articles, however, were academic in style and substance, and the Universal House of Justice eventually responded by criticizing those scholars who "cast the Faith into a mold which is essentially foreign to its nature, taking no account of the spiritual forces which Baha'is see as its foundation."[15] After changes in editorship were made, the project was eventually put on hold, and it remains today in a state of limbo.

The Internet allowed for issues of scholarship to become more widely discussed in a public forum, and with this increased exposure, an atmosphere of distrust and fear began to emerge. As one scholar expressed it in a letter to the Universal House of Justice in 1997: "If left unchecked, I fear the problem threatens not only the unity of the community, but the image of the Bahá'í Faith in the eyes of people of capacity and influence in the world at large."[16] The House's response crystallized the essential difference in approach to the study of the Baha'i religion between its members and more liberal Baha'i intellectuals:

> A related paradigm for the study of religion has gradually consolidated itself in the prevailing academic culture during the course of the present century. It insists that all spiritual and moral phenomena must be understood through the application of

a scholarly apparatus devised to explore existence in a way that ignores the issues of God's continuous relationship with His creation and His intervention in human life and history. Yet, from a Bahá'í point of view, it is precisely this intervention that is the central theme of the Teachings of the Founders of the revealed religions ostensibly being studied.[17]

Some scholars who have supported the House have argued for the adoption of a new paradigm for Baha'i scholarship that would include such elements as: (1) a nonelitist approach to Baha'i Studies whereby scholarship becomes an endeavor accessible to all members of the Baha'i community without exception, (2) an acceptance that the primary motive for Baha'i scholarship should be service to the Cause, (3) support for the proposition that Baha'i scholarship should not cause dissension or disagreement within the community, (4) a belief that one of a Baha'i scholar's duties is to refute arguments against the Faith, (5) an admission that an attempt at religious objectivity for a Baha'i scholar is essentially dishonest, (6) an agreement that Baha'i scholars should not make pronouncements on matters that are not within their areas of expertise or responsibility—for example, criticism of the Baha'i Administrative Order, (7) a denial that Baha'u'llah's Cause is similar to other religions and organizations or that it shares in their inadequacies, and (8) an assent to the proposition that Baha'i sacred texts are beyond the bounds of critical scholarly analysis.[18] Although there has been no official adoption of such a paradigm, sympathy for some of its principles has often been expressed in Internet postings.

For scholars trained in a variety of social science disciplines, many of the above qualifications have been found to be extremely problematic if not unacceptable. One result has been that a number of Baha'i academics have tended to stay away from publishing articles or books dealing with the Faith, and others have learned to exercise a certain discretion in their work. Those who have been more outspoken in their criticism have either been challenged by Baha'i institutions or put in a position where they have felt it necessary to withdraw from the Faith. An example of the former is a Baha'i publisher whose company acted as a distributor and vocal supporter of Cole's *Modernity and the Millennium*. The book, which was well-received in American academia, presented Baha'u'llah's work and writings as one of several efforts by Middle Eastern thinkers to work out a response to the challenges posed by the forces of modernity. It was assailed, however, in a letter sent to the distributor from the Baha'i World Center for its misconception of the nature of Baha'u'llah's mission and its negative depiction of current Baha'i leadership.[19] The letter also claimed that Cole had previously embarked on a deliberate assault against the

Baha'i Cause, in which he had not hesitated to attack its institutions and misrepresent its fundamental teachings. The correspondence then went on to warn the publisher that he should "meditate profoundly on the questions raised in the foregoing, as these issues bear directly on the relationship that binds you to your Lord."[20]

Of all the issues related to Baha'i scholarship, the one that would seem to be most contentious is prepublication review, whereby anything written for publication about the Faith by a believer must be submitted to a Baha'i institution for approval. This policy was first set in place during 'Abdu'l-Baha's leadership, and Shoghi Effendi continued the practice (which he described as temporary) to prevent the spread of distorted versions of the religion's teachings, many of which were rampant at the time. The Universal House of Justice has likewise maintained the convention. The policy did not cause any great degree of controversy through most of the century, but as one contemporary writer has noted, the youth conversions of the early 1970s created a class of bright, intellectually-inclined Baha'is who "naturally chafed at the restrictions placed upon written ideas."[21]

Review has become especially problematic because it constitutes a third-party intervention between the author and the publisher, a process most publishing houses are not willing to accept. Within the Baha'i review process itself, problems arise when the reviewers are not knowledgeable enough about the material to make reasonable judgments or they exceed their boundaries and begin to make editorial evaluations about the suitability of the work for publication.[22] Then there is the personal cost of review for Baha'i academics, which can include, among other things, the loss of credibility in the scholarly community. Supporters of the policy argue that prepublication review is in practice no different than an academic publisher's process of peer review and that the Baha'i community needs to be protected against individuals' misunderstandings and/or projections of their personal agendas into their work. Here, they are essentially defending the explanations of the Universal House of Justice, as found in such documents as *Individual Rights and Freedoms* (discussed below) and several subsequent letters to individuals. In these statements, the House has emphasized that Baha'i scholars should view themselves as involved in a common struggle to achieve Baha'u'llah's purpose for the human race and that their activities should not be seen as set apart from this process or operating on authority outside of it. As they stated in 1993: "The House of Justice believes that part of the difficulty that some Baha'i academics are having with the question of prepublication review may arise from the fact that, in their scholarly work, such believers do not see themselves as full participants in this process, free to act with the spiritual autonomy they exercise in other aspects of their lives."[23] The position in which some Baha'i scholars find themselves is, thus, somewhat reminiscent of the situation that confronted several Mormon intellectuals in the mid-1960s. These scholars perceived themselves as faithful and loyal Mormons rather than dissidents, and most learned to exercise a certain degree of caution in their writings, but some of the more self-conscious and outspoken among them eventually got caught in a systematic clampdown by Morman authorities.[24]

Individual Rights and Freedoms

In December 1988, the Universal House of Justice released a publication directed to the Baha'is of the United States titled *Individual Rights and Freedoms*. The document opened with the following statement:

> We have noticed with concern evidences of a confusion of attitudes among some of the friends when they encounter difficulties in applying Baha'i principles to questions of the day. On the one hand, they acknowledge their belief in Baha'u'llah and His teachings; on the other, they invoke Western liberal democratic practices when actions of Baha'i institutions or of some of their fellow Baha'is do not accord with their expectations. At the heart of this confusion are misconceptions of such fundamental issues as individual rights and freedom of expression in the Baha'i community.[25]

The passage would seem to indicate that for some American Baha'is who were raised with the inherent assumptions found in documents like the Bill of Rights, the Baha'i approach to individual freedom was proving problematic. American individualism appeared to be in conflict with certain Baha'i notions of authority.

The remainder of the document revealed the House's main areas of concern. These were the aforementioned prepublication review, believers' acceptance of Baha'i institutional authority, and Baha'i public criticism of those institutions. The foundation of the House's argument was that despite Baha'u'llah's introduction of certain democratic methods into his religion's administrative institutions and notwithstanding the high importance he gave to individual freedom, Baha'is were still duty-bound to work within the framework of his divinely-conceived Order, whose core principle was "moderation in all things." Thus they concluded: "We come to appreciate that the Administrative Order He has conceived embodies the operating principles which are necessary to the maintenance of that moderation which will ensure the 'true liberty' of humankind."[26]

According to some critics, the importance placed on unity within the American Baha'i community has, at times, created anxiety concerning any expression of dissent. This, in turn, has resulted in severe limits imposed on individual free expression, especially concerning community affairs and institutional decisions.[27] Baha'i leadership responds to such accusations by declaring that Baha'is are welcome to raise such questions at the Nineteen Day Feast or, if necessary, to take those questions or objections to higher institutions. However, as a member of the American National Spiritual Assembly stated in a speech given in Los Angeles in March 1988: "It is something else when whispering campaigns or petitions are sent around for signatures objecting to the activities of the institutions. That also may be something which is countenanced by American democracy but has nothing to do with the Baha'i Faith."[28]

The emphasis given to supporting institutional resolutions goes as far as demanding full compliance, even if there is a significant minority view that a certain decision is wrong. The underlying principle here is that unity in error is better than division over truth, for the former will eventually be understood and changed, while the latter will only result in continued conflict and strife. This principle is even employed between different levels of the Baha'i administrative system. Thus, on very few occasions has the National Spiritual Assembly directly intervened in the working of local spiritual assemblies (though there have been examples of direct intervention, even to the point of dissolving an assembly). While this policy may be helpful in terms of allowing local leadership to gradually mature, it can have the negative effect of permitting strong-willed personalities to dominate communities. Nevertheless, the common advice given to believers is to follow Shoghi Effendi's counsel when he wrote that "all criticisms and discussions of a negative character which may result in undermining the authority of the Assembly as a body should be strictly avoided."[29]

Another traditional Baha'i ideal related to freedom of speech is *hikmat*, the maxim that how and when something is said is as important as what is said. Translated as practical wisdom, *hikmat* has a long standing within Baha'i history stretching back to the time of the Bab. A prominent Baha'i has described the term in these words: "By wisdom is meant taking any praiseworthy action through which the Cause of God may be promoted. Lack of wisdom is to take actions which owing to circumstances result in harming the Faith, even though they may be carried out with the best possible motive."[30] In practice, *hikmat* has involved such acts as misleading people concerning one's Baha'i identity or concealing inconvenient aspects of the Baha'i teachings.[31] Historically, *hikmat* was often used as a means of protecting Baha'is from open and frequently violent hostility. In contemporary America, its application would appear to be related to the requirement of "moderation in all things" in that public criticism of the

Baha'i community is deemed excessive use of a believer's freedom of speech.

The question of freedom of speech in a Baha'i context came to a head in the late 1990s when Canadian fantasy writer Michael McKenny was abruptly removed from the membership rolls for repeatedly raising issues on Baha'i e-mail lists concerning the absence of women on the Universal House of Justice and making statements that were seen as bringing into question the supreme institution's infallibility.[32] In the eyes of his supporters, McKenny was a victim of the arbitrary misuse of power, and they were quick to cite 'Abdu'l-Baha's forbidding of *takfir* (the power to declare someone "not a Baha'i"). From the perspective of the Universal House of Justice and those who agreed with that body's decision, the writer was an example of a few Baha'is who refused to use the proper channels for expressing their discontent. In so doing, McKenny was seen as purposefully arousing disaffection within the community and thereby attempting to change the essential structure and principles of Baha'i administration to be in accord with his own personal notions. It seems apparent, therefore, that in the McKenny case two differing notions of freedom of speech collided: one that emphasized the undoubted right of the individual to declare his conscience and assert his views and another that stressed the prevention of conflict and contention within the community.

Abortion, Capital Punishment, and Homosexuality

Turning to issues that the Baha'i community shares with society at large, three stand out as being especially significant: abortion, capital punishment, and homosexuality.

In his book of laws, *Kitáb-i Aqdas*, Baha'u'llah makes no mention of either contraception or abortion, and 'Abdu'l-Baha was likewise silent on these issues. In the absence of scriptural teachings, Shoghi Effendi used three guiding propositions when writing his commentaries on such matters: (1) the sanctity of human life, (2) the conviction that life begins at conception, and (3) the belief that procreation and the education of children are the primary reasons for the existence of marriage and the family. From these judgments, he determined that contraception could be used within marriage, but that abortion was contrary to the Baha'i teachings. However, since in his role as Guardian Shoghi Effendi had no legislative powers, it was left up to a future Universal House of Justice to make a legal ruling. From an examination of letters written by several Houses of Justice, it is clear that these bodies also considered casual abortion to be prohibited. For example, in a 1983 letter written on behalf of the House of Justice to the National Spiritual Assembly of Ireland, it was stated that surgical operations for the purpose of preventing the birth of unwanted children were forbidden unless there were circumstances that justified such actions on medical grounds.[33] Nevertheless, to this point in time, no Universal House of Justice has used its legislative power to officially forbid the termination of a pregnancy. Consequently, although there is a strong current of anti-abortion sentiment found among Baha'i leadership, the procedure is technically not contrary to Baha'i law, and in the absence of legal prohibition, individuals are called upon to use their own consciences when considering such matters.

Although only anecdotal in scope, it is also important to note that the author has either spoken to or received reports from several Iranian women who stated that until they came to the United States, they had never even heard of abortion as being a community issue, and that the procedure was commonly used by Baha'i women in Iran. If such is the case, the importance given to the issue in the American Baha'i community may well be a result of contemporary Baha'i leadership being influenced by conservative Western attitudes rather than an expression of scriptural authority.

Concerning capital punishment, both views (and the myriad of arguments that surround them) can be found in the American Baha'i community. This is partly a result of the fact that while Baha'u'llah allowed for the ultimate penalty, he did not require its use. It is perhaps telling, however, that in a statement sent to Amnesty International on behalf of the Baha'i International Community, Universal House of Justice member Douglas Martin wrote that the option of applying the death penalty was given support by the Baha'i community on the grounds that when educational methods fail to bring about desired change, civil authority has the right to resort to such measures. Arguing against the notion that capital punishment makes the state guilty of the very crime it abhors, the statement went on to say:

> With only a small minority of dissenting voices, it is universally accepted that civil government has not only the right but the responsibility to defend the population in time of war, recognizing that such defense involves actions many of which are aimed directly at the taking of human life. In the view of the Baha'i community, this principle applies equally to the moral authority of the State in protecting society against attacks on its members from within ... ultimately, it is justice and not forgiveness upon which the social covenant among them is established.[34]

In section 107 of the *Kitáb-i Aqdas*, Baha'u'llah writes: "We shrink, for very shame, from treating of the subject of boys. Fear ye the Merciful, O peoples of the world! Commit not that which is forbidden you in Our

Holy Tablet, and be not of those who rove distractedly in the wilderness of their desires."[35] Over the years, this passage has generally been interpreted as a prohibition against homosexuality. Hence, we find Shoghi Effendi stating: "Homosexuality, according to the Writings of Baha'u'llah, is spiritually condemned. This does not mean that people so afflicted must not be helped and advised and sympathized with. It does mean that we do not believe that it is a permissible way of life."[36] In 1973, the Universal House of Justice in a letter to an individual believer claimed:

> A number of sexual problems, such as homosexuality and trans-sexuality can well have medical aspects, and in such cases recourse should certainly be had to the best medical assistance. But it is clear from the teaching of Baha'u'llah that homosexuality is not a condition to which a person should be reconciled, but is a distortion of his or her nature which should be controlled or overcome.[37]

More recently, several commentators have noted that Baha'u'llah's reference in the *Kitáb-i Aqdas* addresses pederasty rather than homosexuality per se and that Shoghi Effendi's interpretations in the areas of science are not infallible. One provocative essay went so far as to suggest that Baha'u'llah renders gender distinction immaterial as a guide for individual or social action. The author concluded from this premise that "although licit sex is limited to marriage, it could be regarded as a valid reading of the text to consider the sexes of the partners unspecified and irrelevant."[38] Nevertheless, as the following account reveals, the official Baha'i position toward homosexuality can at most be characterized as one of sympathetic disapproval.

At the request of the National Spiritual Assembly, a group of gays, lesbians, and their supporters gathered in Reno, Nevada, in September 1993 to discuss the beliefs and practices of the Baha'i Faith with regard to homosexuality. In the process, they produced and sent a letter to the national body in which they admitted that many of them had been in hiding from their Baha'i communities. They also indicated that they had found no evidence whatsoever that a homosexual could be changed into a heterosexual by medicine or psychological treatments.[39] The National Spiritual Assembly did not respond directly but later approved for distribution a document in which this statement appeared:

> To regard homosexuals with prejudice and disdain would be entirely against the spirit of Baha'i Teachings. The doors are open for all of humanity to enter the Cause of God, irrespective of their present circumstances; this invitation applies to homosexuals as well as to any others who are engaged in practices contrary to the Baha'i Teachings. Associated with this invitation is the expectation that all believers will make a sincere and persistent effort to eradicate those aspects of their conduct which are not in conformity with Divine Law.[40]

Consequently, for the time being, gay and lesbian Baha'is find themselves in an awkward position. On the one hand, they are members of a religion that often represents itself as being socially progressive, yet their community differs from that of other progressive religious denominations in the United States (for example, Unitarians and Episcopalians) when it comes to the question of homosexuality. In practice, this means that gays and lesbians can either leave the Baha'i community, make concerted efforts to change their sexual orientation, or remain closeted when it comes to expressing their sexual preferences.

9

Anti-Baha'i Polemic and Baha'i Responses

In Chapter 5, it was mentioned that from the very early years of its introduction into the United States, the Baha'i Faith encountered cases of verbal
hostility from conservative, evangelical Christians. Thus in October 1899,
Stoyan Krstoff Vatralsky held a meeting in Kenosha, Wisconsin, at which
he delivered an anti-Islamic, anti-Baha'i diatribe titled "The Kenosha Truth
Knowers: the Few Truths They Know and the Many Errors They Teach."

Shortly thereafter, several American newspapers, including the *New York
Times* and the *North American*, painted the Baha'i Faith in negative hues,
speaking of "Babist propaganda" and "oriental cultism." Over the decades,
there have been periodic examples of further anti-Baha'i polemic. Three
of the most recent tracts, though somewhat less virulent in tone, have
been those written by William McElwee Miller, Francis Beckwith, and
Vance Salisbury.

WILLIAM McELWEE MILLER

William McElwee Miller was a Presbyterian clergyman who served in
the Church's Iranian missions for more than forty years. In addition to
his ministerial duties, Rev. Miller spent a great deal of his time writing
and speaking on the subject of the Baha'i Faith. He wrote two books on
the religion and collaborated with the Rev. E. E. Elder on a number of
articles. His most exhaustive tract, *The Baha'i Faith: Its History and Teachings*,
was published in 1974.

Miller's major criticisms of the Baha'i Faith can be categorized under two main headings: political intrigue and misplaced spiritual priorities. In his historical presentation, Miller expended much time and energy describing what he saw as a fundamental flaw in the evolution of community leadership from the Bab to Baha'u'llah. Here he turned his attention to the Bab's appointment of Subh-i-Azal as his vice-regent and the latter's refusal to acknowledge Baha'u'llah's claim to be He whom God shall make manifest. The reverend argued that through his assertion to be a Manifestation of God, Baha'u'llah made a power play and thereby usurped his half brother's legitimate claim to community leadership. In this vein, he wrote:

> All the Babis were convinced that the Bab had been sent by God and was infallible. Then, since Subh-i-Azal had been appointed by the Bab himself as his successor, was not he also sent by God, as they had for sixteen years believed? And did he not possess divine wisdom, and was he not one with the Bab? How then could it be possible that such an one as Subh-i-Azal should be unable to recognize Him-Whom-God-Will-Manifest when he appears?[1]

Miller's view that Baha'u'llah's rise to community leadership was akin to a political coup consequently implied that his claims to revelation were misguided, if not contrived.

Miller's own brand of theology, which emphasized individual salvation through personal faith and understood society to be essentially irredeemable, allowed him to judge the Baha'i emphasis on community organization and social justice as misplaced religious priorities. In this connection, he argued that the Baha'i holy figures' vague doctrines about the nature of the soul and the question of salvation did not provide the spiritual tools required for the enforcement of their ethical teachings. In contrast to Christianity, he claimed that the Baha'i teachings lacked an adequate consideration of man's sinful nature: "Few are the appeals to men to repent of their sins as the prophets of old appealed, few the assurances of God's love for sinners and his promises to them of forgiveness and a new life of holiness."[2] Then Miller went directly to the heart of his position: "In all Baha'i literature can there be found a promise of a Savior from sin? ... Sinners need salvation, and the Baha'i Faith fails to provide a Savior."[3]

FRANCIS BECKWITH

Francis Beckwith's critique of the Baha'i Faith was more straightforward than Miller's and lacked any attempt at historical analysis. In a pamphlet-like publication issued in 1985 and titled *Baha'i: A Christian Response to Baha'ism*, the professor from Simon Greenleaf University in Anaheim,

California, put forward two essential arguments: first, that the Baha'i concepts of Manifestation and Progressive Revelation contained internal contradictions, and second, that Baha'i beliefs related to Jesus Christ were contrary to the teachings found in the Bible.

According to Beckwith, the nature of God as revealed by seven of the recognized Baha'i Manifestations is inconsistent (Beckwith confusedly included Confucius in his list). Thus, he wrote that Moses and Muhammad believed in one God; Krishna and Confucius believed in many gods; Zoroaster was a dualist; Buddha was an agnostic; and Jesus was a strict monotheist who also taught that God was capable of begetting a son. It logically follows, he argued, that not all of the supposed Manifestations could have been correct, and this fact destroys the Baha'i belief in Progressive Revelation. As he adjudged: "For when one examines the doctrine of God's nature, as revealed by the so-called manifestations, there exists a mass of contradictory doctrine."[4]

Beckwith also spent time showing how several of the Baha'i Manifestations were tainted by sin. For example, he reminded his readers that Moses was guilty of murdering an Egyptian, and that the Qur'an speaks of Allah forgiving Muhammad for his past sins. In a rather disrespectful tone, Beckwith concluded that the Baha'i Manifestations were authorities with wax noses—"noses which can be twisted in any way the Baha'i apologist sees fit in order to keep his religious beliefs consistent."[5]

It is when Beckwith came to the Baha'i understandings of Jesus and the Bible that his polemic hit full stride. He flatly stated that the Baha'i Faith denies the chief characteristics attributed to Jesus by scripture. This claim was based on his own tradition's particular understanding of scripture, but that notwithstanding, the professor's primary examples were: (1) that Jesus Christ is God incarnate, (2) this same Jesus Christ rose bodily from the grave, (3) Jesus Christ will return in the skies in bodily form, and (4) Jesus Christ is the only savior for all eternity. It goes without saying that the last of these beliefs cannot in any way be reconciled with Baha'i doctrine. As for the other three, Beckwith had the following things to say:

> After a careful examination of the New Testament the reader becomes aware that Jesus and the biblical writers taught the doctrine of Incarnation....[6] When the text of the New Testament is examined, it becomes clear to the reader that the text teaches the physical resurrection of Jesus....[7] It is crystal clear that the above passage [Acts 1: 9–11] is claiming that Christ will return in the same way He left. He departed via the sky, therefore He will return that way.[8]

Since Baha'i teachings do not take these matters literally but explain them as being examples of the use of religious metaphor, Beckwith concluded that along with the world's other non-Christian spiritual traditions, "Baha'iism" was a false religion.

At one point in the publication, Beckwith introduced an element of scandal by citing two different Baha'i interpretations of a prophecy from the book of Daniel concerning the coming of world peace (Daniel 12:12). Both are attributed to 'Abdu'l-Baha but appear in different editions of the widely disseminated introductory book, *Baha'u'llah and the New Era*. Beckwith implied that the Baha'i Publishing Committee altered the original work when the first prophecy failed to come to pass in 1957. In a somewhat melodramatic fashion, he referred to the incident as the "Baha'i Watergate."[9]

VANCE SALISBURY

Vance Salisbury's criticism of the Baha'i Faith lay in what he saw as the suppression and manipulation of historical materials on the part of twentieth-century Baha'i authors. It should be noted that although Salisbury is a Christian and has established a religiously oriented website, similar charges have also been brought by other Baha'i critics, including the former Baha'i scholar Denis MacEoin. One area where Salisbury viewed this as happening was in Baha'i writings on Babi history. He claimed that Baha'i authors often ignored or distorted certain Babi concepts and conduct that were not in agreement with the teachings of Baha'u'llah or the ideals of the modern Baha'i community. An example of this approach is the way most Baha'i authors have dealt with the Bab's doctrine of *jihad* (holy war), which was later annulled by Baha'u'llah. According to Salisbury, these writers presented Babi jihad as essentially a form of self-defense.

At that point, he quoted Baha'i authors William S. Hatcher and J. Douglas Martin in their book *The Baha'i Faith: The Emerging Global Religion*: "Raised in this Muslim value system, the Babis felt fully justified in defending themselves and their families against the attacks of the mullas. Some may have expected the Bab would reveal his own doctrine of jihad. If so, they were disappointed."[10] From Salisbury's perspective: "This stands in contrast to the writings of the Bab which outline in some detail the waging of Holy War in order to promulgate the cause of his religion and which, toward the end of his life, took on a very hostile tone towards anyone who would not recognize his messianic claims."[11]

When it came to Baha'i history, Salisbury claimed that later editions of certain popular Baha'i books had been selectively revised by administrative editors. These revisions included both posthumous additions and deletions, changes that Salisbury suggested have been attempts at covering up undesirable facts and/or information. Thus, he cited the case of Dr. John E. Esslemont's *Baha'u'llah and the New Era*, where the first edition contained a statement of gratitude to the Baha'i historian 'Abdu'l-Husayn Áyatí (also known as Ávaríh), but in later editions, this acknowledgment was removed. Salisbury's explanation for the change was that since Ávaríh subsequently lost his faith and was eventually declared a covenant-breaker by Shoghi Effendi, words of praise related to his historical learnedness needed to be suppressed.

Salisbury likewise took aim at the issue of the lack of a living Baha'i Guardian, concluding in the process that "the institution of the Guardian of the Cause of God had been the subject of the most widespread bowdlerization of texts."[12] Once again, he pointed to later editorial revisions made to certain popular Baha'i books. Written before Shoghi Effendi's death, these books openly assumed that the position of Guardian of the Faith was divinely ordained and would therefore be permanent in nature. One example that Salisbury cited in this respect was John Ferraby's introductory book, *All Things Made New*. The original edition was published in 1957 and dedicated to Shoghi Effendi as the first Guardian of the Baha'i Faith. In the book's 1987 edition, the word "first," was left out of the dedication, and a number of sentences from 'Abdu'l-Baha's *Will and Testament* that emphasized the importance of a permanent Guardian were removed from the text. For Salisbury, these changes indicated that the failure of the Guardianship to become a lasting institution was, to say the least, a sensitive subject for Baha'i leadership since it raised the problematic paradox of a divinely ordained but defunct institution.

BAHA'I RESPONSES

Baha'is have not remained silent in the face of Christian criticism. As far back as the Vatralsky episode, when Thornton Chase sent a lengthy reply to Kenosha newspapers, there have been Baha'i writers who have countered their critics in print. During the post–Shoghi Effendi phase of Baha'i history, when Christian critiques became more numerous, Baha'i apologetics has become a virtual genre within Baha'i literature.

Although it was originally written in German, a translation of Udo Schaefer's *The Light Shineth In Darkness* was published in 1978 and widely distributed throughout the American Baha'i community. One of the essays in the book, "Answer to a Theologian," confronted many of the doctrinal positions put forth by Christian writers. Schaefer's main argument was that Christian objections to Baha'i beliefs have primarily been based on the teachings of the apostle Paul. However, Schaefer continued, it was upon Peter, not Paul, that Jesus conferred authority. Over the centuries, Christianity has forgotten this fact, and consequently, most of Jesus' followers have actually been disciples of Paul. Schaefer went on to assert that it was Paul, the apostle who never met the historical Jesus, who obscured things. Paul not only made Christianity a religion of sacraments, but, more significantly, also took the phrase "Son of God" and changed it from a Jewish messianic title into a literal truth.[13] Thus, the Church's plan for salvation, which includes such Pauline doctrines as Original Sin, the Incarnation, and the Holy Trinity, are by Baha'i standards deformities of Jesus' original teaching.[14] In effect, Schaefer was saying that Baha'i and traditional Christian theologians exist within two different universes of thought, and as long as the latter maintain their assumptions, Baha'i claims and teachings will remain impossible for them to accept.

In 1978, Douglas Martin wrote an article titled "The Missionary as Historian: William Miller and the Baha'i Faith" that appeared in the journal *Baha'i Studies*.[15] The paper presented William McElwee Miller as a man obsessed with the mission of defaming the Baha'i Faith. At the top of Martin's list of Miller's shortcomings was his misuse of sources. According to Martin, while Miller claimed to have based his work on reliable authors, apart from the works of E. G. Browne, the reverend in fact had depended heavily on anti-Baha'i works, the most notorious being the writings of Jelal Azal, a descendent of Baha'u'llah's half brother and rival, Subh-i-Azal. Thus, it was Martin's assessment that Miller was not primarily interested in the writing of history; rather, he had engaged himself in the spreading of Azali falsehoods.

In addition to his lack of fairness, Martin charged Miller with an ignorance of Baha'i thought. Like Schaefer, Martin concluded that the inability of the Christian clergyman to view religion in conceptual categories other than those of his own tradition made him incapable of writing anything more than religious propaganda. Indeed, Martin went so far as to claim that what was most missing in Miller's book was the Baha'i Faith itself.

Concerning Francis Beckwith's critique, the Baha'i apologist Peter Terry has provided a point-by-point rebuttal titled "Truth Triumphs: A Baha'i Response to Misrepresentations of the Baha'i Teachings and Baha'i History." One of the main issues the Baha'i writer pursued in his 1999 article was the unity of the Baha'i Manifestations. Here he countered Beckwith's charge of differing views of deity by claiming that all Baha'i Manifestations taught the existence of a single God. He noted, however, that "Baha'i doctrine does not take, as its source, the Scriptures ascribed to all of these Manifestations of God, nor the present practice of the religions associated with these Manifestations of God."[16] In other words, from Terry's perspective, Beckwith was not dealing with official Baha'i doctrine but with the traditional understandings of various contemporary religious communities whose own traditions had distorted the teachings of the Manifestations.

On the issue of Beckwith's "Watergate" charge, the Research Department at the Baha'i World Center in Haifa, Israel, responded by asserting that the questionable passage in Dr. Esslemont's book was based on the author's own understanding of what 'Abdu'l-Baha had said concerning the Book of Daniel and was therefore not an official Baha'i statement. In Baha'i terminology, information acquired in this fashion is referred to as a "pilgrim's note," and as such, it is not to be taken as anything but hearsay. However, the Research Department's finding went on to say that 'Abdu'l-Baha did not give the date of the establishment of world peace but rather the worldwide establishment of the Baha'i Faith. Textual changes in subsequent editions were not, therefore, a cover-up, as Beckwith claimed, but an attempt at maintaining the purity of the Baha'i teachings from man-made additions.[17]

Although there have not been to this date any official Baha'i responses of which this author is aware to Vance Salisbury's accusations, similar claims regarding source manipulation have generally been answered in one of two ways: first, that such charges are really cases of much ado about nothing—that is, they are technical ruses designed to mislead and confuse; and second, that in certain instances the withholding of information has not been carried out for deceptive purposes but rather as examples of "wisdom." The first category speaks for itself. As for the second, it will be recalled from Chapter 8 that the Babi and Baha'i communities have had a long history of holding back information on the basis that it can be damaging either to individuals or the Faith as a whole, especially when it is not presented in a proper context. An example of this procedure took place in the early 1980s when Kalimat Press in Los Angeles decided to publish a translation of a memoir written by Baha'u'llah's personal barber, Ustád Muhammad-'Alíy-i Salmání. Just prior to publication, the Universal House of Justice decided that certain passages needed to be omitted. In letters to Kalimat Press and University of Michigan Professor Juan R. I. Cole, the House of Justice claimed that there was no question whatsoever of suppressing information. Rather, it was a matter of having the information placed in a proper relationship to other records and commented upon by experts in the field. The letter to Professor Cole went on to say that when a Baha'i publishing house issues a translation of an original document written by a person who was close to Baha'u'llah, readers will likely assume that actions and statements in that document are accurate portrayals and are approved of by Baha'is. The House therefore concluded that certain of the barber's accounts were misleading and unworthy of present publication.[18]

In closing this chapter, it should be emphasized that many Christian thinkers and organizations are on good terms with the American Baha'i community and often praise the Faith for its high-minded spiritual principles. When it is expressed, anti-Baha'i polemic would appear to be primarily a result of a narrow and exclusivist view of religion, although the Baha'i use of such practices as *hikmat* have produced suspicion among some non-Baha'is, especially in light of the claim that the independent investigation of truth is one of the Faith's essential principles. Although certain antagonists have referred to it as a cult, given changes in the American religious landscape that now sees approximately 4 percent of the country's citizens belonging to non-Christian religions and barring some backlash from Christian extremists, it can be assumed that the American Baha'i community will continue to take its place within the accepted boundaries of the American religious spectrum.

Conclusion

Looking back at the body of material contained in both Parts I and II of this study, a number of important themes and trends become apparent. In general terms, perhaps the Baha'i Faith's most significant dimension is the potential model it offers for a universal form of religious life. In the midst of contemporary globalization, many, if not most, religious communities are still maintaining a narrow form of identification based on the assumption of "the in" and "the out," "the saved" and "the damned." Denying the plurality of religious truth or focusing on the uniqueness of their own traditions, they are attempting to isolate their followers from the spiritual implications of a global worldview. With its belief in the Oneness of Religion, the Baha'i Faith counters such insulation and provides for the possibility of a transformation in spiritual identity that goes beyond not only religious, but also national and ethnic limitations. A danger that the Baha'i community faces in promoting this process is the possibility that it might uphold the historical truths of the world's great religious traditions but then relegate them to the past by denying that they have a creative role to play in the present; that is, the Baha'is might claim that only their religion has the ability to bring about a global transformation. Elements of this type of thinking are currently found not only among the Baha'i rank and file but also at levels of leadership. Should such a Baha'i "triumphalism" prevail, the movement's ability to help create a universalized form of human identity would likely be impaired.

In terms of its administrative organization, the Baha'i Faith promotes a pattern of institutional communication that likewise speaks to a global perspective. Continual consultation and feedback between local, national, and international centers of authority should allow for what sociologist Michael McMullen has referred to as the process of "thinking globally and acting locally." In this respect, he argues that while other religious groups and denominations in the United States are also global in their outreach, the Administrative Order helps shape Baha'i identity and behavior in a way that is distinctly universalist.[1]

The existence of both democratic and more authoritarian methods of decision making within the Baha'i system should also enhance a global outlook in that they ideally provide for a balance between local and international perspectives. Whether the administrative balances that Shoghi Effendi envisioned are actually being maintained has recently become a question of concern for some Baha'is who feel that the Administrative Order is now characterized by a top-down approach to decision making. The extent to which this claim is actually the case will probably determine the religion's future growth in the United States, where democratic assumptions are deeply imbedded in the political culture. Any extensive movement away from these values would likely be detrimental to future expansion.

The question of exactly where the Baha'i Faith is to be situated in the overall panorama of American religious life is another subject worthy of consideration. Initial reflection might cause one to classify the Faith as a new religious movement: that is, a religious group outside of the cultural mainstream whose appearance on the American scene is relatively recent. While such a classification may be sociologically convenient, it is somewhat misleading in that the Baha'i Faith is rooted in a cultural heritage that is close to 1,500 years old. Should the religion then be seen as a modernized form of Islam? There are at least two reasons to reject such a designation. First, at least since Shoghi Effendi's time, Baha'is have denied that they are affiliated with Islam. Moreover, as noted in the body of this text, various Muslim communities have historically seen the Baha'i Faith as being outside Islamic identity. If the Baha'i Faith is neither a new religious movement nor an offshoot of Islam, what exactly is it?

A start to answering this question in terms of its American manifestation may well be found in the pages of an insightful essay by Anthony Lee titled "Reconciling the Other: The Baha'i Faith in America as a Successful Synthesis of Christianity and Islam." Lee argues that as the result of a number of factors, not the least of which has been the ability of the Baha'i Faith to adapt its core teachings to a variety of cultural settings, certain Islamic elements within the religion have been successfully "Christianized," sometimes without American believers even being aware of the process. In Lee's own words:

> I propose that the actual experience and practice of American Baha'is is not a mere imperfect reflection of Islamic contexts, but is a living religion in which the traditions and religious assumptions of both Islam and Christianity have been blended in organic unity. This mix does not arrive from some artificial, deliberate syncretism which has been imposed on the community, but from the unique history of the Baha'i Faith in America and from the lived experience of Baha'is who bring Christian assumptions to their new Faith.[2]

If Lee is correct, the Baha'i Faith is somewhat of an anomaly when it comes to religious classification. The religion would seem to fall into a certain gray area somewhere between a new religious movement and an independent world religion. Its uniqueness would appear to lie in the fact that it is able to adjust its essential teachings to a variety of cultural settings and thereby prove itself capable of speaking a religious language that is both local and universal in orientation. In relationship to its American experience, "Baha'i practices with obvious Islamic roots are lived and experienced by American Baha'is as an extension of Christian piety and a fulfillment of Christian expectations."[3]

While there are difficulties in accurately classifying the Baha'i Faith within the spectrum of American religious life, when it comes to identifying the religious and social backgrounds of those individuals who have joined the Baha'i community over the years, the ground is more solid. As indicated during the examination of the Kheiralla period of American Baha'i history, a large percentage of the initial members had been under the influence of one or the other of two cultural streams: spiritualism (often referred to as the metaphysical movement) and the second-coming traditions (millennialists). Thus, from its earliest years in the United States, the Baha'i community contained theologically diverse elements, since the believers who came from spiritualist or metaphysical backgrounds brought with them more liberal religious ideas while the millennialists tended toward more conservative beliefs. What seems to have allowed the two groups to live in relative harmony with one another was the charismatic leadership provided by both George Ibrahim Kheiralla and 'Abdu'l-Baha. After Kheiralla's departure, liberal Protestants who were attracted to the social and spiritual principles as articulated by 'Abdu'l-Baha began joining the movement in larger numbers, thereby adding a new faction to the American Baha'i community. Again, it was 'Abdu'l-Baha's individual charisma that provided the unifying element.

The 1917 Mason Remey–led purge (recounted in Chapter 5) drove many of the fringe groups out of the American community, but certain theological radicals remained, albeit under more guarded conditions. During the decades of Shoghi Effendi's leadership, the number of believers entering the Faith from mainstream religious backgrounds slowly increased, but with the arrival of the 1960s, the community brought in another wave of liberal believers, many of whom had been influenced by what would come to be known as the youth counterculture. At about the same time, mass teaching in several Southern states saw the conversion of large numbers of rural African Americans who, despite their liberal ideals related to race relations, were by and large theologically conservative, if not fundamentalist, in orientation. The unifying element in the community during this period would appear to have been the social idealism found in the concepts of the Unity of Religion and the Oneness of Mankind. The almost utopian dimensions of human equality and social integration implied by these beliefs appear to have made theological differences relatively insignificant.

With the political backlash of the Reagan years and the arrival of large numbers of Persian Baha'i refugees in the United States following the 1979 Iranian Revolution, the American Baha'i community began to make a conservative turn. During the 1980s and 1990s, issues related to correct belief and proper research methodology took on a more serious posture, and by the arrival of the new millennium, misunderstandings and disagreements between liberals and fundamentalists of the type referred to in Chapters 7 and 8 were becoming more frequent. In their most severe form, these conflicts have been referred to as "the Baha'i culture wars." Whether the two groups can be accommodated to one another remains to be seen, but since vocal and liberal Baha'is of the type mentioned in this study appear to be an ever-decreasing minority, Baha'i leadership may not feel inclined to create a reconciliatory bridge. In this vein, well-read, liberal Baha'is are certainly aware of what took place in 1917, when American Baha'i leadership was capable of using both institutional and community pressure to rid itself of unwanted elements.

In terms of racial, ethnic, and gender composition, the twentieth century witnessed the transformation of the American Baha'i community from an essentially white, middle-class, Protestant group of believers (with a disproportionate number of female members) into a movement characterized by diversity in all of these categories. Starting as early as 1909 with the interracial efforts of individual believers such as Pauline Hannen and Louis Gregory and later expanding into the race amity conferences that characterized Baha'i efforts at social outreach from the 1920s through the 1940s, the groundwork was effectively laid, though not without internal resistance, for the eventual mushrooming of the number of African American followers that would take place in the late 1960s and early 1970s. Then, with the arrival during the latter part of the century of large numbers of both Persian and Southeast Asian Baha'i refugees, as well as the conversion of Latinos and Native Americans, the American Baha'is could boast of a sizable number of well-functioning, culturally and ethnically diverse local communities, of which Baltimore and Atlanta were outstanding examples.

One of the major themes that has characterized the short history of the Baha'i Faith in the United States, and one to which reference has already been made above, is the tension that exists between some of the movement's more liberal religious and social teachings and its assumptions concerning leadership. When placed in the American context, this discrepancy appears to reveal itself as a natural collision between individualism and authoritarianism.

To a considerable degree, the authoritarian aspects of Baha'i leadership can be seen to stem from the religion's Shi'ite cultural roots, where the concept of divinely guided *imáms* is given great reverence. As a self-proclaimed Manifestation of God, Baha'u'llah is believed to have been infallible, and his legitimate heirs to authority, 'Abdu'l-Baha, Shoghi Effendi, and the Universal House of Justice, are, to varying degrees, also seen in this light. What adds emphasis to the Baha'i belief in the unquestionable nature of ultimate authority are the challenges and resulting schisms that have occurred at each stage of leadership change. These events have resulted in an overriding fear of disunity and created widespread suspicion that any disagreement with authority harbors a challenge to community identity. Those who have been the sources of rupture have been labeled as covenant-breakers and given a demonic image.

The authoritarian side of Baha'i leadership began impacting the American Baha'i community at the time of Kheiralla's break with 'Abdu'l-Baha and the latter's promotion of the Doctrine of the Covenant, which he summarized as follows: "Any opinion expressed by the Centre of the Covenant is correct and there is no reason for disobedience by anyone."[4] While the declaration seemingly conflicted with the Faith's more liberal principles, such as the independent search for truth and the primacy of moral behavior over creed or doctrine, many of the early Baha'is embraced the Doctrine of the Covenant because of their love for 'Abdu'l-Baha. Even though at times the degree of devotion shown to him went beyond proper limits, personal attachment to the Master remained of immense importance within the community and for some Baha'is constituted one of the most basic elements of their Faith.[5]

During the last years of 'Abdu'l-Baha's life, the administrative implications associated with the Doctrine of the Covenant had begun to seep into the domain of American Baha'i leadership. In the name of unity, Mason Remey and his supporters were able to declare the Reading Room Baha'is "violators of the Covenant." What is more, they were effectively able to chase a number of less outspoken believers from the community. Consequently, by the time Shoghi Effendi became Guardian of the Baha'i Faith, national Baha'i institutions in the United States were already characterized by certain authoritarian modes of operation.

Although Shoghi Effendi occasionally disapproved of the American National Spiritual Assembly's periodic heavy-handedness, as during the Alfred Lunt crisis of 1933–1934, the emphasis the Guardian gave to the creation of the Baha'i Administrative Order, as well as the perceived threats to his leadership from the likes of Ahmad Sohrab and members of his own family, gave further impetus to the development of the authoritarian side of Baha'i institutional life. It was only after the Guardianship had ended that the pendulum began to swing back toward a less authoritative system. A possible reason for the change may lie in the fact that America's most vocal supporter of the Doctrine of the Covenant, Remey, was himself declared a covenant-breaker. According to this explanation, the challenge to Baha'i belief and the disruption to the Faith's administrative organization that resulted from both Shoghi Effendi's unexpected death and Remey's subsequent claim to be the next Guardian led to a general downplaying of questions related to institutional authority. While the interpretation is only speculative, it can certainly be argued that many of the mass teaching techniques used in the United States in the 1960s and 1970s placed less emphasis on the administrative side of religion. What primarily attracted new converts to the movement during this period were its social principles and/or mystical components. It may well be that *hikmat* (practical wisdom) dictated that, to a generation that seemed to denounce authoritarianism on principle, the wise approach for Baha'i teachers was to focus on the charismatic figures of Baha'u'llah and 'Abdu'l-Baha and their humanitarian teachings while at the same time diminishing the importance given to such issues as institutional infallibility and covenant-breaking.

In connection with the previously alluded to conservative shift that began to take place in the American Baha'i community in the mid-1970s, there was a related reversal back toward an emphasis on institutional authority. This may have resulted from the election of a more conservative Universal House of Justice, or perhaps it was a response to the general societal attitude that the 1960s were over. In either case, the 1979 Iranian Revolution and the Baha'i refugees that it produced fueled the backlash by incorporating into the American Baha'i mainstream elements that were traditionally more conservative when it came to matters of religious authority. Moreover, the attacks on Iranian Baha'is in their homeland helped bring to the surface the ever-present and underlying fear of persecution that has been part of Baha'i history since the time of the Bab. In such situations, a "circle-the-wagons" mentality arises that tends to produce a style of leadership that is more authoritarian than grassroots in nature. It is within this framework that recent Baha'i condemnation of certain Western democratic values must be understood.

Returning to the theme of charismatic leadership, it has been noted by a number of commentators that with the death of 'Abdu'l-Baha, the Baha'i community was left with an emotional void. It should not be surprising, therefore, to find that a desire still existed among the Western faithful for an authority figure upon whom they could transfer their psychological needs. As fate would have it, Shoghi Effendi was neither capable nor desirous of expressing such charisma. Instead, he attempted to fill the spiritual vacuum by creating a cohesive administrative system. Nonetheless, there were still those who demanded a larger-than-life figure to signify Baha'i leadership, and consequently, often against his will, a process of Guardian "idolization" began to unfold. The fact that Shoghi Effendi lived a rather secluded lifestyle and seldom left the confines of Haifa attached an element of mystery to his person that, in turn, added to the growing myth. For example, it was not uncommon to find Baha'is who believed that he had a son who was being kept in hiding. However, with Shoghi Effendi's death and the shocking realization that there would be no more guardians, the charismatic phase of Baha'i leadership came to an end. Although there have been occasional efforts to exalt the Universal House of Justice to an almost supernatural level, the fact that the Faith's leadership was in the hands of an institution rather than an individual inevitably produced what German sociologist Max Weber termed the "routinization" of authority. When routinization takes place, believers begin to look at leadership more as a mechanical process than a dynamic presence. In terms of the American Baha'i community, it can be argued that routinization has led to national institutions obtaining a relatively greater authoritative presence vis-à-vis international institutions than they did in the past. This does not mean that American Baha'is have consciously determined such a shift or that American Baha'i leadership acts independently of Haifa. Rather, it suggests that in the absence of a charismatic center there is often a psychological tendency for both individuals and institutions to gravitate toward those sources of power with which they are most familiar.

Over the period of its historical development in the United States, the
Baha'i Faith has influenced the beliefs and lifestyles of tens of thousands
of Americans. The movement has not only expanded individuals' spiritual
horizons, it has also introduced them to new forms of ritual, devotion,
and religious ceremony. Yet, what of the reverse process? In what ways
has American society and culture affected the contours of the American
Baha'i community?

Perhaps the most obvious impact American religious practice has had
on the Baha'i community has been the Christianization process mentioned
in Lee's article. Early on, such influences were more overt, for example,
the use of specific orthodox Christian beliefs like the doctrine of Jesus'
vicarious atonement and the development of a Christianized Baha'i hymnody. Even though some of these elements were later discarded or reinterpreted, an underlying Christian orientation has remained. One of the
best examples of this process can be seen in the way many American
Baha'is have understood Baha'u'llah and 'Abdu'l-Baha. Both have often
been viewed in the manner of orthodox Christian representations of Jesus.
A prime example is the suffering servant motif. Such perceptions can be
contrasted with the way the holy figures are represented in Persian and
Arabic sources, where they are more often than not portrayed in terms of
themes related to the Prophet Muhammad or the Shi'ite *imáms*. This
process of cross-cultural identification is not unique to Baha'i communities
in the West. Indeed, as has already been stated on more than one occasion, one of the features that has characterized the international expansion
of the Baha'i Faith has been its ability to incorporate local religious concepts into its own belief system. In this connection, the example of India
once again comes to mind, where Baha'u'llah is often surrounded by symbols and concepts related to the popular Hinduism.

In connection to this Christianizing process, Professor Juan R. I. Cole
has suggested that relatively recent conservative attitudes found among
Baha'i leadership at the international level can in part be attributed to
Christian fundamentalist elements both within American society at large
and in the Baha'i community specifically. Thus, he claims that in addition
to the Christian Right's increasing influence in American public life, significant numbers of 1970s converts brought with them Christian fundamentalist approaches to religion. Consequently, by the 1980s, at least 10
percent of the American Baha'i membership likely adhered to some form
of fundamentalist orientation, and since their strict moral codes and theological commitments helped them control local spiritual assemblies, they
have been able to influence individual appointments to such positions as
auxiliary board members and their assistants.[6]

Another area where some Baha'i thinkers feel that the influence of American religious norms have impacted the Baha'i community in the United States is in relationship to what is sometimes called American "civil religion." This term comes from the observation that there exists a distinct religious attitude among Americans that often goes beyond specific denominational affiliations and makes them more like one another than is the case with members of religious communities in Europe, the Middle East, or Asia. As part of the melting pot mentality, civil religion encourages areas of common identity based on a number of social, political, and economic ideals that tend to embody a certain American way of life. Everything from fashion to style of political behavior can be brought under this label. Viewing the American Baha'i community from such a perspective, it can be argued that although Baha'is have their own distinct belief system and manner of community behavior, they have often blurred the distinctions between American and Baha'i lifestyles. By and large, American Baha'is have not maintained a "ghettoized" identity, and their lack of specific external markers (for instance, clothing), distinct political affiliations, or taboos related to modernization prevent them from starkly standing out from their fellow citizens. If such is the case, it might help explain why it has always been so easy for Americans to become Baha'is—and just as easy for them to depart the community. Religious affiliations in America are simply more exchangeable than they are in other parts of the world.

Turning from theology to social principles, whereas Baha'i ideals related to both gender and racial equality are claimed to have originated with Baha'u'llah or 'Abdu'l-Baha, there is evidence to believe that the American Baha'i experience has helped refine these ideals. One need only contrast nineteenth- or early-twentieth-century Middle Eastern Baha'i communities with later American communities. In the former, women's roles were still comparatively restricted, and the ownership of slaves (often referred to in Baha'i literature as servants) was not unknown, while the American communities contained women and blacks who were not only socially active but often outspoken. In this regard, it would be difficult to believe that a movement that claimed gender and racial equality would not have been influenced by both the suffragette movement (and later women's liberation) and the civil rights movement. It will be recalled that it was an American Baha'i woman, Corrine True, whose persistence resulted in 'Abdu'l-Baha finally allowing women to serve on local and national spiritual assemblies, and that following in the footsteps of Louis Gregory, an African American, numerous Baha'is supported integration efforts in the South through their contacts with various groups within the civil rights movement.

Finally, while the stance that Baha'i leadership has taken on such sexually related issues as abortion and homosexuality seems clear, the impact that the constitutionality of the former and the limited but vocal public expression of support for the latter have had on American society in general have likely influenced the thinking of many American Baha'is, at least to the point of raising in their minds a number of legal, scientific, and theological questions.

In closing, a few reflections regarding the future growth of the Baha'i community in the United States would seem appropriate. Historical predictions are inevitably problematic in that they cannot take into account unforeseen circumstances, but since the issue of community expansion has received a great deal of attention from American Baha'is themselves, certain possibilities can at least be posited in light of some of the community's own conclusions.

It is a well-known fact among insightful American Baha'is that except for immigrant additions, in recent years community growth has remained relatively stagnant. A decline in the number of lasting enrollments following the end of large scale mass teaching efforts in the South plus the rapidly aging nature of the community as a result of the next generation of Baha'is (children of the baby boomers) not joining in large numbers or accepting the level of community responsibility assumed by their parents has brought the situation to a point of crisis. How do Baha'is account for this development, and what plans do they have to overcome it?

The range of explanations is quite wide. At one extreme, there is what might be termed "the guilt explanation." According to this perspective, the Baha'is themselves are to blame in that they are either failing to live exemplary Baha'i lives or they have not given enough attention to their teaching responsibilities. A related explanation points to Western decadence. In this view, the lifestyles of materialistic Western countries are seen to have reached a point where they are virtually beyond the pale of historical redemption. Thus, the majority of Westerners are no longer able to commit to the spiritual forces unleashed by Baha'u'llah's revelation. This approach has also been known to be expressed at the international level of Baha'i leadership, and its implications for future teaching strategies is clear: primary emphasis needs to be given to the Baha'i communities in the developing world whose current numbers are not only greater but whose potential for growth is also more substantial. On the more liberal side of the analysis is the belief that an overemphasis on the administrative side of community life combined with a narrowing of theological and social vision has caused membership gains to be lost. Here, the problem is seen not only as one of shortsighted expansion goals, where it is argued that if Americans are looking for conservative religion they are more likely to find it in their own evangelical traditions than in a religion of Middle Eastern origin, but also as a question of retaining those individuals who declare their faith in Baha'u'llah. Although there are no official figures available on the number of Baha'is who have either left the community or become inactive, the accurate address statistic cited in Chapter 8 indicates that the number is probably more than 50 percent, and such a high percentage, these critics argue, can only be accounted for by a failure in leadership.

If we look at the most recent teaching plans and compare them with those that used Shoghi Effendi's strategies, one fundamental distinction stands out. While the new Cluster System and the standardized Ruhi teaching method represent efforts to systematize the spread of the Faith, they counter the well-established assumption that underlay previous beliefs about growth; namely, that dispersion of Baha'is to new locations was the key to successful propagation. Does the strategic change represented by the Cluster System signal an admission that in the United States, at least, the original blueprint has been found wanting and that the mere spreading of the message has not only failed to bring about the desired entry by troops but has also caused the Baha'is to be so thinly spread that in the words of a more cynical observer, "the Baha'is are everywhere—and nowhere?" Or is it an indication that the vision of mainstream mass conversion has been found to be unrealistic, and that new circumstances require a fresh approach to expansion?

Whatever the answers to these questions might reveal, it would appear that future growth of the Baha'i community in the Untied States is likely to be gradual. Even if many Baha'is continue to adhere to the "rise of Christianity" model of historical analysis, it should be remembered that it took more than three centuries of relatively slow growth and social adaptation before the Church was in a position to affect large scale conversion, and then only after major political and economic changes had reshaped fundamental contours of the Roman Empire. While similar structural changes in the contemporary world are not impossible, it seems likely that they would become manifest over an extended period of time. Thus, what will be required of any religious movement that deems itself capable of acting as a catalyst for planetary unity is an apprehension of the evolutionary nature of effective religious change. It must not only promote its founders' innovative insights, it must also grasp the nature of surrounding cultural and historical forces and creatively adapt to them. Perhaps most importantly, it must have the ability, when necessary, to admit its own shortcomings. Historically, Baha'i leadership has on several occasions demonstrated such a capacity when facing difficult political and/or cultural challenges. The Bab's decision not to fulfill traditional apocalyptic prophecies in a literal manner by refusing to return to Karbala after his pilgrimage to Mecca, Baha'u'llah's moderation of Babi militancy, and 'Abdu'l-Baha and Shoghi Effendi's respective inclusions of Krishna and the Buddha as Manifestations of God are all examples of this kind of adaptability. The ability of future Baha'i leadership to manifest such wisdom will likely determine its future growth both in the United States and worldwide.

Notes

FOREWORD

1. See, for example, Regina M. Shwartz, *The Curse of Cain: The Violent Legacy of Monotheism* (Chicago: University of Chicago Press, 1997).

2. I am drawing here on a lecture that I heard Mark Juergensmeyer deliver in the fall of 1996 at the annual meeting of the American Academy of Religion, when he was working his way toward his pioneering *Terror in the Mind of God: The Global Rise of Religious Violence* (Berkeley: University of California Press, 2000).

3. See especially the recent work of Paul Berman, *Terror and Liberalism* (New York: W.W. Norton, 2003) and Sam Harris, *The End of Faith: Religion, Terror, and the Future of Reason* (New York: W.W. Norton, 2004). The latter book is especially interesting for its proposal that the most hopeful "end of faith" is, in fact, a form of nondual empirical mysticism indebted to India and confirmed by contemporary neuroscience.

4. I am perfectly aware that it is the brain, in response to the different natural and social environments of history, that has produced such software, such mythologies and worldviews, in the first place. The analogy, then, breaks down, as the brain is not a computer and cultural systems have evolved in tandem with biological and social needs within a kind of feedback mechanism.

5. Jack Miles, "Global Requiem: The Apocalyptic Moment in Religion, Science, and Art," *CrossCurrents* 50 (Fall 2000), 296–97.

6. Friedrich Nietzsche, *Thus Spoke Zarathustra: A Book for All and None*, trans. and pref. Walter Kaufmann (New York: The Modern Library, 1995), 130.

7. For an extended discussion of this concept as a model for the study of religion, see Jeffrey J. Kripal, "Comparative Mystics: Scholars as Gnostic Diplomats," *Common Knowledge* 10 (Fall 2004): 485–517. Ideally speaking, the present Foreword should be read in the context of this same essay.

8. Beverly J. Lanzetta, *The Other Side of Nothingness: Toward a Theology of Radical Openness* (Albany: SUNY, 2001), 53, 57.

INTRODUCTION

1. On the question of American Baha'i numbers, the 2001 American Religious Identification Survey of 50,000 households by telephone estimated 84,000 Baha'is. See http://www.religioustolerance.org/us_rel3.htm.

2. Baha'u'llah, *Gleanings from the Writings of Baha'u'llah*, rev. ed., trans. Shoghi Effendi (Wilmette, IL: Baha'i Publishing Trust, 1969), 288.

CHAPTER 1

1. Abbas Amanat, *Resurrection and Renewal: The Making of the Babi Movement in Iran, 1844–1850* (Ithaca, NY: Cornell University Press, 1989), 136.

2. ['Abdu'l-Baha], *A Traveler's Narrative Written to Illustrate the Episode of the Bab*, vol. 2, trans. and ed. E. G. Browne (Cambridge: Cambridge University Press, 1891), 11.

3. H. M. Balyuzi, *The Bab* (Oxford: George Ronald, 1973), 134n.

4. "The Ecclesiastical Sentence (fatwá) of the 'Ulama of Tabriz,'" in *Materials for the Study of the Babi Religion*, ed. E. G. Browne (Cambridge: Cambridge University Press, 1961), 259.

5. Peter Smith, *The Babi and Baha'i Religions* (Cambridge: Cambridge University Press, 1987), 23.

6. Amanat, *Resurrection and Renewal*, 396.

7. See "An Austrian Officer's Account of the Cruelties Practised on the Babis Who Suffered in the Great Persecution of 1852," in Browne, *Materials for the Study of the Babi Religion*, 265–71.

8. Smith, *Babi and Baha'i Religions*, 31–47.

9. Denis MacEoin, "Hierarchy, Authority, and Eschatology in Early Babi Thought," in *Studies in Babi and Baha'i History: In Iran*, vol. 3, ed. Peter Smith (Los Angeles: Kalimat Press, 1986), 125–26.

10. Baha'u'llah, *Kitáb-i Íqán*, 2nd ed., trans. Shoghi Effendi (Wilmette, IL: Baha'i Publishing Trust, 1970), 250–51.

11. 'Abdu'l-Baha, *Traveler's Narrative*, xxxviii–xl.

12. H. M. Balyuzi, *'Abdu'l-Baha* (London: George Ronald, 1971), 73.

13. Balyuzi, *'Abdu'l-Baha*, 141.

14. 'Abdu'l-Baha, *Paris Talks: Addresses Given by 'Abdu'l-Baha in Paris in 1911–1912*, 11th ed. (London: Baha'i Publishing Trust, 1969), 136.

15. Quoted in Alan L. Ward, *239 Days: 'Abdu'l-Baha's Journey in America* (Wilmette, IL: Baha'i Publishing Trust, 1979), 167.

16. Peter Smith, "The American Baha'i Community, 1894–1917: A Preliminary Survey," in *Studies in Babi and Baha'i History*, vol. 1, ed. Moojan Momen (Los Angeles: Kalimat Press, 1982), 101–102.

17. Shoghi Effendi, *The World Order of Baha'u'llah*, rev. ed. (Wilmette, IL: The Baha'i Publishing Trust, 1969), 134.

18. Estimates of the number of Baha'is at the time of 'Abdu'l-Baha's death range from 100,000 to 1 million, most of whom resided in Iran. For example, see Peter Smith, "A Note on Babi and Baha'i Numbers in Iran," *Iranian Studies* 17 (1984).

19. Mary (Rúhíyyih Khánum) Maxwell, "Twenty-Five Years of the Guardianship," *Baha'i Library Online* at http://bahai-library.com/?file=khanum_25_years_guardianship.html, 6.

20. During the early years of administrative development, assemblies were often assigned to areas or regions rather than specific countries, thus the National Spiritual Assembly of Central America and others.

21. *The Baha'i World: An International Record*, vol. 12 (Wilmette, IL: Baha'i Publishing Trust, 1956), 253.

22. William Garlington, "Baha'i Conversions in Malwa," in *Studies in Babi and Baha'i History: From Iran East and West*, vol. 2, eds. Juan R. Cole and Moojan Momen (Los Angeles: Kalimat Press, 1984), 167.

23. The Universal House of Justice, "Message of July, 1964," in *Wellspring of Guidance: Messages from the Universal House of Justice* (Wilmette, IL: Baha'i Publishing Trust, 1970), 28.

24. Smith, *Babi and Baha'i Religions*, 165.

25. *A Wider Horizon. Selected Messages of the Universal House of Justice 1983–1992* (Riviera Beach, FL: Palabra Publications, 1992), 138–39.

CHAPTER 2

1. Baha'u'llah, *Gleanings from the Writings of Baha'u'llah*, 3–4.

2. Baha'u'llah, *Kitáb-i Íqán*, 98.

3. Baha'u'llah, *The Hidden Words of Baha'u'llah*, rev. ed., trans. Shoghi Effendi (Wilmette, IL: Baha'i Publishing Trust, 1963), 4.

4. Juan Ricardo Cole, *The Concept of Manifestation in the Baha'i Writings* (Ottawa: The Association for Baha'i Studies, 1982), 20.

5. 'Abdu'l-Baha, *Tablets of 'Abdu'l-Baha 'Abbas*, vol. 3 (New York: Baha'i Publishing Committee, 1940), 538.

6. Cole, *Concept of Manifestation in the Baha'i Writings*, 23.

7. 'Abdu'l-Baha, *Some Answered Questions*, rev. ed., trans. Laura Clifford Barney (Wilmette, IL: Baha'i Publishing Trust, 1968), 178.

8. Dann J. May, "The Baha'i Principle of Religious Unity: A Dynamic Perspectivism," in *Studies in the Babi and Baha'i Religions: Revisioning the Sacred*, vol. 8, ed. Jack McLean (Los Angeles: Kalimat Press, 1997), 11.

9. Exactly who the Sabians were is problematic. The *Qur'an* refers to them as a People of the Book (and thus, perhaps, Shoghi Effendi's inclusion of them in his list). Other Islamic sources identify them with followers of John the Baptist or the pagan Sabaeans of Harran.

10. May, "Baha'i Principle of Religious Unity," 8.

11. See Christopher Buck, "Baha'i Universalism and Native Prophets," in *Studies in the Babi and Baha'i Religions: Reason and Revelation*, vol. 13, eds. Seena Fazel and John Danesh (Los Angeles: Kalimat Press, 2002), 173–201.

12. *Baha'i World Faith: Selected Writings of Baha'u'llah and 'Abdu'l-Baha*, 2nd ed. (Wilmette, IL: Baha'i Publishing Trust, 1966), 46–47.

13. 'Abdu'l-Baha, *Paris Talks*, 80.

14. 'Abdu'l-Baha, *Some Answered Questions*, 301–2.

15. For an excellent discussion of Baha'i views on evolution, see *Evolution in Baha'i Belief*, ed. Kevin Brown (Los Angeles: Kalimat Press, 2001).

16. Baha'u'llah, *Gleanings from the Writings of Baha'u'llah*, 218.

17. *Baha'i World Faith*, 238.

18. Juan R. I. Cole, *Modernity and the Millennium* (New York: Columbia University Press, 1998), 167.

19. Cole, *Modernity and the Millennium*, 177.

20. Universal House of Justice. *Women: Extracts from the Writings of Baha'u'llah, 'Abdu'l-Baha, Shoghi Effendi and the Universal House of Justice* (Thornhill, Ontario: Baha'i Canada Publications, 1986), 46.

21. Baha'u'llah, *Gleanings from the Writings of Baha'u'llah*, 95.

22. Shoghi Effendi, *World Order of Baha'u'llah*, 203.

23. For example, see Sen McGlinn, "Theocratic Assumptions in Baha'i Literature," in Fazel and Danesh, *Studies in the Babi and Baha'i Religions: Reason and Revelation*, 173–201.

24. Baha'u'llah, *Epistle to the Son of the Wolf*, trans. Shoghi Effendi (Wilmette, IL: Baha'i Publishing Trust, 1969), 138.

25. "Turning Point for All Nations: A Statement of the Baha'i International Community on the Occasion of the 50th Anniversary of the United Nations, October, 1995," at http://www.ibiblio.org/Bahai/Texts/English/Turning-Point-For-All-Nations.html.

26. Baha'u'llah, *Hidden Words of Baha'u'llah*, 3.

27. 'Abdu'l-Baha, *The Secret of Divine Civilization*, 2nd ed., trans. Marzieh Gail (Wilmette, IL: Baha'i Publishing Trust, 1970), 24–25.

28. Shoghi Effendi, *Directives From the Guardian* (New Delhi: Baha'i Publishing Trust, 1973), 20.

29. Cited in J. E. Esslemont, *Baha'u'llah and the New Era*, 3rd ed. (Wilmette, IL: Baha'i Publishing Trust, 1970), 142.

CHAPTER 3

1. John Walbridge, "The Nineteen Day Feast," *Baha'i Academics Resource Library*, at http://bahai-library.org/encyclopedia/feast.html.

2. In the largest Baha'i communities, there are sometimes several district feasts. Such is the case in Los Angeles and Atlanta.

3. Baha'u'llah, *Gleanings from the Writings of Baha'u'llah*, 210.

4. *Baha'i World Faith*, 368.

5. *Baha'i Prayers* (Wilmette, IL: Baha'i Publishing Trust, 1967), 117.

6. *Baha'i Prayers*, 132.

7. See Chapters 3 and 4, R. Jackson Armstrong-Ingram, *Music Devotions and Mashriqu'l-Adhkár* (Los Angeles: Kalimat Press, 1987).

8. William Garlington, "Baha'i *Bhajans*: An Example of the Baha'i Use of Hindu Symbols," *Occasional Papers in Shaykhi, Babi and Baha'i Studies* 2 (January, 1998), at http://www.h-net.msu.edu/-bahai/bhpapers.htm.

9. 'Abdu'l-Baha, *Paris Talks*, 176–77.

10. The Universal House of Justice. *A Synopsis and Codification of the Kitáb-i Aqdas* (Haifa: Baha'i World Center, 1973), 62.

11. See Linda Walbridge, "Rituals: An American Baha'i Dilemma," *Baha'i Studies Review* 5 (1995).

12. Baha'u'llah, "The Ridván Tablet," in *The Baha'i Revelation: A Selection from the Baha'i Holy Writings and Talks by 'Abdu'l-Baha*, rev. ed. (London: Baha'i Publishing Trust, 1970), 145–46.

13. The Baha'i day begins and ends at sunset. Therefore, although the official date given for the celebration of the Declaration of the Bab is May 23, it is actually celebrated during the evening of May 22.

14. For accounts of this interesting episode, see *The Martyrdom of the Bab: A Compilation* (Los Angeles: Kalimat Press, 1992).

15. Balyuzi, *'Abdu'l-Baha*, 523n9.

16. Shoghi Effendi, *God Passes By* (Wilmette, IL: Baha'i Publishing Trust, 1965), 311.

17. Baha'u'llah, *Kitáb-i Aqdas*, 91.

18. "The Lotus of Bahapur," *National Spiritual Assembly of the Baha'is of India Website*, at http://www.bahaindia.org/temple/sabha.htm.

19. Technically speaking, in Baha'i scriptures there is difference between hajj, or pilgrimage to Baghdad and Shiraz, and visitation (*ziyarat*) to Haifa. American Baha'is, however, tend to call them both "pilgrimage."

20. For a succinct look at Baha'i pilgrimage, see G. M. Viswanathan, "Baha'i Pilgrimage to Israel," at http://www.ibiblio.org/Bahai/Pilgrimage/pilgrimage.html.

21. David S. Ruhe, *The Door of Hope* (Oxford: George Ronald, 1983), 112.

22. *Synopsis and Codification of the Kitáb-i Aqdas*, 61.

23. Baha'u'llah, *Epistle to the Son of the Wolf*, 25.

24. For a moving account of a Baha'i medic's experiences in Vietnam, see David Langness, "A Baha'i Goes to War," in *Circle of Peace: Reflections of the Baha'i Teachings*, ed. Anthony Lee (Los Angeles: Kalimat Press, 1985).

25. Baha'u'llah, *Kitáb-i Aqdas*, 21.

26. Anthony A. Lee, "Choice Wine: The Kitáb-i Aqdas and the Development of Baha'i Law," *Baha'i Library Online*, at http://bahai-library.org/conferences/wine.html.

27. "Guidelines for Teaching," in *Compilation of Compilations* (Sydney: Baha'i Publications Australia, 1991), 295.

CHAPTER 4

1. Quoted in Shoghi Effendi, *Baha'i Administration* (Wilmette, IL: Baha'i Publishing Trust, 1968), 21.

2. Shoghi Effendi, *God Passes By*, 331.

3. Shoghi Effendi, *Baha'i Administration*, 65.

4. Shoghi Effendi, "National Spiritual Assembly—National Convention," *Baha'i Library Online*, at http://bahai-library.org/compilations/nsa.html#II.

5. Shoghi Effendi, *Baha'i Administration*, 39.

6. "Letter of the Universal House of Justice to the National Spiritual Assembly of Colombia, June 23, 1971," in *Lights of Guidance: A Baha'i Reference File*, 3rd rev. ed., comp. H. Hornby (New Delhi: Baha'i Publishing Trust, 1994), 165.

7. "Memorandum From the Department of the Secretariat, September 8, 1991," *Baha'i Library Online*, at http://bahai-library.org/uhj/translation.and.review.html.

8. Baha'u'llah, "The Tablet of Ishráqát," trans. Shoghi Effendi, in *Baha'i Revelation*, 159.

9. 'Abdu'l-Baha, *Will and Testament of Abdu'l-Baha*, trans. Shoghi Effendi (Wilmette, IL: Baha'i Publishing Trust, 1994), 20.

10. Baha'u'llah, "Words of Paradise," in *Baha'i World Faith*, 182.

11. *The Constitution of the Universal House of Justice* (Haifa: Baha'i World Center, 1972), 5–6.

12. "1995: Four-Year Plan Messages to Baha'is of the World and to the Continental Board of Counselors," *Baha'i Library Online*, at http://bahai-library.org/?file=uhj_four-year_plan_messages.html.

13. Udo Schaefer, "Infallible Institutions?" in Fazel and Danesh, *Studies in the Babi and Baha'i Religions: Reason and Revelation*, 15.

14. "Letter From the Universal House of Justice to the International Teaching Center, October 10, 1976," in *Lights of Guidance*, 330.

15. "Letter From the Universal House of Justice to the International Teaching Center, October 10, 1976," 331.

16. "Elucidation of the Nature of the Continental Boards of Counselors, April 24, 1972," *Baha'i Library Online*, at http://bahai-library.org/uhj/counselors.html.

17. Shoghi Effendi, *World Order of Baha'u'llah*, 148.

18. Shoghi Effendi, *World Order of Baha'u'llah*, 150.

19. This was the claim that Mason Remey made regarding the position taken by the Persian Hands of the Cause during that group's meetings in Haifa following Shoghi Effendi's death. See "Who's Who in the Baha'i Faith—Mason Remey," *Baha'i Faith Network*.

20. Shoghi Effendi, *World Order of Baha'u'llah*, 151.

21. "Comments on the Guardianship and the Universal House of Justice," *Baha'i Library Online*, at http://bahai-library.com/?file=uhj_guardianship_uhj_infallibility.html.

22. "The Universal House of Justice's Power of Elucidation," in *Messages from the Universal House of Justice: 1963–1986, The Third Epoch of the Formative Age*, comp. Geoffrey W. Marks (Wilmette, IL: Baha'i Publishing Trust, 1996), 646.

23. Moojan Momen, "The Covenant and Covenant-breaker," *Baha'i Library Online*, at http://bahai-library.com/?file=momen_encyclopedia_covenant.html.

24. Quoted in Shoghi Effendi, *God Passes By*, 238.

25. For a good example of this approach, see Terry Culhane, *I Beheld a Maiden* (Los Angeles: Kalimat Press, 2001), 37.

CHAPTER 5

1. Peter Smith, "The American Baha'i Community," in Moman, *Studies in Babi and Baha'i History*, 88.

2. Kheiralla's first wife died, and his second marriage ended in divorce.

3. Quoted in Robert Stockman, *The Baha'i Faith in America: Origins 1892–1900*, vol. 1 (Wilmette, IL: Baha'i Publishing Trust, 1985), 22–23.

4. Browne, *Materials for the Study of the Babi Religion*, 117.

5. Richard Hollinger, "Ibrahim George Kheiralla and the Baha'i Faith in America," in Cole and Momen, *Studies in Babi and Baha'i History: From Iran East and West*, 103.

6. Robert Stockman, "Love's Odyssey: The Life of Thornton Chase," *Baha'i Library Online*, at http://bahai-library.com/books/t.chase/ch.chapt12.html.

7. Stockman, *Baha'i Faith in America: Origins*, 117.

8. Regarding the social and religious backgrounds of believers in the early Chicago community see Stockman, *Baha'i Faith in America: Origins*, 100–104.

9. Stockman, *Baha'i Faith in America: Origins*, 142.

10. Anton Haddad, "Outline of the Baha'i Movement in the United States: A sketch of its promulgator [Ibrahim Kheiralla] and why afterwards he denied his Master, Abbas Effendi," *Baha'i Library Online*, at http://bahailibrary.com/?file=haddad_outline_bahai_movement.html, 19.

11. Lady Bloomfield, *The Chosen Highway* (Wilmette, IL: Baha'i Publishing Trust, 1940), 235–36.

12. Quoted in Balyuzi, *'Abdu'l-Baha*, 70.

13. Hollinger, "Ibrahim George Kheiralla and the Baha'i Faith in America," 115.

14. Hollinger, "Ibrahim George Kheiralla and the Baha'i Faith in America," 116.

15. William P. Collins, "Kenosha, 1893–1912: History of an Early Baha'i Community in the United States," in Momen, *Studies in Babi and Baha'i History* 234.

16. Haddad, "Outline of the Baha'i Movement in the United States," 16.

17. Abdel Karim Effendi Teherani (Abdu'l-Karím Tihrání), *Addresses Delivered before the New York and Chicago Assemblies*, trans. Anton Haddad (Chicago: Behais Supply and Publishing Board, 1900), 16.

18. Stockman, *The Baha'i Faith in America: Origins*, 176.

19. Juliet Thompson, *The Diary of Juliet Thompson* (Los Angeles: Kalimat Press, 1983), 6.

20. Smith, "American Baha'i Community," 107.

21. Robert Stockman, *The Baha'i Faith in America: Early Expansion, 1900–1912*, vol. 2 (Wilmette, IL: Baha'i Publishing Trust, 1995), 83.

22. 'Abdu'l-Baha, *Some Answered Questions*, trans. Laura Clifford Barney (Wilmette, IL: Baha'i Publishing Trust, 1964), 120–21.

23. Stockman, *Baha'i Faith in America: Early Expansion*, 97.

24. Stockman, *Baha'i Faith in America: Early Expansion*, 126.

25. Stockman, *Baha'i Faith in America: Early Expansion*, 111.

26. Smith, "American Baha'i Community," 139.

27. Smith, "American Baha'i Community," 149.

28. Stockman, *Baha'i Faith in America: Early Expansion*, 338.

29. Gayle Morrison, *To Move the World* (Wilmette: Baha'i Publishing Trust, 1982), 32.

30. Stockman, *The Baha'i Faith in America: Early Expansion*, 245.

31. Armstrong-Ingram, *Music, Devotions and Mashriqu'l-Adkhár*, 49–50.

32. Quoted in Balyuzi, *'Abdu'l-Baha*, 204.

33. Quoted in Balyuzi, *'Abdu'l-Baha*, 206.

34. Quoted in Balyuzi, *'Abdu'l-Baha*, 288.

35. Allan L. Ward, *239 Days*, 77.

36. Quoted in Balyuzi, *'Abdu'l-Baha*, 270.

37. Thompson, *Diary of Juliet Thompson*, 233.

38. Peter Smith, "The Baha'i Faith in the West: A Survey," in *Studies in the Babi and Baha'i Religions: Baha'is in the West*, vol. 14, ed. Peter Smith (Los Angeles, Kalimat Press, 2004), 9.

39. Smith, "American Baha'i Community," 190.

40. Smith, "American Baha'i Community," 200.

41. Smith, "American Baha'i Community," 170.

42. Morrison, *To Move the World*, 70.

43. Anthony A. Lee, Peggy Caton, et al., "The Service of Women on the Institutions of the Baha'i Faith," *Documents on the Shaykhi, Babi and Baha'i Movements* 3, no. 2 (May, 1999) at http://www.h-net.msu.edu/-bahai/docs/vol3/wmnuhj.htm.

CHAPTER 6

1. Maxwell, "Twenty-Five Years of the Guardianship," 9.

2. Shoghi Effendi, *World Order of Baha'u'llah*, 97.

3. Richard Hollinger, "Introduction," in *Studies in the Babi and Baha'i Religions: Community Histories*, vol. 6, ed. Richard Hollinger (Los Angeles: Kalimat Press, 1992), xxv.

4. Maxwell, "Twenty-Five Years of the Guardianship," 6.

5. Loni Bramson-Lerche, "Some Aspects of the Development of the Baha'i Administrative Order in America, 1922–1936," in Momen, *Studies in Babi and Baha'i History*, 262.

6. Loni Bramson-Lerche, "Some Aspects of the Establishment of the Guardianship," in *Studies in the Babi and Baha'i Religions: Studies in the Honor of the Late Hasan M. Balyuzi*, vol. 5, ed. Moojan Momen (Los Angeles: Kalimat Press, 1988), 269.

7. Shoghi Effendi, *World Order of Baha'u'llah*, 16–17.

8. Peter Smith, "Reality Magazine: Editorship and Ownership of an American Baha'i Periodical," in Cole and Momen, *Studies in Babi and Baha'i History: From Iran East and West*, 146.

9. Smith, *Babi and Baha'i Religions*, 124.

10. Mirza Ahmad Sohrab, "The Baha'i Cause," in *Living Schools of Religion*, ed. Vergilius Ferm (Ames, IA: Littlefield, Adams & Co., 1956), 314.

11. Smith, *Babi and Baha'i Religions*, 125.

12. Ruth White, *Is the Bahai Organization the Enemy of the Bahai Religion?* (New York, Ruth White, 1929), 8.

13. Bramson-Lerche, "Some Aspects of the Development of the Baha'i Administrative Order in America," 282.

14. Shoghi Effendi, *Messages To America* (Wilmette, IL: Baha'i Publishing Trust, 1947), 56.

15. All statistical information in the following section is taken from Smith, "American Baha'i Community," 118–21.

16. Smith, "American Baha'i Community," 121.

17. Arthur Hampson, "The Growth and Spread of the Baha'i Faith" (PhD dissertation, University of Hawaii, 1980), 345.

18. Shoghi Effendi, *Messages to America*, 87.

19. Shoghi Effendi, *Messages to America*, 88.

20. Robert Stockman, "Baha'i Membership Statistics," *Baha'i Library Online*, at http://bahai-library.com/?file=stockman_bahai_membership_statistics.html. [Note: "Baha'i Membership Statistics" was the title of a post sent to the Baha'i Studies listserv on November 1, 1998. It is an unofficial list compiled by Dr. Robert Stockman, who is coordinator of the Research Office at the United States Baha'i National Center.]

21. *Star of the West*, 10 (October 16, 1919): 230.

22. R. Jackson Armstrong-Ingram, "Horace H. Holley (1887–1960). Author, Baha'i Administrator, Hand of the Cause," *Research Notes in Shaykhi, Babi and Baha'i Studies* 1 (June, 1997) at http://www.h-net.org/-bahai/notes/holley.htm.

23. Armstrong-Ingram, "Horace H. Holley."

24. Morrison, *To Move the World*, 46.

25. Shoghi Effendi, *Citadel of Faith: Messages to America 1947–1957* (Wilmette, IL: Baha'i Publishing Trust, 1965), 163.

26. Quoted in Dorothy Freeman Gilstrap, *From Copper to Gold: The Life of Dorothy Baker*, 2nd ed. (Wilmette, IL: Baha'i Publishing Trust, 1999), 484.

27. There are a number of recorded statements by 'Abdu'l-Baha in which he speaks of African tribal peoples in less than complementary tones. For example: "If man is left in his natural state, he will become lower than the animal and continue to grow more ignorant

and imperfect. The savage African tribes of central Africa are evidences of this. Left in their natural condition, they have sunk to the lowest depths and degrees of barbarism, dimly groping in a world of mental and moral obscurity." *The Promulgation of Universal Peace* (Wilmette, IL: Baha'i Publishing Trust, 1982), 308.

28. Quoted in Shoghi Effendi, *The Advent of Divine Justice* (Wilmette, IL: Baha'i Publishing Trust, 1963), 31.

29. Christopher Buck, "Alain Locke: Baha'i Philosopher," *The Baha'i Studies Review* 10 (2001/2002): 19.

30. Buck, "Alain Locke: Baha'i Philosopher," 33.

31. Du Bois insisted that his wife dissociate herself from the Baha'i Faith because the secretary of the National Spiritual Assembly, Horace Holley, had authorized a segregated meeting in Nashville. See Morrison, *To Move the World*, 260–62.

32. Quoted in Morrison, *To Move the World*, 138.

33. Shoghi Effendi, *Baha'i Administration: Selected Messages 1922–1932*, 7th rev. ed. (Wilmette, IL: Baha'i Publishing Trust, 1974), 129.

34. Morrison, *To Move the World*, 210.

35. Shoghi Effendi, *Advent of Divine Justice*, 33.

36. Richard W. Thomas, *Racial Unity: An Imperative for Social Progress*, rev. ed. (Ottawa: Association for Baha'i Studies, 1993), 143.

37. Morrison, *To Move the World*, 294.

38. Roger Dahl, "History of the Kenosha Baha'i Community," in Hollinger, *Studies in the Babi and Baha'i Religions: Community Histories*, 28.

39. Dahl, "History of the Kenosha Baha'i Community," 41.

40. Dahl, "History of the Kenosha Baha'i Community," 43.

41. Deb Clark, "The Baha'is of Baltimore, 1898–1990," in Hollinger, *Studies in the Babi and Baha'i Religions: Community Histories*, 131.

42. Clark, "Baha'is of Baltimore, 1898–1990," 138.

43. Peggy Caton, "The Sacramento Baha'i Community, 1912–1987," in Hollinger, *Studies in the Babi and Baha'i Religions: Community Histories*, 257–59.

44. Caton, "The Sacramento Baha'i Community, 1912–1987," 260.

45. Michael McMullen, *The Baha'i: The Religious Construction of a Global Identity* (Piscataway, NJ: Rutgers University Press, 2000), 159. [At the time Oakshette created his church, there was no requirement that Baha'is withdraw their memberships in other religious organizations. When Shoghi Effendi made this a requirement, Oakshette consulted with the National Spiritual Assembly over the matter, and the body allowed him to maintain his church. He died shortly thereafter.]

46. McMullen, *The Baha'i*, 161.

47. McMullen, *The Baha'i*, 163.

CHAPTER 7

1. Most of the data for this section comes from the unpublished notes of Professor Juan R. I. Cole, which he has kindly shared. His information is based to a large extent on personal interviews. Subsequent footnotes will be cited as "Cole, Unpublished Notes on the Baha'is and the Civil Rights Movement."

2. Cole, Unpublished Notes on the Baha'is and the Civil Rights Movement.

3. Cole, Unpublished Notes on the Baha'is and the Civil Rights Movement. [In response to being ruled out of order, Blackwell proffered his resignation and announced his intention to return to Haiti, where he had already served as a pioneer.]

4. Anthony A. Lee, "Introduction," in *Circle of Unity: Baha'i Approaches to Current Social Issues*, ed. Anthony A. Lee (Los Angeles: Kalimat Press, 1984), xvi.

5. Cole, Unpublished Notes on the Baha'is and the Civil Rights Movement.

6. Deb Clark, "Baha'is of Baltimore, 1898–1990," in Hollinger, *Studies in the Babi and Baha'i Religions: Community Histories*, 140.

7. Personal Correspondence with Richard Hollinger, December 23, 2003.

8. Marks, *Messages From The Universal House of Justice 1963–1986*, 33.

9. Sidney E. Ahlstrom, "The Moral and Theological Revolution of the 1960s and Its Implications for American Religious History," in *The State of American History*, ed. Herbert J. Bass (Chicago, Triangle Books, 1970), 104.

10. Marks, *Messages From The Universal House of Justice 1963–1986*, 39.

11. Cited in Arthur Hampson, "Growth and Spread of the Baha'i Faith" (PhD Dissertation, University of Hawaii, 1980), 234.

12. Hampson, "Growth and Spread of the Baha'i Faith," 233.

13. Robert Stockman, "United States of America: History of the Baha'i Faith," unpublished entry written for possible inclusion in *A Short Encyclopedia of the Baha'i Faith*, an ongoing project of the United States National Spiritual Assembly. Currently available at *Baha'i Library Online*, at http://bahai-library.com/?file= stockman_encyclopedia_usa.html.

14. Except for Merie, whose conversion story is taken from Sandra Kahn, "Encounter of the Two Myths: Baha'i and Christian in the Rural American South—A Study in Transmythicization" (PhD dissertation, University of California, Santa Barbara, 1977), the following conversion accounts make use of pseudonyms, and in some cases locations have also been changed.

15. From personal interview conducted January 22, 2004.

16. From personal interview conducted April 22, 2004.

17. Information related to John was obtained from the personal files of freelance writer Karen Bacquet (April, 2004).

18. From personal interview conducted December 20, 2003.

19. Kahn, "Encounter of the Two Myths," 269.

20. Kahn, "Encounter of the Two Myths," 271.

21. June R. Wyman, "Becoming a Baha'i: Discourse and Social Networks in an American Religious Movement" (PhD dissertation, The Catholic University of America, 1985), 79.

22. Wyman, "Becoming a Baha'i," 79.

23. Kahn, "Encounter of the Two Myths," 246.

24. Kahn, "Encounter of the Two Myths," 248.

25. From personal interview with David Langness conducted April 17, 2004. For support of this claim, see Nancy Hardesty, "Masks of the Sacred: Religious Pluralism in South Carolina," in *Religion in South Carolina*, ed. Charles H. Lippy (Columbia, SC: University of South Carolina Press, 1993).

26. Kahn, "Encounter of the Two Myths," 260.

27. From personal interview with David Langness conducted April 17, 2004.

28. Kahn, "Encounter of the Two Myths," 263.

29. From personal interview with David Langness conducted April 17, 2004.

30. From personal interview with Anthony Lee conducted April 29. 2004.

31. From personal interview with Anthony Lee conducted April 29, 2004.

32. From personal interview with Bob Ballenger conducted April 11, 2004.

33. From personal interview with Bob Ballenger conducted April 11, 2004.

34. Hampson, "Growth and Spread of the Baha'i Faith," 345.

35. For statistics related to American Baha'i membership in the 1970s, see http://www. h-net.org/-bahai/docs/vol2/usstats1.htm.

36. Universal House of Justice, *Promise of World Peace* (Haifa: Baha'i World Center, 1985), 2.

37. Kahn, "Encounter of the Two Myths," 276.

38. "Letter to Iranian Expatriates Following 1979 Iranian Revolution," trans. Ináyat Rawhání, in *Baha'i World*, vol. 18 (Haifa: Baha'i World Centre, 1986), 360.

39. From personal interview with Payam Afsharian conducted May 12, 2004.

40. Wyman, "Becoming a Baha'i," 133.

41. From personal interview with Payam Afsharian conducted May 12, 2004.

42. Frank Lewis and Puran Stevens, *Iranian Refugees in America: A Cross-Cultural Perspective* (Wilmette, IL: U. S. Baha'i Refugee Office of the National Spiritual Assembly of the Baha'is of the United States, 1986), 19.

43. Ron Kelley and Jonathan Friedlander, eds., *Irangeles: Iranians in Los Angeles* (Los Angeles: University of California Press, 1993), 130.

44. "Los Angeles Baha'i Study Class Newsletter" (November 9, 1976), 2, *Documents on the Shaykhí, Babi and Baha'i Movements* 4, no. 4 (November, 1998), at http://www.hnet. msu.ed u/-bahai/docs/vol2/lastudy/lastudy1.htm.

45. Juan R. I. Cole, "Fundamentalism in the Contemporary Baha'i Community," *Review of Religious Research* 43 (March, 2002): 209.

46. From personal interview with Steve Scholl conducted December 22, 2003.

47. "President George Bush's Letter to the American Baha'is," *Baha'i NYC*, at http://www.bahainyc.org/presentations/worldcongress/bush.html.

48. "Letter From the National Spiritual Assembly of the Baha'is of the United States to the American Baha'i Community, November 23, 1997," *Baha'i Library Online*, at http://bahai-library.com/nsa/regional.election.html.

49. Robert Stockman, "United States of America History of the Baha'i Faith," *Baha'i Library Online*, at http://bahailibrary.com/?file=stockman_ encyclopedia_usa.html.

50. Juan R. I. Cole, "The Baha'i Faith in America as Panopticon, 1963–1997," *The Journal for the Scientific Study of Religion* 37 (June 1998): 246.

51. For an account of this episode, see K. Paul Johnson, "Baha'i Leaders Vexed by On-Line Critics," *Gnosis Magazine* 42 (Winter 1997): 9–10.

52. At a later date, Cole made a public statement that included the following: "However, in the meantime I have continued to read, meditate on, study and translate the works of Baha'u'llah and the other holy figures, and I continue to find nothing in any of this material that would in any way justify what was done to me and others on talisman@indiana. edu in 1996. And I found that that old love I had conceived for Baha'u'llah in August, 1972, just would not flicker out. I therefore feel the obligation publicly to say that I feel myself a believer in and a follower of Baha'u'llah.... And that I formally disavow my earlier disavowal of Him.... As for the rest, I know very well by now what the reactions and expectations of many will be. All I can say is this: I probably do not mean 'believe in' or 'follower' in the sense most conservative Baha'is would take the terms to connote." In Juan R. I. Cole, "Personal Statement on Baha'u'llah, 3 Years On," at http://www-personal. umich.edu/-jrcole/bahai/1999/persdec.htm.

53. Quoted in Johnson, "Baha'i Leaders Vexed by On-Line Critics," 10.

54. Ian Kluge, "A Review of Juan Ricardo Cole's 'The Baha'i Faith in America as Panopticon, 1963-1997,'" point # 18, *Baha'i Library Online* at http://bahai-library.com/reviews/panopticon.kluge.html#1.

55. "Religious Leaders Issue Plea for Peace," *Dayton Daily News*, September 16, 2001, in 2001 *Baha'i Newsletter Archives* at http://www.uga.edu/bahai/News/091601-5.html.

56. "The Destiny of America and The Promise of World Peace," *New York Times*, December 23, 2001 (Sunday edition), 29.

57. Universal House of Justice, "Letter to the World's Religious Leaders, April 2002," *Baha'i Library Online* at http://bahai-library.com/?file=uhj_religious_leaders_2002.html.

58. Universal House of Justice, "Letter to the World's Religious Leaders, April 2002."

59. Roger Dahl, "History of the Kenosha Baha'i Community," in Hollinger, *Studies in the Babi and Baha'i Religions: Community Histories*, 46.

60. Clark, "Baha'is of Baltimore, 1898–1990," 143.

61. Clark, "Baha'is of Baltimore, 1898–1990," 145.

62. Caton, "Sacramento Baha'i Community, 1912–1987," 265–66.

63. Caton, "Sacramento Baha'i Community, 1912–1987," 269.

64. Caton, "Sacramento Baha'i Community, 1912–1987," 271.

65. Michael McMullen, *The Baha'i: The Religious Construction of a Global Identity* (Piscataway, NJ: Rutgers University Press, 2000), 168.

66. McMullen, *The Baha'i*, 171.

67. Ellen Wheeler, Assistant Director of the Office of Public Information for the Baha'is of the United States, *The Pluralism Project* at http://www.pluralism.org/resources/statistics/index.php.

CHAPTER 8

1. Robert Stockman, "The American Bahá'í Community in the Nineties," in *America's Alternative Religions*, ed. Timothy Miller (Albany, NY: SUNY Press, 1995). Available at *Baha'i Library Online*, at http://bahai-library.com/?file=stockman_american_community_nineties.html.

2. "Speech given by Douglas Martin in Raleigh, North Carolina, April 10, 2004," transcribed by John Bradley, April 12, 2004, Mt. Airy, NC.

3. "2003 Ridván Message From the Universal House of Justice," *Baha'i Library Online*, at http://bahai-library.com/published.uhj/ridvan/2003.html.

4. Quoted in "Letter of the Universal House of Justice to the National Spiritual Assembly of New Zealand, May 31, 1988," *Baha'i Library Online*, at http://bahai-library.com/id.php?item.new=1395.

5. "Letter written on behalf of Shoghi Effendi, July 28, 1936," *Baha'i News*, no. 105 (February 1937): 2.

6. Quoted in Lee, Caton, et al., "The Service of Women on the Institutions of the Baha'i Faith."

7. "Letter of the Universal House of Justice to the National Spiritual Assembly of New Zealand, May 31, 1988," *Baha'i Library Online*, at http://bahai-library.com/id.php?itemnew=13 95.

8. "Letter of the Universal House of Justice to an Individual on the Infallibility and Historical Knowledge of the Guardian, July 25, 1974," *Baha'i Library Online* at http://bahai-library.com/?file=uhj_ infallibility_history_guardian.html.

9. "Letter of the Universal House of Justice to an Individual on the Infallibility and Knowledge of 'Abdu'l-Baha," *Baha'i Library Online*, at http://bahailibrary.com/?file=uhj_ infallibil ity_abdulbaha.html.

10. "Letter of Counselor Stephen Birkland to a Baha'i Intellectual and Publisher," at http://www-personal.umich.edu/-jrcole/bahai/1999/bhcouns2.htm.

11. Schaefer, "Infallible Institutions?" 20.

12. "The Universal House of Justice's Power of Elucidation October 25, 1984," in Marks, *Messages From The Universal House of Justice: 1963–1986*, 646.

13. Moojan Momen, "Fundamentalism and Liberalism," in Fazel and Danesh, *Studies in the Babi and Baha'i Religions: Reason and Revelation*, 149.

14. Cole, "Fundamentalism in the Contemporary Baha'i Community," 214

15. Quoted in Cole, "Fundamentalism in the Contemporary Baha'i Community," 206.

16. "Letter from Dr. Susan Stiles Maneck to the Universal House of Justice, May 10, 1997," *Baha'i Library Online*, at http://bahai-library.com/?file=uhj_scholarsinternet.html.

17. "Letter from the Universal House of Justice to Dr. Susan Stiles Maneck, July 20, 1997," *Baha'i Library Online*, at http://bahai-library.com/?file=uhj_scholarsinternet.html.

18. See John Parris, "Scholarship in the Baha'i Community," *Bahá'í Studies Review* 1 (1991).

19. "Letter of Douglas Martin regarding Modernity and the Millennium, via the BWC Secretariat, 3 August 1999," at http://www-personal.umich.edu/-jrcole/bahai/ 2002/ fulltext.htm.

20. "Letter of Douglas Martin regarding Modernity and the Millennium."

21. Karen Bacquet, "Enemies Within: Conflict and Control in the Baha'i Community," *Cultic Studies Journal* 18 (2001): 154.

22. In this regard, see Barney Leith, "Baha'i Review: Should the "red flag" law be repealed?" *Bahá'í Studies Review* 5, no. 1 (1995).

23. See "Issues Related to the Study of the Baha'i Faith: Extracts from Letters written on behalf of the Universal House of Justice," published as a supplement to the May 1998 issue of *Baha'i Canada* by the National Spiritual Assembly of the Baha'is of Canada.

24. Richard and Joan Ostling, *Mormon America: The Power and the Promise* (New York: Harper Collins, 1999), 352.

25. Universal House of Justice, *Individual Rights and Freedoms* (Haifa: Baha'i World Center, 1988), 1.

26. Universal House of Justice, *Individual Rights and Freedoms*, 17.

27. Bacquet, "Enemies Within," 142.

28. Quoted in Juan R. I. Cole, "Race, Immorality, and Money in the American Baha'i Community: Impeaching the Los Angeles Spiritual Assembly," *Religion* 30 (2000): 121.

29. Quoted in Universal House of Justice, *Individual Rights and Freedoms*, 33.

30. Adib Taherzadeh, *The Revelation of Baha'u'llah*, vol. 4 (Oxford: George Ronald, 1987), 320.

31. See Susan Stiles Maneck, "Wisdom and Dissimulation: The Use and Meaning of Hikmat in the Baha'i Writings and History," *Baha'i Studies Review* 6 (1996).

32. A similar fate would likewise befall New Zealand Baha'i Alison Marshall, who was summarily removed from the Baha'i rolls in 1996, apparently for criticisms she made over the Internet concerning the Universal House of Justice.

33. "Letter Written on the Behalf of the Universal House of Justice to the National Spiritual Assembly of Ireland, March 16, 1983," in Hornby, *Lights of Guidance*, 345.

34. "Statement on Capital Punishment From the Baha'i International Community to Amnesty International," *Baha'i Library Online*, at http://bahailibrary.com/published.uhj/capital.punishment.html.

35. Baha'u'llah, *Kitáb-i Aqdas*, 58.

36. "Letter Written on Behalf of Shoghi Effendi to an Individual Believer, May 21, 1954," in Hornby, *Lights of Guidance*, 365.

37. "Letter From the Universal House of Justice to an Individual Believer, January 2, 1973," in Hornby, *Lights of Guidance*, 366.

38. R. Jackson Armstrong-Ingram, "The Provisions for Sexuality in the *Kitáb-i Aqdas* in the Context of Late Nineteenth Century Eastern and Western Sexual Ideologies," *Baha'i Library Online*, at http://bahai-library.org/conferences/sex.aqdas.html.

39. "Letter Containing Recommendations to the National Spiritual Assembly of the Baha'is of the United States From a Gay-positive Group," *Baha'i Academics Resource Library*, at http://bahai-library.com/letters/gays.html.

40. Roger Reini, "The Baha'i Faith and Homosexuality: A Compilation From the Baha'i Writings," *Baha'i Academics Resource Library*, at http://bahai-library.com/unpubl.compilations/homosexuality.comp.html.

CHAPTER 9

1. William McElwee Miller, *The Baha'i Faith: Its History and Teachings* (South Pasadena, CA: William Carey Library, 1974), 99–100.

2. Miller, *Baha'i Faith: Its History and Teachings*, 356.

3. Miller, *Baha'i Faith: Its History and Teachings*, 357.

4. Francis Beckwith, *Baha'i: A Christian Response to Bahaism* (Minneapolis: Bethany House Publishers, 1985), 16.

5. Beckwith, *Baha'i: A Christian Response to Bahaism*, 19.

6. Beckwith, *Baha'i: A Christian Response to Bahaism*, 21.

7. Beckwith, *Baha'i: A Christian Response to Bahaism*, 25.

8. Beckwith, *Baha'i: A Christian Response to Bahaism*, 24.

9. Beckwith, *Baha'i: A Christian Response to Bahaism*, 37.

10. William S. Hatcher and J. Douglas Martin, *The Baha'i Faith: The Emerging Global Religion* (San Francisco: Harper and Row, 1985), 13.

11. Vance Salisbury, "A Critical Examination of 20th Century Baha'i Literature," *Baha'i Library Online*, at http://bahai-library.com/?file=salisbury_critical_examination_literature.html.

12. Salisbury, "Critical Examination of 20th Century Baha'i Literature," *Baha'i Library Online*.

13. Udo Schaefer, *The Light Shineth In Darkness* (Oxford: George Ronald, 1977), 82.

14. Schaefer, *Light Shineth In Darkness*, 87.

15. See Douglas Martin, "The Missionary as Historian: William Miller and the Baha'i Faith," *Baha'i Studies* 4 (December, 1978).

16. Peter Terry, "Truth Triumphs: A Baha'i Response to Misrepresentations of the Baha'i Teachings and Baha'i History," *Baha'i Library Online*, at http://bahai-library.com/unpubl.articles/truth.triumphs.html.

17. "Memorandum From The Research Department to The Universal House of Justice, November 6, 1990," *Baha'i Library Online*, at http://bahai-library.com/uhj/beckwith. html.

18. "Letter From the Universal House of Justice to Juan Cole, December 2, 1982," *Baha'i Library Online*, at http://216.239.57.104/custom?q=cache:4OyxTUWGGGsJ:bahai-library.com/uhj/salmani.letters.html+Salmani&hl=en&ie=UTF-8.

CONCLUSION

1. Michael McMullen, *The Baha'i*, 177.

2. Anthony Lee, "Reconciling the Other: The Baha'i Faith in America as a Successful Synthesis of Christianity and Islam," *Occasional Papers in Shaykhi, Babi and Baha'i Studies* 7 (March, 2003) at http://www.h-net.org/~bahai/bhpapers/vol7/reconc.htm.

3. Lee, "Reconciling the Other."

4. 'Abdu'l-Baha, *The Promulgation of Universal Peace*, comp. H. MacNutt, 2nd ed. (Wilmette, IL: Baha'i Publishing Trust, 1982), 386.

5. Smith, *Babi and Baha'i Religions*, 110.

6. See Juan R. I. Cole, "Fundamentalism in the Contemporary Baha'i Community." It should also be noted that Michael McMullen's polling in Atlanta suggests that fundamentalists are more than 10 percent of the population.

Selected Bibliography

'Abdu'l-Baha. *Paris Talks: Addresses Given by 'Abdu'l-Baha in Paris in 1911–1912*. 11th ed. London: Baha'i Publishing Trust, 1969.

———. *The Promulgation of Universal Peace*. 2nd ed. Compiled by Howard MacNutt. Wilmette, IL: Baha'i Publishing Trust, 1982.

———. *The Secret of Divine Civilization*. 2nd ed. Translated by Marzieh Gail. Wilmette, IL: Baha'i Publishing Trust, 1970.

———. *Some Answered Questions*. rev. ed. Translated by Laura Clifford Barney. Wilmette, IL: Baha'i Publishing Trust, 1968.

———. *Will and Testament of 'Abdu'l-Baha*. Translated by Shoghi Effendi. Wilmette, IL: Baha'i Publishing Trust, 1994.

Ahlstrom, Sidney E. "The Moral and Theological Revolution of the 1960s and Its Implications for American Religious History." In *The State of American History*, edited by Herbert J. Bass. Chicago: Triangle Books, 1970.

Amanat, Abbas. *Resurrection and Renewal: The Making of the Babi Movement in Iran, 1844–1850*. Ithaca, NY: Cornell University Press, 1989.

Armstrong-Ingram, R. Jackson. *Music Devotions and Mashriqu'l-Adhkár*. Los Angeles: Kalimat Press, 1987.

Bacquet, Karen. "Enemies Within: Conflict and Control in the Baha'i Community." *Cultic Studies Journal* 18 (2001): 140–71.

Baha'i Prayers. Wilmette, IL: Baha'i Publishing Trust, 1967.

Baha'i World Faith: Selected Writings of Baha'u'llah and 'Abdu'l-Baha. 2nd ed. Wilmette, IL: Baha'i Publishing Trust, 1966.

Baha'u'llah. *Epistle to the Son of the Wolf*. Translated by Shoghi Effendi. Wilmette, IL: Baha'i Publishing Trust, 1969.

———. *Gleanings from the Writings of Baha'u'llah*. rev. ed. Translated by Shoghi Effendi. Wilmette, IL: Baha'i Publishing Trust, 1969.

———. *The Hidden Words of Baha'u'llah*. rev. ed. Translated by Shoghi Effendi. Wilmette, IL: Baha'i Publishing Trust, 1963.

———. *Kitáb-i Aqdas*. Haifa: Baha'i World Center, 1992.

———. *Kitáb-i Íqán*. 2nd ed. Translated by Shoghi Effendi. Wilmette, IL: Baha'i Publishing Trust, 1970.

Balyuzi, H. M. *'Abdu'l-Baha*. London: George Ronald, 1971.

———. *The Bab*. Oxford: George Ronald, 1973.

———. *Baha'u'llah, the King of Glory*. Oxford: George Ronald, 1980.

Beckwith, Francis. *Baha'i: A Christian Response to Bahaism*. Minneapolis, MN: Bethany House Publishers, 1985.

Bramson-Lerche, Loni. "Some Aspects of the Development of the Baha'i Administrative Order in America, 1922–1936." In *Studies in Babi and Baha'i History*, Vol. 1, edited by Moojan Momen. Los Angeles: Kalimat Press, 1982.

———. "Some Aspects of the Establishment of the Guardianship." In *Studies in the Babi and Baha'i Religions: Studies in the Honor of the Late Hasan M. Balyuzi*, Vol. 3, edited by Moojan Momen. Los Angeles: Kalimat Press, 1988.

Brown, Kevin, ed. *Studies in the Babi and Baha'i Religions: Evolution in Baha'i Belief*, Vol. 12. Los Angeles: Kalimat Press, 2001.

Browne, E. G., ed. *Materials for the Study of the Babi Religion*. Cambridge: Cambridge University Press, 1961.

Buck, Christopher. "Alain Locke: Baha'i Philosopher." *The Baha'i Studies Review* 10 (2001/2002): 7–50.

———. "Baha'i Universalism and Native Prophets." In *Studies in the Babi and Baha'i Religions: Reason and Revelation*, Vol. 13, edited by Seena Fazel and John Danesh. Los Angeles: Kalimat Press, 2002.

Caton, Peggy. "The Sacramento Baha'i Community, 1912–1987." In *Studies in Babi and Baha'i History: Community Histories*, Vol. 6, edited by Richard Hollinger. Los Angeles: Kalimat Press, 1992.

Clark, Deb. "The Baha'is of Baltimore, 1898–1990." In *Studies in Babi and Baha'i History: Community Histories*, Vol. 6, edited by Richard Hollinger. Los Angeles: Kalimat Press, 1992.

Cole, Juan R. I. "The Baha'i Faith in America as Panopticon, 1963–1997." *The Journal for the Scientific Study of Religion* 37 (June 1998): 234–48.

———. *The Concept of Manifestation in the Baha'i Writings*. Ottawa: The Association for Baha'i Studies, 1982.

———. "Fundamentalism in the Contemporary Baha'i Community." *Review of Religious Research* 43 (March 2002): 195–217.

———. *Modernity and the Millennium*. New York: Columbia University Press, 1998.

Collins, William P. "Kenosha, 1893–1912: History of an Early Baha'i Community in the United States." In *Studies in Babi and Baha'i History*, Vol. 1, edited by Moojan Momen. Los Angeles: Kalimat Press, 1982.

Culhane, Terry. *I Beheld a Maiden*. Los Angeles: Kalimat Press, 2001.

Dahl, Roger. "History of the Kenosha Baha'i Community." In *Studies in Babi and Baha'i History: Community Histories*, Vol. 6, edited by Richard Hollinger. Los Angeles: Kalimat Press, 1992.

Esslemont, J. E. *Baha'u'llah and the New Era*, 3rd ed. Wilmette, IL: Baha'i Publishing Trust, 1970.

Garlington, William. "Baha'i Conversions in Malwa." In *Studies in Babi and Baha'i History: From Iran East and West*, Vol. 2, edited by Juan R. Cole and Moojan Momen. Los Angeles: Kalimat Press, 1984.

———. "The Baha'i Faith in Malwa." In *Religion in South Asia*, edited by G. A. Oddie. New Delhi: Manohar, 1977 .

Gilstrap, Dorothy Freeman. *From Copper to Gold: The Life of Dorothy Baker*, 2nd ed. Wilmette, IL: Baha'i Publishing Trust, 1999.

Hampson, Arthur. "The Growth and Spread of the Baha'i Faith." PhD dissertation. Honolulu, HI: University of Hawaii, 1980.

Hatcher, William S., and J. Douglas Martin. *The Baha'i Faith: The Emerging Global Religion.* San Francisco: Harper and Row, 1985.

Hollinger, Richard. "Ibrahim George Kheiralla and the Baha'i Faith in America." In *Studies in Babi and Baha'i History: From Iran East and West*, Vol. 2, edited by Juan R. Cole and Moojan Momen. Los Angeles: Kalimat Press, 1984.

Johnson, K. Paul. "Baha'i Leaders Vexed by On-Line Critics." *Gnosis Magazine* 42 (Winter 1997): 9–10.

Kahn, Sandra. "Encounter of the Two Myths: Baha'i and Christian in the Rural American South—A Study in Transmythicization." PhD dissertation. Santa Barbara, CA: University of California, 1977.

Kelley, Ron, and Jonathan Friedlander, eds. *Irangeles: Iranians in Los Angeles*. Los Angeles: University of California Press, 1993.

Lee, Anthony, ed. *Circle of Unity: Baha'i Approaches to Current Social Issues*. Los Angeles: Kalimat Press, 1984.

Leith, Barney. "Baha'i Review: Should the "red flag" law be repealed?" *Baha'i Studies Review* 5 (1995): 27–35.

Lights of Guidance: A Baha'i reference file. 3rd rev. ed. Compiled by. H. Hornby. New Delhi: Baha'i Publishing Trust, 1994.

MacEoin, Denis. "Baha'i Fundamentalism in the Academic Study of the Babi Movement." *Religion* 16 (1986): 57–84.

———. "Hierarchy, Authority, and Eschatology in Early Bab Thought." In *Studies in Babi and Baha'i History: In Iran*, Vol. 3, edited by Peter Smith. Los Angeles: Kalimat Press, 1986.

Maneck, Susan Styles. "Wisdom and Dissimulation: The Use and Meaning of Hikmat in the Baha'i Writings and History." *Baha'i Studies Review* 6 (1996): 11–23.

Martin, Douglas. "The Missionary as Historian: William Miller and the Baha'i Faith." *Baha'i Studies* 4 (December 1978), http://bahai-library.com/?file=martin_missionary_historian_miller.

May, Dann J. "The Baha'i Principle of Religious Unity: A Dynamic Perspectivism." In *Studies in Babi and Baha'i History: Revisioning the Sacred*, Vol. 8, edited by Jack McLean. Los Angeles: Kalimat Press, 1997.

McGlinn, Sen. "Theocratic Assumptions in Baha'i Literature." In *Studies in Babi and Baha'i History: Reason and Revelation*, Vol. 13, edited by Seena Fazel and John Danesh. Los Angeles: Kalimat Press, 2002.

McMullen, Michael. *The Baha'i: The Religious Construction of a Global Identity.* Piscataway, NJ: Rutgers University Press, 2000.

———. "Women and the Baha'i Faith." In *Religion and Women*, edited by Arvind Sharma. Albany, NY: State University of New York Press, 1994.

Messages from the Universal House of Justice: 1963–1986, The Third Epoch of the Formative Age. Wilmette, IL: Baha'i Publishing Trust, 1996.

Miller, William McElwee. *The Baha'i Faith: Its History and Teachings.* South Pasadena, CA: William Carey Library, 1974.

Momen, Moojan. "Fundamentalism and Liberalism." In *Studies in Babi and Baha'i History: Reason and Revelation*, Vol. 13, edited by Seena Fazel and John Danesh. Los Angeles: Kalimat Press, 2002.

———. *Islam and the Baha'i Faith.* London: George Ronald, 2000.

———. "Relativism: A Basis for Baha'i Metaphysics." In *Studies in the Babi and Baha'i Religions: Studies in Honor of the Late Hasan Balyuzi*, Vol. 5, edited by Moojan Momen. Los Angeles: Kalimat Press, 1988.

Morrison, Gayle. *To Move the World.* Wilmette, IL: Baha'i Publishing Trust, 1982.

Nabil, Zarandi, and Shaykh Muhammad. *The Dawn-Breakers: Nabil's Narrative of the Early Days of the Baha'i Revelation*, translated and edited by Shoghi Effendi. Wilmette, IL: Baha'i Publishing Trust, 1932.

Ostling, Richard, and Joan Ostling. *Mormon America: The Power and the Promise.* New York: Harper Collins, 1999.

Parris, John. "Scholarship in the Baha'i Community." *Baha'i Studies Review* 1 (1991).

Schaefer, Udo. "Infallible Institutions?" In *Studies in the Babi and Baha'i Religions: Reason and Revelation*, Vol. 13, edited by Seena Fazel and John Danesh. Los Angeles: Kalimat Press, 2002.

———. *The Light Shineth In Darkness.* Oxford: George Ronald, 1977.

Shoghi Effendi. *The Advent of Divine Justice.* Wilmette, IL: Baha'i Publishing Trust, 1963.

———. *Baha'i Administration: Selected Messages 1922–1932.* 7th rev. ed. Wilmette, IL: Baha'i Publishing Trust, 1974.

———. *Citadel of Faith: Messages to America 1947–1957.* Wilmette, IL: Baha'i Publishing Trust, 1965.

———. *Directives From the Guardian.* New Delhi: Baha'i Publishing Trust, 1973.

———. *God Passes By.* Wilmette, IL: Baha'i Publishing Trust, 1965.

———. *Messages To America.* Wilmette, IL: Baha'i Publishing Trust, 1947.

———. *The World Order of Baha'u'llah.* Wilmette, IL: Baha'i Publishing Trust, 1969.

Smith, Peter. "The American Baha'i Community, 1894–1917: A Preliminary Survey." In *Studies in Babi and Baha'i History*, Vol. 1, edited by Moojan Momen. Los Angeles: Kalimat Press, 1982.

———. *The Babi and Baha'i Religions.* Cambridge: Cambridge University Press, 1987.

———. "The Baha'i Faith in the West: A Survey." In *Studies in the Babi and Baha'i Religions: Baha'is in the West*, Vol. 14, edited by Peter Smith. Los Angeles: Kalimat Press, 2004.

———. "Reality Magazine: Editorship and Ownership of an American Baha'i Periodical." In *Studies in Babi and Baha'i History: From Iran East and West*, Vol. 2, edited by Juan R. Cole and Moojan Momen. Los Angeles: Kalimat Press, 1984.

Sohrab, Mirza Ahmad. "The Baha'i Cause." In *Living Schools of Religion*, edited by Vergilius Ferm. Ames, IA: Littlefield, Adams & Co., 1956.

Stockman, Robert. "The American Baha'i Community in the Nineties." In *America's Alternative Religions*. Edited by Timothy Miller. Albany, NY: State University of New York Press, 1995.

———. *The Baha'i Faith in America: Early Expansion, 1900–1912*, Vol. 2. Wilmette, IL: Baha'i Publishing Trust, 1995.

————. *The Baha'i Faith in America: Origins 1892–1900*, Vol. 1. Wilmette, IL: Baha'i Publishing Trust, 1985.

Taherzadeh, Adib. *The Revelation of Baha'u'llah.* four vols. Oxford: George Ronald, 1987.

Thomas, Richard W. *Racial Unity: An Imperative for Social Progress.* rev. ed. Ottawa: Association for Baha'i Studies, 1993.

Thompson, Juliet. *The Diary of Juliet Thompson.* Los Angeles: Kalimat Press, 1983.

Universal House of Justice. *Individual Rights and Freedoms.* Haifa: Baha'i World Center, 1988.

————. *Wellspring of Guidance: Messages from the Universal House of Justice.* Wilmette, IL: Baha'i Publishing Trust, 1970.

Walbridge, John. *Sacred Acts, Sacred Space, Sacred Time.* Oxford: George Ronald, 1996.

Walbridge, Linda. "Rituals: An American Baha'i Dilemma." In *Baha'i Studies Review* 5, (1995), http://bahai-library.com/?file=walbridge_rituals_american_dilemma.

Ward, Alan L. *239 Days: 'Abdu'l-Baha's Journey in America.* Wilmette, IL: Baha'i Publishing Trust, 1979.

White, Ruth. *Is the Baha'i Organization the Enemy of the Baha'i Religion?* New York: Ruth White, 1929.

Wyman, June R. "Becoming a Baha'i: Discourse and Social Networks in an American Religious Movement." PhD dissertation. Washington, D.C: Catholic University of America, 1985.

Index

About the Author

WILLIAM GARLINGTON taught history and religious studies in the United States and Australia for over twenty-five years.